LAUNCHING
LEARNERS
in Science, PreK–5

LAUNCHING *LEARNERS* in Science, PreK–5

How to Design
Standards-Based
Experiences and
Engage Students
in Classroom
Conversations

Kerry C. Williams
George E. Veomett

Skyhorse Publishing

Skyhorse Publishing books may be purchased in bulk at special discounts for sales promotion, corporate gifts, fund-raising, or educational purposes. Special editions can also be created to specifications. For details, contact the Special Sales Department, Skyhorse Publishing, 307 West 36th Street, 11th Floor, New York, NY 10018 or info@skyhorsepublishing.com.

Skyhorse® and Skyhorse Publishing® are registered trademarks of Skyhorse Publishing, Inc.®, a Delaware corporation.

Visit our website at www.skyhorsepublishing.com.

10 9 8 7 6 5 4 3 2 1

Library of Congress Cataloging-in-Publication Data is available on file.

Cover design by Rose Storey
Cover photo credit Lisa Riley

Print ISBN: 978-1-62914-663-8
Ebook ISBN: 978-1-63220-018-1

Printed in China

Contents

Preface

While taking pictures for this book, we watched as a first grader figured out that she could turn her scissors into a magnet by rubbing another magnet on the blades. As we celebrated this finding with her, she looked over and said confidently, "I guess I was just made for science." Yes, Jessie, you were made for science, and so are your teachers, although they might not know it yet.

It's funny that we often think about teaching young children as a hands-on, minds-on, emotional experience requiring choices and materials to manipulate, yet, when we think about how to help teachers move toward structures that will permit these experiences, we often give them activities and tell them what to do. As this book was created, we thought about young children learning science, and about the learners reading this book: teachers.

Just as we could give young children facts and expect them to understand science, we could give you activities and expect you to teach science. You might try a few and then go back to your normal routines. However, we want children to experience and use science throughout their lives, and we want you to do more than a few activities. We want you to make science education something you understand, feel excited about, and continue to improve. This requires more than activities. It requires knowing what science really is, knowing how children learn, and knowing the flexible structures that facilitate that learning.

This book revolves around those three ideas. Teaching science is as much about learning what it means to do science as it is about the pedagogy of teaching. In order to teach science well, you need to be, in a sense, a scientist. This book provides opportunities for you to observe, share, experiment, organize, and hypothesize not only about science content but also about teaching science and about the students you will be teaching. It describes the principles of and requirements for the active learning of science and identifies the key ingredients that should be practiced by students for their development as young scientists and as learners in general. In other words, this book is full of tools that you can use to make science in your classroom meaningful, exciting, and enduring.

The late Dr. Robert L. Egbert, who put us on the path of writing this book, said that teaching is about telling stories and asking questions. We hope you will become a learner and a reflector as you read the stories and think about the questions. We hope that you can use the tools in this book, your school district's science curriculum, and your students' ideas and interests to make science a wonderful experience in your classroom. We hope that by the time you're done reading this book, like Jessie, you will be inspired and confident—you will believe that you, too, are "made to teach science."

■ ACKNOWLEDGMENTS

I (KCW) would like to acknowledge all of the teachers in my life. My first teachers, my mom and dad, have really taught me about learning and have made me believe in myself as a teacher and a person. I could not have done this without their love, support, and energy for this project. I would like to acknowledge Jen and Mike for being my teachers of science. They let me "play" with science and help me to understand what doing science means. I would like to acknowledge George Veomett and Robert Egbert for helping me to understand what life-long learning really means and looks like. Thanks to George for his questions and his kindness throughout this crazy process. I certainly will miss our meetings with mocha. I have many inspiring teachers to thank. Thank you to Carla Farley, Mary Jo Kraus, Lisa Stiles, and Josh Snyder for letting me be a part of their exceptional classrooms where science is happening in wonderful ways. Thank you to my friends Wendy, Sue, Deann, Cheryl, Carla, and Kelly who teach me that laughter and a shoulder to cry on can help you get through anything. I would like to acknowledge Jean Ward and the other wonderful editors from Corwin who taught me about the process of writing a book and were eager, understanding, and gentle at the same time. Finally, I would like to thank John, Ryan, and Tyler who teach me every day about what is really important in life.

I (GEV) would like to acknowledge the inspiration and assistance of all those teachers and students with whom I've worked. Foremost among these are Kerry Williams, my coauthor, whose spirit and views molded mine forever, and Dr. Robert Egbert who brought us together, centered on this work. In addition, I would like to specifically recognize Kathy Jacobitz, Jim Landon, and David Crowther who pioneered the HHMI preservice teacher program at the University of Nebraska-Lincoln, introduced me to constructivism, and set me on the path I have followed ever since. The many students who have shared their journey into biology and science education over the many years of my association with "Hands-on Biology for Elementary Education Majors" have inspired me with their creativity and dedication to the education of the future leaders of our country. Finally, I would like to acknowledge the assistance, inspiration, and love of Marilyn Veomett, a superb teacher, counselor, and my personal educator.

We gratefully acknowledge the contributions of the following reviewers:

Paul Adams
Anschutz Professor of Education and Professor of Physics
Fort Hays State University
Hays, KS

Susan Illgen
Early Childhood/Family Education Coordinator II
Oklahoma State Department of Education
Oklahoma City, OK

Linda Kallam, PhD
Professor of Mathematics
Southeastern Oklahoma State University
Durant, OK

Felicia M. Moore, PhD
Assistant Professor, Science Education
Teachers College, Columbia University
New York, NY

Rose M. Pringle
Associate Professor
University of Florida
Gainesville, FL

Christine Anne Royce, EdD
Assistant Professor
Shippensburg University
Shippensburg, PA

About the Authors

© The Picture People

Kerry Curtiss Williams is a former elementary teacher, methods instructor, and supervisor of student teachers. She was educated at the University of Nebraska–Lincoln and was named one of the college's "Ninety Notables." She currently works with inservice teachers pursuing their master's degree through Wayne State College within a learning community format. Dr. Williams specializes in pedagogical structures that help all levels of learners construct knowledge. Her research interests include thinking routines, math and science education, and learning community structures. A native Nebraskan, Williams and her husband live in Omaha with their two sons.

George E. Veomett was educated at the University of Rochester, Rochester, NY (AB in Biology) and the University of Colorado, Boulder (PhD in Biology). He has taught embryology, developmental biology, and cell biology at the University of Nebraska–Lincoln since 1977. His interest in elementary and middle school science education was enhanced when he codirected experimental programs sponsored in part by the Howard Hughes Medical Institute. A college-wide teaching award winner, he has taught general biology to preservice elementary and middle school teachers for more than 12 years. He has received a College of Arts and Sciences Distinguished Teaching Award from the University of Nebraska and has been recognized for service and teaching numerous times by the Parents Association and the Teaching Council, by Mortar Board and the Greek system. He is a member of numerous honorary and professional associations; among these are Phi Beta Kappa, Sigma Xi, the American Society for Cell Biology, the National Science Teachers Association, The National Association of Biology Teachers, the Nebraska Association of Teachers of Science, and the Nebraska Academy of Sciences (of which he is a past president).

This book is dedicated to

John (KCW)
&
Marilyn (GEV)

PART I

Welcome to *Launching Learners in Science*

In a sense, the ideas for this book began long ago. They began as John Dewey wrote about changes in education in the 1890s and as administrator David Weikart worked to provide an effective education for at-risk students in the 1960s and developed a curriculum that promoted decision making, cognitive development, and student involvement. The ideas grew in college classrooms with Robert Egbert of the University of Nebraska in the 1980s and within the National Science Education Standards of the 1990s. They continue to grow within science courses for elementary teachers with George Veomett and in elementary classrooms with Kerry Williams. The ideas in this book are meant to challenge your thinking about science, about children, and about yourself as a teacher. We want these ideas to nudge you to take risks and to help you create the best learning environment possible for children. The ideas discussed here are connected and powerful, yet they aren't step-by-step recipes for teaching science. Instead, they are meant to help you understand how effective learning takes place, what experiences are needed for students to learn science, and how to facilitate safe science classrooms. In short, this book offers a way of thinking about science and about learning.

We believe that people—adults as well as children—learn best when they participate actively in their own learning. So as you read this book, you will find questions to ponder and problems to solve. You will be asked to share your thoughts with colleagues or friends. In other words, we want you to read this book actively! There are stories and metaphors, science content, and history to help you make sense of science in the context of active learning. As you read, continually make connections between the information presented and your own science experiences and your classroom. As you begin to teach, revisit relevant sections of the book. Different sections will take on new meaning as you begin to apply the ideas and strategies presented.

Chapter 1 explores the "roots" beneath our science education approach and will help you to develop an understanding about the depth behind our three components to teaching science. Chapter 2, "The Nature of Science," will lead you to clarify your own understanding of what science is and will help you structure your classroom in a way that encourages children to explore science actively. The final chapter in this section will help you understand how your prior beliefs and feelings about science as well as about your own efficacy in science affect how you teach. Let's get started!

1

The Origin of *Launching Learners in Science*

A new approach to learning science can look very promising; it can offer refreshing new ideas and innovative strategies. Yet too often the approach does not really take root in the classroom. Like a plant with no roots, different approaches to teaching and learning science come and go as if they were blown over by gusting winds. Given too little time and support to truly understand the ideas surrounding the approach, teachers often give up on them and go back to something more familiar, or they go on to the next promising approach they are expected to use. Fully embracing and valuing an approach to teaching science requires understanding the theories and research behind it and thinking about your beliefs about teaching science, thus growing some roots!

The approach to teaching science described in this book is not a curriculum but rather a way of thinking about teaching and learning science that can be incorporated into curricula presented by individual schools, districts, or states. It is based on the broader constructivist approach, especially as presented in the *National Science Education Standards* (*NSES*) of the National Research Council (NRC), and it consists of three main components. These components are (1) knowing science, (2) knowing children and how they learn, and (3) knowing flexible structures that facilitate learning and teaching science in an environment where individual learners' and local, state, and district needs are met. Note that in each component the word "knowing" is used rather than "knowledge." What is the difference? Although subtle, the difference is important. For us, "knowing" implies a continued journey within the domain being learned whereas "knowledge" implies an ending. One of the professional development standards cited in the *National Science Education Standards* is "The development of the understanding and ability for lifelong learning" (NRC, 1996, p. 4). Indeed, we hope you continue to learn about science, children learning science, and teaching science throughout your career as an educator.

Each of the three components within this approach is a vital piece of teaching science, and each is grounded in experience, theory, and ongoing research. In other words, each component has a purpose and an origin. You might wonder why someone who teaches science would need to know about the origin of these components. Why not merely give teachers a list of lessons and content to do in their classrooms with directions to follow? If you look back at the components listed above, each of them is very broad and yet personalized to individual teachers. Your understandings of science are different from those of your colleagues. The students that you teach have different understandings of science as well as different levels of maturity. Your schools, school districts, and states each have different requirements for teaching science. Following a list of directions will not allow you to meet the needs of your students, your school, or your self. Truly knowing what you believe about science, children learning science, and teaching science will help you meet all of these individual needs. Take some time to think

Figure 1.1   Growing Roots

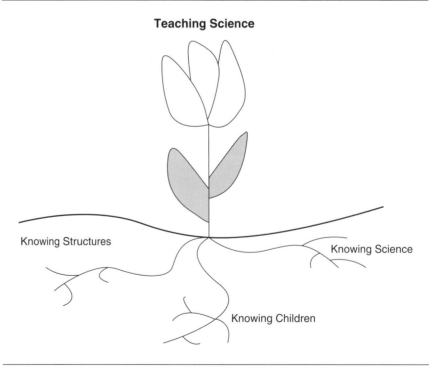

Teaching science requires some "roots" including knowing structures that facilitate learning, knowing children, and knowing science.

about what you believe about teaching and learning science now. Where did *your* beliefs originate? Who or what influenced those beliefs?

The components surrounding this text originated from a great variety of sources and experiences including everything from working in actual science laboratories to reading about maturation according to Piaget to teaching all levels of students. And, although the components are our "roots" keeping us grounded when new ideas come along, they are also always growing, and we are always learning.

Perhaps one of the most influential sources of the three components of this text is the *National Science Education Standards*. These standards provide a great deal of structure and direction with regard to knowing science, knowing children and how they learn science, and knowing flexible structures to teach science effectively. However, they also provide much choice and decision-making responsibility for teachers and students. "The content embodied in the Standards can be organized and presented with many different emphases and perspectives in many different curricula. They bring coordination, consistency, and coherence to the improvement of science education" (NRC, 1996, p. 3). Make sure to look at the outline of the Standards presented at the end of this chapter.

Other important influences include several educational researchers both past and present. John Dewey's writings help us advocate learning as an active process of constructing knowledge (Dewey, 1938). Jean Piaget's research helps us weave child development into thinking and planning for classrooms, and Vygotsky's research helps us think about child development in the context of social learning. More recently, Ron Ritchhart helps us develop thinking routines to empower students in classrooms to actually think rather than just take in information. Rich Stiggins promotes assessment *for* learning rather than *of* learning, helping us to design effective assessment tools.

Our vision of the structures needed to teach science in classrooms comes from newly developed brain research and theorists such as Gardner, Perkins, and others who have helped us realize that intelligence is about more than language and mathematical ability. Our vision comes also from recreating the scientific method, transforming it into more than a step-by-step process, and from actually using routines such as the 5E cycle and plan-do-review (plan-do-review is a routine rather than an approach. It is a thinking routine promoted in Chapter 8) in classrooms. These theories, among many others, provide the origins for our ideas, both theoretical and practical, and you will see these ideas come through as you read each section.

In addition, we have been influenced by our own experiences in laboratories and in classrooms. The stories told throughout this book really happened and will hopefully encourage you to trust and learn from your own experiences. We hope that the stories, theories, and Standards are an origin for many great science experiences to come for you! *Teaching is a thinking profession,* and you must do the thinking about science, children, and structures in order to create meaningful science experiences with your students.

Let's begin with the content area we are addressing: science. What does it mean to know science? Who needs to know science?

■   **KNOWING SCIENCE**

At first glance, you might think knowing science means being able to answer science questions, or maybe you envision someone who does well in science courses. Take some time to think about this component from another angle. *Why* would someone who teaches science need to "know science?" How will knowing science influence how you teach?

My understanding of "knowing science" was influenced a great deal during one experience with my sister. Perhaps her words will help you as well. In the snowy mountains of Colorado on vacation, my family sat in a lodge while taking a break from skiing. We talked about what my sister Jennifer would do after finishing her PhD in biology. We eagerly offered our suggestions—I thought she would be a great biology teacher at a college, my mother suggested applying to a college where she could teach and do research, and my father suggested a small college where there would not be as much pressure to write grants. As the three of us excitedly talked about the possibilities, we suddenly realized that Jennifer's face was crinkled and doubtful. The world stopped for a moment, and everything got quiet. Jennifer said quietly and with conviction, "But . . . I want to *do* science." She did not want to be in the background of science, learning knowledge from others and then dispensing it. She wanted to come up with her own questions and design experiments to answer them. She wanted to wonder and plan and discover. She wanted to actively do science. And that is what she did. Jennifer went on to do a post-doc in a laboratory in Germany, carrying out a great deal of scientific research. I became an elementary teacher who learned a lot of science with my students. Those six words my sister had practically whispered forever changed how I think about teaching. Learners, like scientists, need to *do* science, too.

Knowing science is much more than being able to answer test questions about scientific facts. It is about knowing enough about the science topic to be able to ask good questions, helping children find possible answers through creative experimentation, and giving children opportunities to share what they find. Teachers and learners of science must have a "familiarity with a discipline's concepts, theories, and models; an understanding of how knowledge is generated and justified; and an ability to use these understandings to engage in new inquiry"(Bransford & Donovan, 2005, p. 398). The key words there are *"engage in new inquiry."* Einstein emphasized the importance of imagination as a tool creating opportunities to go beyond observation (Bransford & Donovan, 2005). Knowing science must be novel, creative, and imaginative rather than a set of steps to follow.

The *National Science Education Standards* states, "Teachers must have theoretical and practical knowledge and abilities about science, learning and teaching science" (NRC, 1996, p. 28). This book is designed to help you begin knowing science both as a topic and as a way into inquiry. Instead of dispensing knowledge to students in your classroom, be an active inquirer with them! Wonder aloud with your students! Try out experiments! Be a learner of science!

The component of knowing science surfaces throughout this book in places like Chapter 2, "The Nature of Science," where you will begin to think about science as a noun and a verb; in Chapter 3 where you will begin to look at your own content and concept knowledge within science and how these may influence how you teach science; and in Chapter 9 where you will begin to put your understandings to work as you develop science workshops. Those chapters, however, are the places where the component of knowing science is most obvious. Look for the component "knowing science" throughout the book!

As of right now, begin to think of yourself as a learner or researcher. What questions do you have about teaching science? How will knowing science and what it means to do science change your classroom? How will you become an inquirer about the students you work with?

KNOWING CHILDREN AND HOW THEY LEARN ■

Sometimes we teachers forget what teaching is all about. We come up with fantastic lesson plans and opportunities for learning but neglect our roles as learners of children. We, as educators, must know who our students are as people, who they are developmentally, and who they are scientifically before we can create opportunities for them to learn science. "Actions of teachers are deeply influenced by their understanding of and relationships with students" (NRC, 1996, p. 29).

Photo 1.1   Relationships With Children

Mrs. Farley shares in this student's excitement while observing snails.

In order to create the best opportunities for students to learn science, we must build relationships with them. "Teaching becomes figuring out how to see and listen to each kid, one kid at a time, so that the kid can reach the goals for himself or herself" (Littky, 2004, p. 13). What is the student interested in studying? Does the student reflect best through writing, drawing, or talking about experiences? What experiences have students had with rocks, light, or animals? What kinds of support and messages do they receive at home about learning in general and specifically about science? Did they get breakfast this morning? Of course, there are a million questions, and, with many students in classrooms, knowing students individually may take some time. However, taking time to consciously listen and consciously think about each as an individual as you plan science lessons is invaluable.

Another important piece to know about your students is where they are in their journey of maturation. Indeed, there will be a wide range of levels of development in each grade. However, there will also be large ranges within single classrooms and within different activities. Jean Piaget, an educational psychologist, developed stages of development discussed in Chapter 4. Many times, teachers use the stages as a way of opting out of certain activities. For example, you may hear statements like, "That is not developmentally appropriate for young children" or "That will be too easy for students at this level." We would like to advocate development as another way to *know* students rather than as a deterrent to their learning. Knowing how a student thinks about objects in the world will help provide you with information about what questions to ask, why students might not understand something, and how to proceed so that they can begin to understand. It will also help you guide them as you inquire about science topics.

Students come to science with preconceptions that are important for you to know as well. "Students bring conceptions of everyday phenomena to the classroom that are quite sensible, but scientifically limited or incorrect" (Bransford & Donovan, 2005, p. 399). In a video produced by the Harvard-Smithsonian Center for Astrophysics, 21 of 23 randomly selected Harvard students gave the wrong answer to the question, "What causes the seasons?" (Littky, 2004). Their preconceived, but incorrect, ideas involved the earth being closer to the sun during summer and further from it during winter. Their experiences would seem to support their preconceptions. After all, our experiences support the idea that distance from a heat source affects temperature. The closer we stand to sources of heat, the greater is the heat (Bransford & Donovan, 2005). The important aspect of this example is not that students gave wrong answers but that they had misconceptions. It is important that we as teachers know our students and their ideas about science well enough to help them have experiences that question their incorrect or incomplete ideas and give them opportunities to amend them.

In addition to knowing students individually, it is important to know what you believe about how students learn in general. Just as knowing science influences how you develop lessons in a classroom, so does knowing what it means to learn. There are many beliefs about how people learn. As stated earlier, this book is formed around the principals of constructivism. Constructivism is the belief that learners must construct or develop their own knowledge through experience. Grounded in the work of Piaget, Vygotsky, Bruner, and Dewey, the constructivist model of learning emphasizes active construction of meaning rather than a passive collection of information. Knowledge is not given to the learner, but rather the learner creates meaning through actively experiencing and then thinking about those experiences. "Learning science is something students do, not something that is done to them" (NRC, 1996, p. 20).

You will find more information about knowing students and how they learn in many of the chapters of this book including all of Part II: Construction Ahead: Influences on Learning. In the chapters that make up that section, you will learn more about maturation and its influence on learning science, more about social interaction and the importance of a balance between adult and student control, and more about what it means to learn actively. All of these topics are vital to teaching science well.

If you believe that learning requires individual construction of knowledge fostered through experience and inquiry, the question then becomes what the teacher needs to know about creating structures so that this happens. What is different about teaching within the constructivist paradigm? How might your classroom look if you believe teachers need to be learners and that learning involves the active construction of knowledge?

KNOWING STRUCTURES THAT FACILITATE LEARNING AND TEACHING SCIENCE

In many science classrooms today, routines are often about making sure everyone is on the same page or about remembering the same facts. The *National Science Education Standards* (NRC, 1996) encourage less emphasis on rigidly following curriculum and treating all students alike and more emphasis on selecting and adapting curriculum and understanding and responding to individual student needs.

Changing Emphases

Take some time to think about how and where you learn best. What structures are in place? What did the teacher do to facilitate your needs? Littky (2004) believes that "We learn best when we care about what we are doing, when we have choices. We learn best when the work has meaning to us, when it matters. We learn best when we are using our hands and minds" (p. 28). How does this translate into the classroom?

Many, many structures and environments facilitate learning science. The environment and structures put into place in one science classroom may look very different from those in another, yet both teachers may have the same goals in mind. The point is not to have classrooms that look and sound the same or to have every teacher using the same techniques. The point is to know that the structures you choose *will* influence learning. If you believe that students learn science best by participating physically, how will you structure that in a classroom? In other words, *why* are you using the structures you are using?

The structures presented in this book (see Part III and IV) are based on brain research, constructivist principles of learning, and the individual needs of learners and teachers. They are flexible and allow teachers to be creative and thoughtful. However, they also provide a strong structure for classroom management, assessment, and meeting the needs of all individual learners.

Recently, there has been much research done on brain-based learning, (see Jensen, 2005.) With new technologies available, many researchers have been able actually to see connections being made and changes happening in the brain at different stages of maturity. Brain research is in its

Table 1.1   Changing Emphasis

Less Emphasis On	More Emphasis On
Treating all students alike and responding to the group as a whole	Understanding and responding to individual student's interests, strengths, experiences, and needs
Rigidly following curriculum	Selecting and adapting curriculum
Focusing on student acquisition of information	Focusing on student understanding and use of scientific knowledge, ideas, and inquiry processes
Presenting scientific knowledge through lecture, text, and demonstration	Guiding students in active and extended scientific inquiry
Asking for recitation of acquired knowledge	Providing opportunities for scientific discussion and debate among students
Testing students for factual information at the end of the unit or chapter	Continuously assessing student understanding
Maintaining responsibility and authority	Sharing responsibility for learning with students
Supporting competition	Supporting a classroom community with cooperation, shared responsibility, and respect
Working alone	Working with other teachers to enhance the science program

SOURCE: *National Science Education Standards*, by the National Research Council, 1996, Washington, DC: National Academy Press, p. 52. Reprinted courtesy of the National Science Foundation.

early stages, but theorists believe that one way to implement brain friendly strategies is to have an environment in which students feel good. Lighting, atmosphere, and surroundings should convey messages of safety and commitment to learning. Students should be immersed in complex experiences with a lot of stimuli. Students should actively analyze their experiences and use their knowledge out in the world. And, above all, students should be able to review and repeat experiences (Franklin, 2005).

The work in the field of brain-based learning connects nicely to the principles of constructivism. "Using knowledge in the world" and "reviewing and repeating experiences" allows for much knowledge to be constructed, and the atmosphere and safe places to learn provide opportunities for all students to construct that knowledge. Many teachers I have spoken to talk about constructivism as a method. They talk about hands-on materials and their students actively participating. When it comes right down to it, constructivism is not a method. It is a way of thinking about learning. Constructivist classrooms look very different at times. Reading a book or answering (some) worksheet questions can be helping students to construct knowledge. What is the difference between reading a book or answering worksheet questions constructively and non-constructively?

Photo 1.2   Experiencing Magnetism

Students construct knowledge about magnets.

In some sense, the activity itself does not make something constructivist or not. However, the order of events does matter within constructivist learning structures. Why might this be the case? Note the difference between a lesson in which the teacher gives the students a set of wires, a battery, and some lightbulbs and teaches them how to put these together to light the bulb versus a lesson in which the teacher gives the students a set of wires, a battery, and some lightbulbs and asks them how many different ways there are to get the bulb to light. The activity is the same, the materials are the same, but the order is different. How? In the first lesson, the students are given the procedure and then asked to repeat it. In the second lesson, students are asked to experience the physical and mindful manipulation before they are asked to understand it.

Providing structures for learning that create opportunities for children to construct knowledge helps and, in a sense requires, individualization of learning. Students who have had more experiences with electricity, for example, will be able to work creatively on more than one way to light the bulb while students who have never had experiences with electricity will be able to learn the more basic concepts. Both of these students are doing the same lesson at the same time, and their needs are being met.

The specific structures within this book include key science experiences (Chapter 7), thinking routines (Chapter 8), and workshops (Chapter 9). The key experiences were developed as a way to help you create lessons that promote the processes of science as well as to help you assess students' strengths and needs in science. Thinking routines (Ritchhart, 2002) help students become aware of the thinking they are doing and allow them to gain thinking dispositions such as the sensitivity to know when there is a problem, the ability to know and do science, and the inclination to keep learning (Williams, 2004). Finally, workshops were developed to help you create science opportunities that revolve around specific science content, that promote effective classroom management, and that emphasize individual differences. In addition, there are also structures in Part IV that will help you develop both assessment opportunities and a physical setting that promotes learning.

Throughout this chapter, we have talked about roots and origins, flexible structures, and constructing knowledge. Now we need to address the other structures in place that teachers deal with daily. Those structures are the ones created through district, state, and national standards. Perhaps this discussion is key to understanding the entire book! We have created this book to give you a way "in to" teaching science. Just like a swimmer, a teacher needs a place to dive in; this book is that place. After reading the book, you must make this approach to teaching science your own based on your beliefs about knowing science, knowing students, knowing structures that promote learning, and combining those beliefs with your district, state, and national standards. Chapter 12 will help you sift through all of these ideas and begin to create a place where all students can learn science with you!

Before "jumping in," reflect on the ideas presented so far. Think of the *National Science Education Standards,* the theories and visions of the researchers who influenced the pieces of this book, and add to this what you believe about learning. Try to construct a picture in your mind of what a science classroom developed around these ideas looks like, sounds like, and feels like. What components of the approach do you already use? Which ones seem to stand out as particularly valuable for elementary science? What other questions do you need to have answered before you continue reading?

■ OUTLINE OF THE NSES SCIENCE CONTENT STANDARDS

I. Unifying Concepts and Processes

U1 *Systems, Order, and Organization*

1. Goal is to think and analyze in terms of systems

2. Types and levels of organization provide useful ways of thinking about the world

U2 *Evidence, Models, and Explanation*

1. Evidence consists of observations and data on which to base scientific explanations

2. Models are tentative schemes corresponding to real objects, events, or classes of events that have explanatory power

3. Scientific explanation incorporates scientific knowledge and new evidence (from observations, experiments, or models) into internally consistent, logical statements

U3 *Constancy, Change, and Measurement*

1. Most things change but some are constant (e.g., "c," charge on electron, etc.)

2. Energy can be transferred

3. Changes can be quantified; different systems of measurement

4. "Scale includes understanding that characteristics, properties, or relationships within a system might change as its dimensions are increased or decreased"

5. Rate: comparing one quantity with another or change of one quantity with the whole

U4 *Evolution and Equilibrium*

1. Evolution is series of changes accounting for present form, function, or characteristics

2. Equilibrium is state in which forces and changes occur in opposite and off-setting directions

U5 *Form and Function*

1. Form and function are complementary aspects of objects, organisms, and systems in the natural and designed world

IIA. Science as Inquiry

A1 *Abilities to Do Science*

1. Asking questions about objects, organisms, and events in environment

2. Plan and conduct a simple investigation

3. Employ simple equipment and tools to gather data and extend senses

4. Use data to construct a reasonable explanation

5. Communicate investigations and explanations

A2 *Understandings About Scientific Inquiry*

1. Review and ask question about results of other scientists' work

IIIB. Physical Science Content Standards

B1 *Properties of Objects and Materials*

1. Objects have many observable properties—size, weight, color, shape, etc.

2. Objects are made of one or more materials that have properties

3. Materials can exist in different states—gas, liquid, solid

B2 *Position and Motion of Objects*

1. Locate objects relative to others or the background
2. Motion can be described by tracing position over time
3. Position and motion changed by push and pull
4. Sound produced by vibration

B3 *Light, Heat, Electricity, and Magnetism*

1. Light travels in straight lines; reflection, refraction, absorption
2. Heat produced in many ways; transferred by conduction
3. Electricity in circuits produces light, heat, sound, magnetism
4. Magnets attract and repel each other and certain materials

IIIC. Life Science Standards

C1 *Characteristics of Organisms*

1. Basic needs
2. Different structures for growth, survival, and reproduction
3. Behavior influenced by internal and external cues

C2 *Life Cycles of Organisms*

1. Organisms have different life cycles
2. Plants and animals resemble their parents
3. Characteristics are inherited and others are the result of interactions with some environment

C3 *Organisms and Their Environments*

1. All animals depend on plants
2. Organisms depend on biotic and abiotic factors; when these change, organisms change
3. All organisms change their environment
4. Humans depend on their environment

IVD. Earth and Space Science

D1 *Properties of Earth Materials*

1. Materials are solid rocks and soils, water, and gases of the atmosphere
2. Soil properties such as color, texture, water retention, etc.
3. Fossils provide evidence for life and environments of long ago

D2 *Objects in the Sky*

1. Sun, moon, stars, clouds, birds, airplanes

2. Sun provides light and heat to maintain temperature of earth

D3 *Changes in Earth and Sky*

1. Surface of earth changes—slow and fast (e.g., erosion and landslides)

2. Weather changes daily and over seasons

3. Objects in sky have patterns of movement

VE. Science and Technology

E1 *Abilities of Technological Design*

1. Identify a simple problem

2. Propose a solution

3. Implement proposed solutions

4. Evaluate a product or design

5. Communicate a problem, design, and solution

E2 *Understanding About Science and Technology*

1. Understanding the basis of and need for the above "abilities"

2. Ability to distinguish between natural objects and objects made by humans

VIF. Science in Personal and Social Perspective

F1 *Personal Health*

1. Safety and security are basic needs of humans

2. We have some responsibility for our own health

3. Nutrition is essential to health

4. Different substances can damage the body and its functions

F2 *Characteristics and Changes in Populations*

1. Human populations include groups living in a particular location

2. Population sizes can increase or decrease

F3 *Types of Resources*

1. We get resources from biotic and abiotic sources

2. Resources can be natural, man-made, or non-material (peace, quiet, safety, etc.)

3. Resources can be limited

F4 *Changes in Environments*

1. Environments are space, conditions, and factors affecting survival

2. Changes can be natural or induced by humans (But if all organisms change their environments, then is it not "natural" for humans to change theirs?)

3. Environments change at different rates

F5 *Science and Technology in Local Challenges*

1. Continuously inventing new ways of doing things, solving problems, and doing work

2. Science and technology have greatly improved food quality and quantity

VIIG. History and Nature of Science

G1 *Science as a Human Endeavor*

1. Science has been practiced for a long time

2. Men and women have made contributions throughout history

3. While much has been learned, much remains to be learned

4. People choose science as career

Conversation Starters

-   How are the National Science Education Standards connected to knowing science, knowing children and how they learn, and knowing flexible structures that facilitate learning and teaching science in an environment where individual learners' and local, state, and district needs are met? Create a web showing the connections.

-   Where do your beliefs about teaching science come from? Make a timeline of important events leading to these beliefs.

-   What does it mean to know science? What does someone know who is scientifically literate?

-   Write a definition of learning.

-   List all of the structures that might influence learning science in a classroom.

-   Take a science lesson and change the order so that it allows students to construct their own knowledge. Take a lesson that does this and change the order so that students are merely receiving information.

-   What is your definition of a standard? Share it with two other people who defined a standard. What were the differences? Similarities? Why is it important to know what a standard is?

2

The Nature of Science

O n a bright, somewhat breezy spring afternoon, my wife and I (GV) were taking a walk in the park and enjoying the beauty of the day. Several of our neighbors had brought their children to the park to enjoy the outdoors after being shut in, first by the winter weather and then by the wind and rain—our annual spring "monsoons," as we call them.

Leaning against the monkey bars in the playground area, we stopped and surveyed the scene. A short distance away, near where the sidewalk met the brief lawn that separated it from the sand on the playground, a young child was walking, staring at the ground. The youngster may have been four or five years old—a preschooler or kindergartner who was obviously intrigued by something on the ground. At first, I couldn't make out what it was. I did not see any toys or flowers that might capture her attention. She crouched as only the young can, bending at the knees and bouncing a little bit. On closer inspection, I saw a little black dot moving in the sand toward a mound of dirt that looked like miniature peas. Obviously, an ant had been found. As the child watched the ant, I could sense the fascination that comes when one observes worker ants going about their jobs. The child picked up a tiny stick and put it in front of the ant. The dot simply went right up and over the impediment as if the twig, hardly the size of a leaf stem, wasn't there. Our little investigator then found a slightly larger twig, the size of a pencil or one of those large pens with a rubber grip, and put that in front of the ant. About this time, someone called the child's name; she looked up and then trotted off, ending the session with the ant.

At the other end of the playground were the swings. Feeling that one is never too old to swing, my wife and I worked our way over to them to enjoy a brief return to our own childhood. Two elementary-aged children were already on the swings and were pumping their way to that height at which there is enough thrill balanced by a feeling of security. A younger child—maybe kindergarten age—was seated on the third swing. This child was in the somewhat awkward transition between needing to be pushed and being able to pump. Although he was trying to get the swing moving, it wasn't gaining the typical pendulum-like movement. Stopping, the child watched the two older children intently. After a minute or so, he moved his feet forward and leaned backward, then put his head forward and legs back. Making that transition was a bit awkward, but, after several trials, his motions became a little smoother. The swing gained momentum, sending the child higher and higher.

Photo 2.1   Child Swinging

Wyatt works to pump his legs on the swings in the park.

Both of these children were engaged in science—an investigation of their physical world. The first child was observing the world and, apparently, pursuing answers to questions such as what effect a barrier would have on the movement of an ant. Placing the tiny stick in the path of the ant was the child's first experiment. After seeing the results, the child tried a second experiment, seemingly to find out if the ant would respond differently to a larger barrier. Now I do not know whether these suppositions of mine are true, but they seem consistent with the observations. In fact, as I think about it, I wasn't as good a scientist that day as the child; I did not try to test my hypothesis by asking the child any questions or finding out what she was thinking. I made observations and reached conclusions, but I did nothing to verify those conclusions. The second child may not have been trying to learn facts, but he was using and learning some scientific methods—observing, experimenting (e.g., trying various pumping techniques), assessing, modifying, and trying the technique again.

Both of these examples illustrate that children learn the *process* of science—science as a verb—much earlier than they master science as a *body of knowledge.* In fact, in some ways, learning science as a body of facts may be an inaccurate concept, since our everyday understanding of "fact" is different from what it is understood to be in science. In this chapter, we will consider the nature of science, its place in elementary education, and how it affects the elementary teacher.

WHAT IS THE NATURE OF SCIENCE?   ■

The term *nature of science* has multiple meanings and raises multiple questions. We have referred to science as both a body of knowledge and a process. As a set of facts and "a way of knowing," what distinguishes science from language arts, history, mathematics, and so on? Are these distinguishing characteristics important for you as a person and as a teacher? Are they important for your students and others in our society? Have these distinctions become more important now than they were in the past? Why all this emphasis on the nature of science in science education reform movements?

The nature of science also encompasses the process of science, that is, science as a verb. How one gathers information and understanding about the physical world is a part of the nature of science. Is there a "scientific method"? What are the steps in the process of doing science? Are all steps found in all science investigations?

For educators, the nature of science also includes its role in education in general and in elementary education in particular. There are important questions to ask regarding this role. Why should we even teach science to elementary school children? Is it more important to teach science facts or a science process? Can one really afford to spend time teaching science when society and administrators are placing so much more emphasis on reading, writing, and arithmetic? Is science important for students or only for science educators?

We will discuss the nature of science from these perspectives in the remainder of this chapter. Before we do that, you may want to look again at the questions above, ponder them, and give your own answers. If you have been educated in the American school system, you probably learned answers to these questions the same way I did. Your perspectives are probably very similar to those of your classmates or the mothers and fathers of your students. Many of us may not have given these questions a lot of thought. You may want to begin by describing what science is to you. How did you learn science? What are the characteristics of scientists?

As we consider the nature of science from the perspectives mentioned above, keep in mind that its true nature is a blend of these and several other views. Indeed, if you consider the nature of science as described by the National Science Teachers Association, by the National Research Council (NRC) in *National Science Education Standards* (*NSES*), in various textbooks, and so on, you will see that each presents a unique view in which all the various characteristics of science are discussed together. Nevertheless, there is value in considering each aspect independently.

■ SCIENCE AS A BODY OF KNOWLEDGE

Science may be considered a description of the physical world and how it works—how the different parts of that world interact with one another. This description consists of facts, hypotheses, and theories. A scientific *fact* is an observation that is agreed upon by many people. Note two components of this definition. It is an observation—meaning it consists of data collected from sensory (e.g., visual, auditory, tactile) input—and many agree on that observation.

A *hypothesis* is an interpretation of the observations, of the facts. The hypothesis reflects how the world works and is only as valid as its reflection and explanation of the world. A hypothesis is always tentative, subject to revision and reconsideration. This implies that hypotheses are always being tested by comparing them to the world as we see and experience it. It is this constant testing of scientific hypotheses that distinguishes knowledge in the scientific world from knowledge in other disciplines, such as language arts. An operatic aria, a Broadway musical song, and a painting in an art museum are not hypotheses constantly being compared to reality to see if they are "correct." On the other hand, that a book falls when released from an outstretched hand, that genes pass information from one generation of organisms to the next, that the orbits of the earth and moon determine solar eclipses are all hypotheses constantly being tested.

Because science describes the world for us at a unique time in history and in the unique culture in which we live, that description is always open to modification. Indeed, some explanations that we know are incorrect still serve as descriptions. For example, we say that the sun "rises" in the east and "sets" in the west. This appears obvious to us and served as an explanation of the phenomenon of morning and night for many of our ancestors. However, most of us realize that, in reality, the earth is turning on its axis of rotation and that we "see" the sun rise in the east because the earth is turning in that direction. This hypothesis is a better explanation of events that we can measure and see; it supplants the old explanation and gives us a better description. However, I still tell myself that the sun rises in the east and sets in the west, especially when I'm using the sun to determine directions!

One of the reasons that one explanation replaces another in science is the new explanation's ability to explain some event more accurately or predict some observation. The future event or observation is something that one can see, measure, calculate, and so on. It must be consistent with other observations and hypotheses. In fact, many science discoveries arise from the need for consistency in explanations. For example, helium was "discovered" in the sun before it was discovered on earth; the existence of an unknown element was postulated to account for observations of some of the properties of sunlight.

Another feature of science arising from its being a description of nature is that competing explanations arise and can be held simultaneously. More than one hypothesis may be consistent with the known data, and there may be no compelling reason to choose one explanation over another. Competing explanations exist in our everyday life. For example, the success of an outstanding sports team—one that seems to stand out above its competitors—can be attributed to better athletes on the team, better coaching, an easier game schedule, and so on. We do not normally think of competing ideas—hypotheses—as occurring in science, but they do. At scientific meetings, research leaders with opposing views often heatedly argue their interpretations—their hypotheses. Although they share certain perceptions and agree on certain observations, they disagree on what those perceptions and observations mean. However, each viewpoint contributes to our knowledge and provides a framework for understanding our world.

Well, how does this discussion of science as a body of knowledge fit into our discussion of elementary-level science? Most school systems have a prescribed science curriculum, which indicates, of course, expectations for science experiences and the types of knowledge students are expected to have. Many states have adopted a set of science education standards that teachers and administrators in that state have adapted from the *National Science Education Standards* (*NSES*). One part of these standards is a description of the types of factual knowledge expected of students. These expectations tend to be phrased in rather general terms that allow teachers and students considerable latitude in teaching and learning. As an example, there are three content areas in the *NSES*. Below is an example of one piece of information from each of these areas that students are expected to understand:

- "Properties of objects and materials: Objects have many observable properties, including size, weight, shape, color, temperature, and the ability to react with other substances." [A K–4 Physical Science Standard, NRC, 1996, p. 127]
- "Organisms and their environment: All animals depend on plants. Some animals eat plants for food. Other animals eat animals that eat plants." [A K–4 Life Science Standard, NRC, 1996, p. 129]
- "Objects in the sky: The sun, moon, stars, clouds, birds, and airplanes all have properties, locations, and movements that can be observed and described." [A K–4 Earth and Space Science Standard, NRC, 1996, p. 134]

While these standards indicate both the content and concept areas and the general type of information children are expected to know, much is left up to the teacher and students as to *how* the information will be learned. What is learned and the ease with which learning occurs depend on each child's developmental stage and the social support and nature of the adult-child interactions in the classroom. The progression in science understanding tends to be from observation and description to more generalized but supported explanations for those observations. Young children in the preoperational stage of development generally focus on observing and describing what they see. Their "facts" may be an assembly of observations with few, if any, hypotheses or explanations. As children gain experience and develop cognitively, hypotheses will become incorporated into the body of knowledge they are gaining, and they will gradually see how these hypotheses are formed into theories and how theories are used to describe the world. See Chapter 4 for a discussion of growth and development as it affects children's learning in general and the learning of science concepts in particular.

■ SCIENCE AS PROCESS

Science is more than an accumulation of descriptions and explanations. It is also a process for arriving at those explanations and descriptions. Many of us were taught the "scientific method" in school; however, there really is no single method employed by all scientists. Most scientific studies do have certain features in common, but how these features were attained, the order in which experiments are done, and so on are generally characteristic of a particular investigator or laboratory. Two reasons that a uniform process—a scientific method—may seem to exist are, first, the work of Sir Francis Bacon and, second, the convention whereby results are communicated to other scientists and to the outside world. Scientific papers have a general format: Introduction (including observations and hypothesis), Materials and Methods (the experiment), and Results and Discussion/ Conclusion (often with predictions). This format has been used so widely and appears to be so logical that it has often been interpreted as "the method."

Elements of the Scientific Process

Let's look at some of the common features of scientific experimentation, beginning with *observation*. When we observe, we see or encounter some aspect of the physical world. This is our initial contact with the physical world; this is how we know the world is there. We receive the information through our senses, both those we can readily identify and are aware of and those that are automatic, often neglected by our conscious selves. We are usually aware of what we see, hear, smell, touch, and taste. But are we aware of the proprioceptors in our body that sense carbon dioxide levels, pH, glucose levels, and so on? Of course, we often become acutely aware of these sensors when something goes wrong, when we are ill or injured, or when the environment changes dramatically. We may also be more aware of our senses in general when we encounter a person unable to utilize them, that is, when someone has a disability in one of the senses.

Although we like to think of our observations as being unbiased, most of us realize that, however objective we try to be, our observations will nevertheless always be biased. We pay particular attention to certain parts of the environment that we have been conditioned or trained to pay attention to, and we interpret what we see based partly on what we expect to see.

Our observations, therefore, are influenced by our training, our culture, our education. Again, we're familiar with these cognitive "facts." You may already be familiar with what are called optical illusions. What accounts for the illusion, of course, is not our eyeball or sensory apparatus or the physical structure of the optical system but rather our interpretive system, the brain's attempt to make sense of what we see based on our past experiences. We generalize certain properties of physical perspective and reach faulty conclusions.

Following the observations comes a period of *asking questions* and *looking for patterns and relationships*. Each of these tasks can be an art. Many a scientist has said that the real problem is to know what question to ask! Good questions take into account many possibilities and are answerable. What causes the sky to appear blue? What accounts for the phases of the

Photo 2.2   Science Terms

Science words on the wall in a classroom.

moon? What is it about being a female cat that increases the likelihood of being calico? Often we pose questions that appear to be beyond the realm of science; they are, nevertheless, often considered when science is discussed. Many *why* questions, for example, are questions science can't really answer—why does quantum mechanics describe the world of small objects and subatomic particles better than Newtonian mechanics? Why are there three stop codons in the biological genetic code instead of two or four? For many such questions, there is no "test" that can be made or proposed. Quantum mechanics does describe the world better, but we do not really know why the world is like that. Trying to find answers to these questions is more the realm of philosophy than science. Scientific questions should be answerable by investigating the physical world rather than the metaphysical one.

Asking questions often leads to *formulating hypotheses,* in other words, to ideas about the answers to those questions. To account for our observation or to explain a phenomenon, we propose an answer, a hypothesis. In science, the hypothesis must be able to be examined in the physical world. By comparing our explanation to the world as it is or to the world after we manipulate it (i.e., after we perform an experiment), we should obtain information that is either consistent with or contradictory to the hypothesis. Scientific hypotheses can never really be "proven," only shown to be false (Karl Popper). Since a hypothesis is an explanation of the real world, we may find better, more complete explanations later to replace our present one.

An explanation that accounts for many different hypotheses and also makes predictions is often called a *theory.* Similar to a hypothesis, a theory offers predictions, is (or has been) tested empirically, and can be falsified. However, a theory is much broader than a hypothesis, explaining more types of phenomena. Since many hypotheses are explained by one theory, a viable theory has been tested many, many times—more than any single hypothesis that it attempts to explain. Yet, as in all of science, any conclusions reached remain tentative. The theory must explain observations in the real world and must make predictions about what is observed in the real world.

Formulating a hypothesis often suggests *tests for the hypothesis*. A scientific hypothesis—or potential explanation—should make some kind of prediction, which must be tested. The testing of a hypothesis is one of the hallmarks of science, and the test must match reality if the hypothesis is to be believed. However, we have to understand what is meant when we talk about testing a hypothesis, for tests can be of many different types.

Most people think that the test for a scientific hypothesis is always an experiment—a deliberate manipulation of the physical world that opens the possibility of proving a particular prediction to be false. For example, we have a hypothesis that the genetic material of an organism is a nucleic acid. If we find a new organism, we test this hypothesis by determining its genetic material. If the genetic material is DNA or RNA, it is consistent with our hypothesis; if it is protein, then it is inconsistent, and we either have to discard the hypothesis regarding the nature of genetic material or modify it. The test, however, is based on our manipulation of the environment and the organism involved.

However, not all tests are experiments that demand manipulation of the physical environment. Some tests are predictions of what should be observed in the real world if the hypothesis is correct. For example, one of the predictions of Einstein's theory of gravity, special relativity, is that light should be bent by gravity. In fact, the theory predicts that there should be *black holes*, objects in space that are so massive, have so much gravity, that light becomes trapped and cannot escape. When one looks in the real world for evidence of black holes (predicted by special relativity), one does see light bending as it passes by a large celestial body.

Also, large, dark, massive bodies (consistent with ideas concerning black holes) have been detected in a number of galaxies. Special efforts are made to observe the light and to detect the location of its source, and measurements of the mass of black holes are made by calculating the orbital speed of stars and gases around them. In neither of these cases is nature being manipulated the way it normally would be during an experiment; the observations remain, however, a test of the hypothesis!

The important part of this aspect of the scientific process is that the predictions arising from the hypothesis are being tested; they are being compared with what occurs in the world. If the prediction corresponds to what is observed, the hypothesis is tentatively accepted. The larger the number of predictions upheld, the stronger the evidence that the hypothesis is correct. *All* predictions that can reasonably be checked should be—even those that seem readily apparent or obvious. What *should* be true because it is apparent nevertheless needs to be tested. After all, it's obvious that the sun rises in the east!

After doing an experiment or making an observation, we *compare what we observe with what we predicted*. If the observation is very similar to our prediction, we conclude that the results of the test are consistent with the hypothesis. Notice the relative terms in the previous sentence. What, precisely, is "very similar"? How similar should the observations be to the circumstances predicted by the hypothesis for us to conclude that they are "consistent" with the hypothesis? People must answer these questions for themselves; however, most scientists will tell you what they consider "very similar." In most instances, they want to be right (i.e., have their observations match their predictions) at least 95% of the time; in other words, they are willing to be wrong less than 5% of the time. Some scientists set stricter limits and are willing to be wrong less than 1% of the time, for example. Determination of these risks is the realm of statistics and statisticians. Being aware of the risks and openly stating them reinforces the tentative nature of the conclusions that are reached in science.

Often, the degree of certainty about a hypothesis that is required or considered necessary is dependent on the consequences; if the consequences of being wrong are very serious, then one wants to be more certain. This concept is illustrated in our daily lives. We may be willing to go outside without an umbrella if there is a 50% chance of rain, but are we willing to forgo medical tests if there is a 50% chance we have cancer? The consequences of being "wrong" are very different in these cases; in the first, we may get wet, but, in the second, we may die. We may be willing to walk across a 4″ × 4″ beam on the floor for pocket change but be unwilling to walk across the beam for $1 million and risk our life if it is suspended between the twenty-fifth floor of two buildings. Differences in consequences really do influence the risks we are willing to take.

Whatever we conclude about our observations and predictions, we must always look for alternative explanations. Our hypothesis may explain the real world and be consistent with what we and others have observed in other circumstances, but it may not necessarily be the only explanation. You may be familiar with the story about a person investigating the causes of drunkenness. The individual went to a bar and noted that people drinking beer from a glass got drunk, that those drinking wine from a glass got drunk, and that those drinking whiskey from a glass got drunk. The individual concluded that since all those who got drunk drank from glasses, the glass must be what made them drunk! Now we all see the fallacy in this case, but, many times, it is difficult to see alternative explanations in our own experiments. The story illustrates the necessity for scientific controls, for holding as many elements as possible constant so that we do not fool ourselves. It also illustrates the necessity for testing the hypothesis. After all, we like our explanation; that is why we proposed it. We must rule out as many explanations as possible, realizing that there may be an explanation—perhaps the real one—that we simply have not thought about or ruled out. Examining only a few variables in our experiments, ideally one at a time, helps eliminate alternative explanations.

One more element of the scientific process is mandatory. We must *communicate our studies*—our hypotheses, tests of the hypotheses, and conclusions. We do this first with those with whom we work. Science is a collegial enterprise, contrary to what many people think; we discuss our ideas with our colleagues and check one another's explanations. When we are satisfied with our explanations and the tests we have devised for them, we communicate both our hypotheses and our tests to others in the field so that they may also examine them. We can communicate our work in written form, in a publication, or we can communicate orally through a presentation such as a symposium lecture or through a combination of oral, visual, and written communication known as a poster presentation.

A poster presentation involves a succinct written description of the hypothesis and the testing of it, which is put on display at a meeting. The author is available at specific times to answer questions from and discuss the issues with meeting participants who have examined the work. Many times, the work presented in poster presentations is work in progress and somewhat incomplete, for example, work in which some experiments are being done but the results are not yet known. Regardless of the communication method chosen, two criteria are extremely important: The explanation presented must explain the phenomenon, and it must be consistent with other factors known to be "true."

A Historical Example

To help you see how the elements of scientific investigation discussed in the text are applied in real life, we present here a short story about a very interesting early nineteenth-century physician. As you read, try to identify these elements: making observations, dealing with bias, searching for patterns and relationships, formulating a question, making a hypothesis, testing the hypothesis, comparing the results of the test to the prediction, and communicating the results.

Physician John Snow (1813–1858) made major contributions in both anesthesiology and epidemiology. He was among the first in England to use ether and chloroform as anesthetics for operations and childbirth. However, here we want to examine his contributions to epidemiology—the study of the causes and control of epidemics. Snow's name is forever linked to the study of cholera in mid-nineteenth-century London. Cholera can be a very virulent disease. It has a short incubation period, from less than 1 day to 4 or 5 days. Someone with cholera generally develops a painless, copious diarrhea that can rapidly dehydrate the person. Often the initial stages are also accompanied by nausea and vomiting. Unless immediate steps are taken to rehydrate the person, death can occur rapidly—even within a day. Cholera is caused by a bacterium, *Vibrio cholerae.* During Snow's day, however, the existence of bacteria was not really known. Although Anton van Leeuwenhoek and others had observed microscopic organisms called "animalcules," including bacteria, in the 1600s, the role of these organisms in disease was unclear. Only in the 1880s would the role of microorganisms in disease be accepted through the efforts of Louis Pasteur and Sir Robert Koch. So, in the 1830s–1850s, the cause of cholera was unknown. The most widely accepted theory was that it was caused by an effluvium—contaminated vapors and odors coming from sewers, decaying material, and those afflicted with the disease.

Snow did not believe that cholera was transmitted through an effluvium. Several features of the disease suggested that it was transmitted through contact with material from those having the disease. For example, doctors and nurses who attended cholera victims did not necessarily contract the disease despite their being in a room where effluvia should be prevalent. On the other hand, people at a distance (that is, not exposed to an effluvium) could get cholera if they came into contact with materials from a victim. One of the cases cited by Snow in his 1855 paper "On the Mode of Communication of Cholera" illustrates the point. A family living six miles northwest of York contracted cholera without apparent contact with anyone known to have the disease. The first person to contract the disease in that area seemed to be the source for other cases in that area. But how did that first person come down with the disease? It was discovered that this individual's sister lived in London and had died from cholera; those attending her estate had sent her clothes (without washing them) to her sole living relative, who contracted cholera within 24 hours. The contaminated clothing seemed to be the route of transmission.

From histories similar to those cited above, John Snow concluded that people somehow ingested the agent that caused cholera and that death was associated with dehydration. He noted, for example, that people who had collapsed from the disease were able to sit up and seemed to be well (for a period of time) if they had a saline solution injected into their veins. Snow concentrated on the mode of transmission, favoring ingestion through contaminated water.

In 1854, cholera broke out in London in a district fairly close to where Dr. Snow lived, giving him an opportunity to test his hypothesis. This outbreak was especially virulent, causing the death of over 500 people within 10 days in a single neighborhood. When the incidence of cholera began to increase in the neighborhood, Snow studied the times and locations of the deaths. He noticed that the outbreak seemed to start on a particular day; the onset of fatal attacks went from 4 on one day to 47 the next. Snow then examined the victims' addresses. He plotted the deaths on a map of the neighborhood and noted that they clustered around the Broad Street pump. At that time, people in London got their drinking water from public pumps that served certain geographical regions. Each pump got water either from its own well or from the Thames River via underground pipes. The area served by the Broad Street pump seemed to be the major affected area. Snow's pictorial representation of the distribution of deaths was an extremely effective tool for analysis.

Snow went to the local regulatory board and convinced the members to remove the pump handle from the Broad Street pump. The number of deaths quickly subsided. However, when all the data were collected, it was apparent that the deaths were already declining and that removal of the pump handle probably had little effect on the course of the epidemic.

Snow continued to pursue his hypothesis that water was the main route by which cholera spread. In a subsequent epidemic, Snow showed that the locality of deaths correlated very highly with the water source for that area. He also showed that apparent exceptions to this really were not exceptions and that individuals dying in other areas probably had drunk water from the affected area. However, there was strong societal resistance to Snow's reasoning. The public health board did not believe that transmission of cholera had anything to do with the water supply. Only years later would this mode of disease transmission be recognized.

SCIENCE AS PROCESS IN ELEMENTARY SCHOOL

Elementary students need to encounter and experience science "as a verb" (i.e., as a process) in the classroom. Although science as process has been stressed in a number of recent science education reform movements, it is

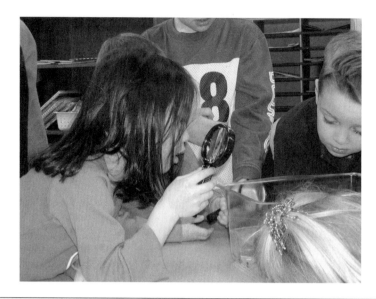

Photo 2.3   Girl Looking With Magnifying Glass

This student is observing using a tool—a magnifying glass.

often neglected in the curriculum from elementary school through college. Science as process is discussed in several places in the *NSES:* It appears in the Content Standards as "science as inquiry" (Chapter 6), in the Assessment Standards that stress analyzing children's achievements (including inquiry) and doing so in an authentic way (Chapter 5 and pp. 39–41), and in the Science Teaching Standards (Chapter 3). The message in all these sections is that, yes, science as a process should be taught in the elementary grades.

What can you expect to see from your students when they engage in the process of science? One of the first things students do is observe. They can be very good observers, using all their senses, from the earliest grades through the remainder of their lives. Observation is a skill that can be developed with practice, and students should practice it frequently. It is important that their observations be labeled as science for reasons discussed later in this chapter. As children make observations, they should also make representations of them in some form—written descriptions, drawings, photographs (from any type of camera, including digital), or other, more novel representations.

A second skill that children can develop from the very earliest years is to ask questions. In fact, asking questions is something young children do naturally. The questions they ask often reflect their curiosity about their physical world: Why is the sky blue? Why do birds sing? Why do robins have red breasts? What is lightning? Why does oil float? And so on and so on. Children's ability to observe and to ask questions should receive frequent reinforcement, even though, early on, they may have difficulty focusing on a question and pursuing it towards answers. As their other skills develop, we can encourage them to experiment and try to answer their own questions. As children gradually become more adept at reasoning, they will move from explanations such as "It's magic" to ones involving complex cause and effect reasoning. This is a major step for the maturing intellect; having logical reasons for thinking in a specific way is a hallmark of scientific growth. We will have more to say about the development of children's thinking in Chapter 4 and 5.

REVIEWING THE NATURE OF SCIENCE IN ELEMENTARY EDUCATION

Students engaged in science activities in the elementary classroom learn that science is both a verb and a noun, that it is both process and supported hypothesis. By incorporating science into their lives during this critical developmental period, students will construct their own schemata, which will include their direct participation in science. Science will be a part of their everyday experience rather than something external.

Many students preparing to be elementary school teachers report few memories of science from their own elementary years. Often, their earliest science memories are from middle school. The lack of memories from elementary school may reflect a scarcity of activities identified as science, the presence of stronger or more recent memories of science, or some other underlying factor. We suspect that students' perception of themselves as *not* being "scientists" may indicate that they were not encouraged to view themselves as such when they were younger. If they really were not introduced to science until grade 5 or later, then they may have already constructed their own self-image, one that did not include them doing "science."

Students often begin to play musical instruments quite early; they use drums and other simple pieces even in preschool. Even though most do not plan to become professional musicians, they learn the basics of playing an instrument. Yet we often fail to give these same students an opportunity to experience the basics of *doing* science. As a result, students believe that unless they are going to be professional scientists there is no reason to really learn the subject.

Dr. Douglas Duncan, an astronomer at the University of Chicago, teaches an introductory general education class in astronomy primarily to arts and sciences majors. Dr. Duncan has polled students on their views of science and scientists and on the reasons these very able students have not pursued a science as a major. According to the surveys, the most common reason for not being attracted to a science major was students' desire to do something creative; in their view, science was not an outlet for creativity! Apparently, these students felt they would be unable to express their individuality and uniqueness in a scientific setting. This finding surprised Dr. Duncan and would likely surprise the vast majority of our scientific colleagues. We see creativity as being one of the major traits of scientists. In fact, a scientist's reputation depends in large part on how clever, unique, and creative his or her experiments are and how creative and encompassing the explanations of natural phenomena.

Three other reasons that Dr. Duncan's students listed for their lack of interest in science were that they did not like math and couldn't do science, that they wanted to do something relevant to their lives, and that they wanted to do something involving other people—something social.

We believe that, if young children do science, they will come to realize that they *can* do science, that it *is* relevant to their lives, and that science involves working closely with other people, that it is *social*. Indeed, we have written this book because we believe all children can express their creativity in ways relevant to their lives and in a vibrant social environment that involves science.

Conversation Starters

- Try this experiment: Survey the room for all its contents, paying special attention to those that are blue but looking at everything. After one to three minutes move to the next step: Write down a list of everything that is red. What effect did paying attention to the blue items have on your ability to recall red items?

- Do you use the plan-do-review process frequently? Think over the past week and identify when you used it—or at least when you used the "plan" and "do" parts!

- Use the plan-do-review process to plan a get-together with a friend, significant other, or spouse. How is this like doing science?

- What is your earliest memory of science in a school setting? Ask your friends the same question and compare your responses. How would you hope your own child or student answers this question?

- Describe the images that the word *scientist* brings to mind. How did you arrive at these images? How stereotypical are they?

- Write 50 questions you have about science. After you have 50, categorize them using the outline of the *National Science Education Standards* in Chapter 1 of this book. Do some questions fit more than one place? How would you go about finding answers to the questions using science as a noun and science as a verb?

- How will you, as a teacher, continue to learn science as a noun and as a verb?

3

Prior Beliefs, Efficacy, and Teaching Science

By now, you have read about the three components guiding the information compiled in this text. You have also read about the nature of science and explored what it means to understand science as a verb and as a noun. These topics are vital to your understanding of using an inquiry-based approach to teaching science. However, we do not want you to stop there. This chapter is all about *your* view of science—your prior experiences with it and your view of yourself as a teacher of science. According to the *National Science Education Standards*, "The actions of teachers are deeply influenced by their perceptions of science as an enterprise and as a subject to be taught and learned" (1996, p. 28). Your views of science affect the decisions you make and your ability to improve your science instruction. Read the following section to see why your views of science, which reflect your experiences and attitudes, are so important to your teaching, and then take some time to reflect on your personal experiences of learning and teaching science and on how those experiences are subsequently reflected in your views.

■ INFLUENCE OF EXPERIENCES AND BELIEFS ON PRACTICE

Personal histories, experiences, and beliefs greatly influence how and what teachers teach (Ball, 1988; Ernest, 1989; Gudmundsdottir, 1990; Holt-Reynolds, 1992; Knowles & Holt-Reynolds, 1991; Krasnow, 1993; Schempp, Sparkes, & Templin, 1993). In fact, Stoddart, Connell, Stofflett, and Peck (1993) found that teachers tend to teach the way they themselves were taught. If your elementary teachers did not spend much time on science or your science lessons consisted of reading a text and answering questions, you are more likely to do the same with your students.

Although previous experiences can have a positive influence on instruction, sometimes these experiences keep teachers from finding more effective ways to teach. Teachers often dismiss ideas or methods that do not match their own experiences, and they use personal histories to test pedagogical choices (Holt-Reynolds, 1992). Consequently, when choosing how to teach science, teachers may reject ideas that did not work for them as learners. If you were unable to figure out physics experiments in science class, you are more likely to avoid them with your own students. When teachers focus on strategies that worked best for themselves, they may unintentionally ignore differences in individual students (Holt-Reynolds, 1992; Smith, 1991). In addition, teachers are influenced by "good or bad" teachers from the past: if your favorite teacher did not teach science but instilled in you a love of reading, teaching science may not be a high priority for you.

Beliefs and experiences are such strong influences for several reasons. First, a lack of attention to what one believes about teaching helps perpetuate a cycle of teaching as one was taught just because it is familiar. Second, beliefs and experiences can create obstacles to reflection. In other words, teachers have trouble thinking about methods of instruction in any other way than how the method affected them in the past. Often teachers are unable to picture a method or approach that they haven't experienced (Smith, 1991). Finally, the number of decisions teachers must make, the variety of tasks they face, and the demands of teaching in general often create an instinctive reaction to problems. Teachers do whatever it takes to "get through" a lesson. Often, when something new doesn't work immediately, it is easiest to return to what is familiar, even if doing so is not effective (Schempp et al., 1993). Why do you teach the way you do? What topics do you just "get through"?

■ EFFICACY

In addition to past experiences with science, feelings of low self-efficacy can keep teachers from effectively teaching science. *Self-efficacy* is a judgment of one's ability to perform a task within a specific domain (Bandura, 1997). There are two kinds of efficacy within the domain of education— teaching efficacy and personal teaching efficacy. *Teaching efficacy* is the belief that teaching and education in general have a positive effect on students. *Personal teaching efficacy* is the belief that you personally can positively influence students (Woolfolk & Hoy, 1990). One can feel efficacious

Photo 3.1   Teacher in classroom

Miss Kraus facilitating a science discussion in her first-grade classroom.

in one area and not in another. For example, you might feel confident in your ability to teach reading but doubt your skills in teaching science. It is important that you reflect on your personal teaching efficacy. How do you feel about teaching science? Are you a good science teacher, or, if you are not yet teaching, do you think you will be? Is science valuable for elementary students? Your honest answers to these questions will greatly influence how you teach science.

Feelings of self-efficacy also influence the classroom environment and teachers' selection of activities. They can enhance or undermine performance and are highly correlated to locus of control in the classroom. That is, teachers who have high self-efficacy tend to have student-centered classrooms; teachers who have low self-efficacy run teacher-centered classrooms in which they make all or most of the decisions (Bandura, 1997; Woolfolk & Hoy, 1990). Highly efficacious teachers feel that their work with students is important and meaningful. They plan carefully so that students are successful in constructing knowledge, they set goals for themselves and their students, and they brainstorm specific ways to assist students in achieving these goals. In addition, highly efficacious teachers feel that students should be involved in decision making, and they are more likely to use new curriculum materials and to change instructional strategies than are low-efficacy teachers (Poole, Okeafor, & Sloan, 1989; Smylie, 1988).

In contrast, teachers with low efficacy expect that students will fail, and they often feel frustrated and discouraged about teaching. They lack specific goals and thus do not plan strategies to achieve any goals; they may merely rely on guidelines they are given and on their own experiences. "To disguise their anxieties about science, most elementary school science teachers have hidden behind textbook-centered lessons that stress vocabulary and memorization of facts" (National Research Council, as quoted in Crowther, 1996, p. 16). Teachers with low self-efficacy also impose decisions on pupils without involving them in the process (Ashton, 1994).

Unfortunately, one does not magically achieve self-efficacy in science, or in any other area. However, feelings of effectiveness can be enhanced through observation and study of different models, hands-on experiences, and reflection on one's beliefs and practices (Bandura, 1981; Crowther, 1996; Gibson & Dembo, 1984).

In this chapter, we want you to reflect on what you believe about teaching science, what you actually do in classroom situations, and how you would like to change in both beliefs and practice. Although there is much to be gained by reading what others have written about teaching, it is mostly through reflection on one's own practice that new insights about teaching develop (Hewson et al., 1999). Discarding everything you believe about teaching science and starting from scratch with new ideas and methods is neither possible nor even desirable. However, thinking about your beliefs and challenging them with new ideas will help you to better understand teaching and learning science. "Experience needs to be coupled with substantive reflection to have an impact on practice" (Zembal-Saul, Blumenfeld, & Krajcik, 2000, p. 320). To help you increase your self-efficacy, in this chapter we will provide you with models of science instruction, ways to seek out ideas from scientists and good science teachers, and ideas for your own hands-on science experiences.

■ REFLECTING ON THE WALLS OF TEACHING SCIENCE

All of us face intimidating walls in our teaching—barriers that keep us from teaching more effectively. Teaching any subject to any age group is a challenging task; teaching science can be especially challenging. As you think about teaching elementary science, you may feel as if you are facing an insurmountable wall. Depending on your past experience with science and your current beliefs about the nature of science, that wall may be very high or perhaps just a small hurdle. Do not think that you must abandon all of your ideas and beliefs about teaching science in order to climb that wall. Instead, try to think of the wall as a challenge that you can go around with innovative ideas and a deeper understanding of what teaching science means.

Take some time to reflect on the walls that make you uncomfortable with teaching science. What are they? Why are they there? Were they created by a science course you took, an early science experience, perhaps a teaching experience? Understanding why the walls were erected can be an important step in going around them. Do any of the walls below sound familiar?

- I do not know enough science content.
- Students need to know the "right answers."
- I don't have time to teach science.
- Science lessons disrupt my classroom management.

These common barriers keep teachers from delving further into the teaching of science. We'll discuss each of these walls in the next section, along with ways you can conquer them.

GETTING AROUND THE WALLS ■

Wall #1: I Do Not Know Enough Science Content

If you shy away from teaching science because you feel you just do not know enough content, you're not alone. According to Tilgner (1990), "inadequate teacher background in science" was one of "three obstacles to teaching science most frequently cited by elementary teachers" in 1970 and "little has changed" (p. 421). Teachers' personal understanding of the subject matter they teach has a powerful influence on their instructional practice (Ball, 1988; Brickhouse, 1990; Bullough, Knowles, & Crow, 1989; Ernest, 1989; Langdon, Weltzl-Fairchild, & Haggar, 1997; Stoddart et al., 1993). Content knowledge determines teachers' explanations, demonstrations, diagnosis of misconceptions, acceptance of students' own methods, and curriculum decisions (Ernest, 1989). Teachers who do not have much content knowledge generally rely on textbooks and memorization to teach a subject. They avoid answering student questions and limit verbal participation (Bullough et al., 1989; Stoddart et al., 1993). This suggests that teachers who wish to move away from relying on memorization and facts toward pursuing science as inquiry must have an understanding of science content. "If the constructivist model is used in the classroom, teachers of elementary science should possess a sound understanding of basic science concepts to guide the identification, acceptance, self-analysis, and reformulation of students' ideas" (Ginns & Watters, 1995).

As important as content knowledge is, it is difficult to gain quickly and easily. It is easy to see why elementary teachers feel they do not know enough science when you consider how much there is to know. An elementary curriculum consists of biology, physics, ecology, chemistry, astronomy, botany, entomology, and geology, to name a few content areas. Within each of those subjects, teachers must have a grasp of numerous ideas and concepts. In addition, since scientific knowledge is always evolving, teachers must keep up with new discoveries in these fields—not an easy task, as scientists themselves do not even know all there is to know about the many disciplines within science! As if this were not enough, teachers also need to have content knowledge about subjects other than science: children's literature, math, social studies, language arts, art, music, physical education, and health. They must understand educational psychology and child development as well as special education procedures and laws. As you can see, trying to learn everything there is to know about science is not a good way to get around this first wall. If teachers tried to learn everything, they would not have any time to teach!

Knowing all the facts of science is impossible, but understanding the processes of science and how it works in the real world is not. Instead of thinking about all the *content* knowledge you need to have, start thinking about the *concept* knowledge you need. What's the difference? Content knowledge can be memorized or learned and quizzed on a test. We construct concept knowledge using what we know about a topic in relationship to the world, taking in and reflecting on information from a variety of sources and experiences. Clark (2002) defines a concept as "A big idea that helps us make sense of, or connect, lots of little ideas" (p. 94). For example, you can learn the names of plants and animals—content—by reading a book or memorizing a list. However, understanding how those plants and animals affect one another and the world—concept—requires making connections between what you know about each piece of information individually.

In the illustration of content and concept knowledge below, content knowledge is a small part of concept knowledge. You must start with the big picture (the concept and how it relates to the world) and the facts (the content) will come with exploration.

Figure 3.1   Concept Knowledge

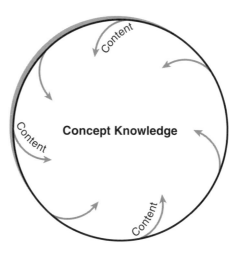

My mom always says, "The world is round and everything is connected." Indeed, as a teacher of scientists, you need to understand these connections. Although content knowledge is important as a way into the concepts, your real intent should be to understand how those bits of content knowledge are connected within concept knowledge.

In order both to do science as a verb and understand science as a noun, you need to understand what the concept is about and how it relates to the world. Doing and understanding science is much more complex than just understanding facts. To make science meaningful and useful, you must begin with concept knowledge and move towards the content. In this way, you will help students to understand why it is important to keep learning rather than teaching them to view learning science as an ending point.

Clark (2002) writes about four different levels of knowledge, including thought systems, concepts, basic ideas, and facts. He compares levels of knowledge with the levels necessary to build a house. The thought systems are the blueprints, the concepts are the frame, the basic ideas are the room dividers, and the facts are the furniture. If we think about this in terms of learning science, we need to begin with the blueprints, not the facts. We would never begin building a house with furniture. As a teacher of science, you do not need to focus on learning facts. You need to focus on the big picture. What is this concept about? What is important within this concept? WHY do kids need to know this?

There are many ways to gain concept knowledge. The important thing is to keep learning and making connections so that you can get around the walls and your students can start doing science! Here are some ideas to help you in your quest for science concept knowledge:

- The Internet is a wonderful resource for learning more about science concepts. Choose some of the topics you will be teaching and search for new information. Remember to read with a critical eye and use more than one source. Questioning what you read as "truth" is important. How is what you find connected to what you already knew?
- Sometimes, looking for lessons is the best way to learn about science. Choose a science topic and find activities from magazines, the Internet, colleagues, or books. Try the activities yourself. What did you find out? What did you wonder as you were doing the activity? How does the activity connect to another activity or fact?
- Go to a local university, college, hospital, or research center, and ask if you can follow a scientist for a day. What do scientists do? How could you make your classroom more like a laboratory during science?
- Observe children in a park or on the school playground. How are they "doing" science?
- Talk to a school librarian about science resources you can get from places like 4-H or one of the state educational service units (which provide services, materials, and other resources for teachers and schools and may be known by a different name in your state). Often these groups have great materials at little or no cost. The resources usually come not only with directions but also with helpful background knowledge and vocabulary.
- Take a risk and design a science lesson you've never taught before. Ask yourself how, out in the world, you could learn about the topic. For example, can you really learn about seeds and plants without actually having access to some?
- Find a variety of children's literature on the subject (see the children's literature resource section). How can the content in a particular book be connected to the larger concept you are researching? How can that content be translated into meaningful science activities?
- Think of a problem you've had, such as a plant in your garden not growing or your car breaking down. What science did you need to know in order to solve those problems? Where did you turn for additional information?
- Ask your students to think of 10 questions about a science topic, and help them find the answers. It's okay to ask someone else or to look it up because doing either will validate your students' questions and encourage them to keep asking.

During my first year of teaching, I was required to teach my students about habitats. I did not know much about habitats, other than the fact that there are different types, such as deserts, forests, oceans, and so on (content knowledge). The students and I asked questions about the different types of habitats and explored the answers together. We made dioramas and learned about the kinds of animals and plants found in various habitats. We asked why certain animals exist in certain habitats, and we made hypotheses and attempted to draw conclusions (concept knowledge).

I knew there must be more to teaching habitats, so the next year I looked for some resources. I found a video called *A Home for Pearl* that discussed urban wildlife, limiting factors, and what each kind of animal required from its habitat. From another teacher who taught habitats, I received some *Project Wild* books, which gave me several ideas for activities. For instance, we created a food chain with plants and animals using paper cards and string, and some of the students became animal predators. We studied some of the same habitats we had the previous year, but this year we made sure that each kind of animal and plant in the dioramas had what it needed to survive).

Each year, I added to my knowledge about habitats, learning from questions the students asked and collecting a variety of resources. During my third year, I found an article in a magazine about a teacher who had built a pond in her room. I made some connections in my mind about the interdependence between plants and animals in different habitats, and, that year, my class made a pond. We gathered information about ponds, and learned what we needed to keep the pond alive. Something happened, however, that I hadn't planned. The plants in the pond began to die after about a week. The students noticed this and asked me what was wrong. I asked them what *they* thought the problem was. The students observed and debated and finally decided that there was not enough sun for the plants. With this hypothesis in mind, we decided to try an experiment. The next week, a student's family brought in a sunlamp for our pond, and the plants thrived. Yippee! Our habitat would survive, and the students learned how vital the sun is!

The next year, I connected some vocabulary to the ideas that the students and I had learned. Some came from a class field trip to a forest, where an educator taught us about consumers, producers, and decomposers. We observed these in the forest and looked for evidence that they were present. We wondered aloud what would happen if one of them were gone. The students and I built our class pond again, but this time we had language to attach to the different types of organisms living there.

I could go on and on about the concept knowledge I learned with my students regarding habitats. Each year I made more connections about the subject, and each year I was a better teacher of it. How did this happen?

I think there were several factors. I started with the concept rather than the content. In other words, even though I didn't know many facts or vocabulary about habitats, I knew why we were studying them—because we live within habitats and the connections between all habitats allow us all to keep living. I was willing to listen both to my wonderfully curious students and to my colleagues. I was willing to take some risks and learn along with my students. The pond, to tell you the truth, smelled and created a mess, and it made the custodians very unhappy. It was a risk, but the students and I learned so much about habitats together. I understood that I did not know very much about habitats to start with, but I was not content to keep doing the same thing year after year. Finally, I think

I became a more successful teacher because I understood the nature of science. My students and I needed to be actively *doing* science, not just gathering science facts.

At this point in my career, I am fairly comfortable with my concept and content knowledge in habitats, solids and liquids, space, insects, and rocks. These science topics I have taught and learned. If I had to teach electricity, I would have to do some studying, but I know I could do it. I know I would need to start with the big picture (why are we studying electricity?); I know that the order of events matters; I know science as inquiry; and I know how to ask questions, be curious, and take risks. You can do the same, too.

Wall #2: Students Need to Know the "Right Answers"

Many teachers feel comfortable with the concept knowledge they have obtained but have reservations about the constructivist nature of science as inquiry. The thought of a teacher having students discover science knowledge themselves rather than feeding them the information they need to know is worrisome. What if students do not get the concepts they need? When do we tell them the "right" answers? If students do not do an experiment correctly, how will they learn anything? These are important questions because they have to do with accountability and student learning. Teachers *do* need to make sure that students learn certain topics. In this section, we want to help you think about how students construct science concept knowledge and how you can help them challenge, debate, and communicate that knowledge. We will start with an illustration of one particular science lesson.

Carla and Tara, two preservice teachers, taught science lessons in a Girl Scout program for one semester. One evening, they presented a lesson on circuits and electricity for 20 girls. Carla and Tara planned the lesson carefully, allowing for exploration and discovery. They read about circuits and batteries ahead of time, so they understood the content behind the lesson. To help the students construct their own knowledge about electricity and circuits, Carla and Tara set up each table with several wires, batteries, lightbulbs, fruits, and vegetables. They did not tell the girls how to make a circuit but instead asked them how they thought they could make the lightbulb glow. The students set to work, and many were able to put the wires, batteries, and lightbulbs together successfully. Then the preservice teachers asked if the girls thought the fruits and vegetables would light the bulbs. Extremely excited about this notion, the girls began poking wires into the lemons, bananas, and cucumbers. They eagerly tried several different ways to light the bulbs and continued to work the entire 30 minutes, even when the fruits and vegetables did not produce any light. Feedback surveys collected after the lesson were very positive and showed that the Girl Scouts had learned from the lesson. However, the preservice teachers were disgusted with the lesson and vowed never to use it in their classrooms. The lemons were supposed to have lit the lightbulbs, and they did not. Carla and Tara considered the experiment a flop because this specific bit of knowledge did not get through to the students.

Photo 3.2   Lightbulb

Meghan works hard to make the lightbulb light.

Carla and Tara may have felt that the students would have learned more if they had simply been told the "right answers." If we think of science only as facts to be learned, then discovery and exploration are not the most efficient methods for learning. However, if we view science as making connections, learning to ask questions, and debating conjectures, we will understand that students can learn from science experiments even when experiments do not turn out exactly as expected. Think about what the students did learn from this activity. They figured out for themselves how to light the bulbs, and they realized that the bulbs would not light without a complete circuit. They learned that some things do not conduct electricity. They experimented to find out whether different fruits would conduct electricity, and, when they were unsuccessful, they challenged themselves to see if the method they were using was the cause. These students debated among themselves and with the teachers about whether or not they thought the fruit worked. They persisted in gathering knowledge even when the bulbs did not light the first time. Carla and Tara learned a lot as well and had some questions of their own, such as what electricity requires and why the bulbs did not light up with the lemon as predicted.

Having children construct knowledge does not mean that the teacher is uninvolved in the process. On the contrary, adult involvement and guidance is vital for helping students make connections to new ideas. "Viewing scientific knowledge as a learner activity rather than an independent body of knowns leads to quite different educational considerations. Rather than identifying the set of skills to be gotten in children's heads, attention shifts to establishing learning environments conducive to children constructing their science in social settings" (Wheatley, 1991, p. 12). Teachers can stretch children's knowledge by presenting new activities that build on prior experiences and by questioning students about their observations and what they think these mean. For instance, Carla and Tara did more than just present students with materials for lighting bulbs. They had to help the students think about why the bulbs lit up and, by extension, why the bulbs in their homes light up. They needed to explore the reasons the lemon should have lit the bulb and why this might be useful to know. Extension activities that shed additional light on what students have learned are also important. What further activity might Carla and Tara have planned to help the Girl Scouts learn more about electricity?

- **Skillful questioning** is a vital part of constructivism and one of the most difficult aspects of teaching to learn. It is an art that takes time and practice to perfect. It is much easier and less time consuming to simply give students facts or explanations rather than to encourage them to reason through questions or problems themselves. Penick, Crow, and Bonnstetter (1996) have developed a system of questioning called HRASE to assist teachers in probing students' thinking. Each component in HRASE—History, Relationships, Application, Speculation, and Explanation—refers to a specific type of question.

- **History questions** help you and the students gather information about what the students did. For example, you might ask the following:
    o What did you do?
    o What happened?
    o What happened next?
    o What did you do first?
    o What procedure did you use?
    o What color (temperature, weight, size) was it?
    o What made you think of doing that?

- **Relationship questions** help students look for relationships and patterns in science.
    o If _____ happened, what happened to _____?
    o Where have you seen something like this before?
    o Did any other students get these same results?
    o What order does that usually follow?
    o What seems to be a common element in all your findings?
    o Where (when, how) do you usually find these?

- **Application questions** are valuable in discerning what students understand.
    o How could you use this?
    o What problems could this solve?
    o Where can we find examples of this in the world?
    o What machine could you build that would do this?

- **Speculation questions** go beyond the data and information and encourage creative thinking.
    o What if you (changed, eliminated, added, mixed, waited)?
    o What would it take to prove that?
    o If you wanted to prevent that from happening, what would you do?
    o If that is true, then _____?

- **Explanation questions** help students convey their observations and conclusions.
    o How does that work?
    o What causes that to happen?
    o How would you change your explanation if I changed _____?
    o How does your explanation fit this other phenomenon?

As you can see, questioning is a valuable way to encourage students to think deeply about what they have done and what they have noticed. It also gives you insight into what students understand so that you can plan additional experiences to help extend their knowledge. Using this method to help students construct content knowledge does, however, require flexibility on your part and a willingness to listen.

If you plan your lessons and entire units ahead of time and are not willing to alter them in response to students' interests, ideas, and discoveries, you might be frustrated with experiments and questioning. However, if you plan activities and then carefully listen to students and observe what they are learning, you can more effectively plan additional activities. "Good teaching is a matter of creating a context that not only allows but vigorously encourages students to become actively involved in their own learning. Good teaching is an art that requires sensitivity, humility, and an infinite confidence in the innate ability of kids to learn about the world in which they live" (Clark, 2002, p. 92).

This aspect of planning is very complex and will take time and patience to develop. Start by reflecting on what you believe about science as a noun. It is easy to have the mindset that everything we know about science is true, especially if we experienced science under a linear, fact-gathering model. Instead, think of science facts as conjectures on which most people agree. For example, we used to think the earth was flat, and now we know that it is round; no one is debating this anymore. Technology has changed many such scientific "facts" over the years. "In learning science, we assume our conjectures are true unless there is some challenge to them from our experience with the world which, of course, includes other persons" (Wheatley, 1991, p. 11).

You might still wonder, "But there *are* certain science facts students need to know. When do I tell them the right answers?" Keep in mind that "knowledge is not passively received, but is actively built upon by the cognizing subject. Ideas and thoughts cannot be communicated in the sense that meaning is packaged into words and sent to another who unpacks the meaning from the sentences. That is, as much as we would like to, we cannot put ideas in students' heads; they will and must construct their own meanings" (Wheatley, 1991, p. 10). This does not mean, however, that we accept students' ideas without challenging them. Challenging means questioning students about their observations and helping them see the contradictions in their ideas; questions such as those above serve to do this. If you focus on providing students with hands-on, minds-on experiences and becoming a partner in the learning quest instead of the giver of knowledge, students will gain the content they need. It will take a conscious effort on your part to ask and guide instead of tell, to dream instead of limit, and to wonder instead of know. But the results are well worth it.

Wall #3: I Don't Have Time to Teach Science

With all that teachers must cover in their classrooms in addition to the focus of many school reforms on reading and math, it may feel as though there isn't time for science. Even if science is a priority, you may feel as though you must move quickly through the objectives rather than spend the time necessary to help kids construct meaning from science activities. There are three ideas that you must consider when thinking about scheduling science into your classroom routine.

1. Why should I teach science?

2. How can I integrate science with other subjects?

3. How can I integrate other subjects with science?

Science is an important piece of any child's education. We believe science should be a part of your classroom routine because it is such an important part of the world our students inhabit. There should be time for some science every day. So much of our lives is entwined with the technology arising from basic scientific research that to be ignorant of science is to be ignorant of our world. Science affects us in a very material way. For example, as I sit composing this sentence on a computer, I am looking at a cathode ray tube, my fingers landing on plastic keys that allow electrical signals to be encoded. I am in an inner room of the building; without electrical lights, I would not be able to see at all.

We are also affected by science in a biological way. I sip instant coffee that has been decaffeinated. I eat snacks prepared from grains that come from fertilized fields treated with pesticides. The grain may have been transported via trains, processed in plants, packaged in plastic, and transported to the nearest store. If the grains have been modified into snacks, they have probably been preserved using chemical additives. Soon, if not already, grains may be modified genetically so that fewer pesticides need to be used.

In addition, more and more of the problems we face in our society are related to science and technology. One of the major problems in our nation is the use of drugs such as cocaine and marijuana, drugs made from biological sources. If drugs are injected into the body using shared needles, users are at a high risk of contracting acquired immunodeficiency syndrome (AIDS). Another problem facing our world and the next generation is the need for new energy sources. If we have students who only know existing science information, but not how to use and do science creatively, who will develop these new sources? All of us need to know science—and how to discover more about specific scientific areas at specific times in our lives.

Science and technology are an integral part of our society. If we are to understand our world and preserve our lifestyle, we must understand science. We make decisions that will affect our own lives and the lives of our children, grandchildren, and future generations. Those decisions should be based on an understanding of the science behind our world, and we should have some understanding of the risks and benefits of those decisions.

There is another reason that science should be a part—a major part—of any school curriculum. We believe that our democratic society depends on the types of skills and habits developed through science education. Democracy is based on shared decision making, and a successful democracy depends on those decisions being good ones. Science as a process requires us to have ideas that are tested, that are based on evidence. Science, like a democratic society, demands that we think for ourselves and share our information with others. While our colleagues test our ideas, we test theirs. This shared communal process is the antithesis of an autocratic state. Scientific hypotheses do not gain their validity by force nor their ability to describe and explain the world by being proclaimed by an authority. Having a population familiar and comfortable with the scientific requirements for evidence and for independent thought is one of the best defenses against threats to democracy.

Young children are absolutely fascinated by their world, making science a natural thing for them to study. "Why" becomes almost a mantra. The answer to one question automatically raises the next, which is "why?" to the first answer. Why is the sky blue? Because we see "blue" light that has been scattered by our earth's atmosphere. Why does the atmosphere scatter light? Why is the scattered light blue? And on and on. This is the perfect model of how science identifies the questions and phenomena to investigate. Acknowledging the validity of asking questions and searching for answers confirms the importance of children's participation in the process.

Science can be integrated with every other subject. Even if you do not believe you have time for an hour of science every day, there are ways to incorporate science into other subjects and portions of the day so that students are doing science as a verb regularly. Doing science daily might be as simple as having something for students to observe when they come into class each morning or having students complete a science project that fits with a book you are reading. For example, in a preschool classroom with teacher Lisa Stiles, the students read the fairy tale *Jack and the Beanstalk*. The students in this preschool read the story (reading) and then grew beans. As the beans grew, they observed them each day (science), measured them using finger lengths (math), and recorded their observations in a logbook (writing). Students shared their ideas at preschool and at home with families (social studies). This kind of planning is often called theme planning and can be used if many of your objectives fit together.

Be careful when taking this approach to finding time for science. It is easy to believe that reading about something scientific during language arts time is incorporating science. Students who are doing science as a verb may be reading, but reading is not science. This approach of integrating science with other subjects works if you can be flexible with your time periods. We don't recommend that science is *only* integrated with other subjects, but instead advocate doing this with a few science objectives. If science is never taught as more than a piece of another subject, students will not learn the science language, processes, and knowledge they need. This approach can be used, however, as a way to add science during particularly busy units within other subjects.

Other subjects can be integrated with science. Ideally, you will create a time for science each day. This does not mean that you will need to cut other things from the curriculum. However, it does mean that you will need to take time to cover some reading, writing, math, and social studies objectives within science lessons. You may be thinking that it is difficult to integrate subjects when objectives are very specific and when the connections within each subject are important. For example, it is valuable to keep concepts in math flowing together so that students can make connections between objectives. Jumping from one subject to the next in math, reading, and writing do not serve students well. But you can take objectives from other subjects and integrate them when it is natural to do so, making it possible to be flexible with time periods and scheduling.

Let's take a moment to make some connections between subjects. What does reading have to do with science? What does math have to do with science? Writing? Social studies? In some sense, science contains all of the subjects. Science is the one subject that utilizes all of the others and vice versa. You can't really do science as a verb and as a noun without reading, writing, and using mathematics and social studies. Look at the three ideas that follow.

1. Students will be able to count to twenty by twos (math).

2. Students will be able to understand cause and effect (reading).

3. Students will be able to write a friendly letter (writing).

Try to think of a science concept that might pull these three ideas together. Indeed, there are probably several concepts in science that would utilize these skills. For example, the three ideas could be incorporated easily into the habitats unit described previously or the rocks workshop listed in Chapter 9. There are many ways to add science to an elementary curriculum. Take some time to think about how it best fits into your schedule.

Wall #4: Active Science Lessons Disrupt My Classroom Management

Does the idea of allowing students to actively pursue science conjure up visions of students running amok, the classroom in shambles, and the principal calling you in to explain what's going on? Many teachers use textbooks and handouts, lectures, and discussions to teach science out of a fear of losing control if they allow students more exploration.

The measure of success for a lesson becomes student behavior rather than student learning. Certainly, teachers need to think about classroom management when teaching any subject. However, keeping students quiet, well behaved, and busy for busyness's sake should not be the goal of a lesson. Instead, we need to think of ways to help students become responsible for both their learning and their classroom. There are several chapters later in this book that will help you develop ideas for managing a science class in a way that fosters deep learning and a positive attitude about science. Here, we want you to begin thinking about the difference between a well-managed classroom in which students are actively learning science and a classroom in which students are only quiet and busy with an assignment. First, imagine an active science setting. What are the students doing? What is the teacher doing? Where are the materials? Next, imagine a classroom where the students are well managed but not necessarily learning. What are the students doing? What is the teacher doing? Where are the materials?

In a classroom of first graders, Beth, a preservice teacher, planned and taught a science lesson on rain. Her lesson included poems about rain, a survey about whether students preferred rainy days or sunny days, and a mobile-making project. Students actively participated in reading and discussing the poems and eagerly asked questions about rain, such as "Why is it cloudy during rain?" and "Where do the raindrops go after they hit the ground?" But Beth, thinking of her survey on their likes and dislikes about rain, carefully guided the students away from these kinds of questions and toward questions such as "What do you like to wear during rainy days?" Catching on to what Beth was looking for, the students began to ask questions that seemed more acceptable to her. Next, the students made umbrella mobiles using premade parts whose color corresponded to students' answers on the survey. For instance, if they liked rainy days, they received a green handle; if not, they received a blue handle. Afterward, Beth reflected on her lesson, feeling it was a great success. She discussed many aspects of classroom management that she felt had gone well and believed the students had learned about rain by reading the poems. This was a lesson Beth would tuck away and use again someday. Think about this lesson. Would you agree with Beth that it was successful?

Yes, the students had fun. They participated in the activities. They were well behaved. But making mobiles is not science. And good classroom management doesn't always mean the students are learning. What did the students learn during this lesson? What do you think Beth's classroom would have looked and sounded like if the students had been actively engaged in science?

In order to understand what classroom management means in an active science setting, you must think deeply about how you believe students learn. It is not enough to consider the noise level of the classroom, the amount of paperwork students turn in, or how tidy the room looks. You may have a quiet classroom, but you won't understand what students are learning and what they aren't.

Students grow and learn in environments that promote interaction with the world. These actual interactions cannot take place under the traditional transmission model, in which students passively receive information from teachers. Instead, they construct an understanding of how their world functions through new experiences, new questions, and new ideas. What does this mean for elementary science? It means that students need to initiate ideas and actively interact with their environment in order for learning to take place. Think back to Beth's lesson: The students were not interacting with one another, with their ideas, or with objects in their world.

If children are interacting in meaningful activities, debating, and questioning, does classroom management fall by the wayside? Does a teacher have to give up having an orderly classroom so that students can interact freely? It depends on your definition of classroom management. If you believe that classroom management can be a framework created by the teacher and students together, with clear expectations, respect for one another and the environment, and consistent routines, then classroom management and actively learning actually go hand in hand.

However, classroom management in an active science classroom may not look or sound like it does in a traditional classroom. For example, many teachers came into my classroom and remarked that it was not "structured." It *was* structured, but in a different way than they were used to. To them, structure meant the students sat quietly in rows, completing paperwork. In an active learning classroom, students may be spread out over the room, engaging in activities that may or may not be identical. Structure in this type of environment involves student choice and initiative along with a firm understanding of routine. The teachers who did not think my room was structured were not able to see that the students knew exactly what to do in the classroom. They knew how to access and handle materials, they knew how to treat other students, and they worked hard.

At times, teachers have a classroom of students who are more difficult to work with. Often teachers in these situations say, "Well, I could do that activity with last year's class, but this year's class just couldn't handle it." In other words, only the "good" or "smart" or "quiet" students are able to participate in active learning experiences. However, many students who have difficulty in traditional classrooms have it *because* they need to be active. Steven, one of my students, was physically unable to sit at his desk for long. He constantly moved around and fell out of his seat often. Many teachers may have believed that activities such as mixing liquids or making taffy, which were the types of science experiences my class engaged in, were inappropriate for a child like Steven. However, these were tasks that captured Steven's attention, met his need for active exploration, and allowed him to be successful in the classroom. When our class made taffy to observe the stages of matter, do you think Steven had any behavior problems? No. How many of the other students do you think were off task? How many do you think did not follow directions? Zero. Zero because they knew what was expected. Zero because they were excited and intrigued with the lesson. Zero because they were able to use their active bodies to help them learn. Was the room a mess? Yes. Was it noisy as students got excited about what they were observing? Yes. The students cleaned the room. I talked to the other teachers ahead of time, so they were prepared for a little noise. Most important, will the students ever forget the stages of matter? I doubt it.

Many elementary teachers, because of their personalities, past experiences, or pressure from administrators, find it difficult to give up some of their perceived control in the classroom. One such teacher was a colleague of mine named Carol. Carol conducted a very quiet classroom; her students worked diligently on projects that she devised for them. Carol and I often discussed and debated educational issues, which helped us both to grow. She had to pass my room whenever she left hers and often commented that my students were "all over the floor" working on projects. I talked excitedly about what my students were learning and encouraged her to take a risk in teaching science. One day she took the challenge. During a unit on space, Carol's students planned and carried out their own space projects. She brought in large boxes for students who wanted to create a space shuttle, and other students designed space suits. Some students worked together, and others had individual projects. One afternoon during Carol's space unit, I looked up to see her standing at my door, looking frazzled and tired. Before I could ask what was wrong, she blurted out, "I do not know how you can stand the chaos!" I walked with Carol into her room and looked around. I asked her how many students were not engaged in meaningful learning about their space topic. Carol looked around and said, "None." Then I asked her if any of the students looked bored. "No." Finally, I asked her what she heard the students talking about and what they were learning. As Carol rattled off a long list, her eyes sparkled and she smiled. She was very proud of what she saw happening among the students. I was proud of *her*. She had taken a huge risk and created an environment in which the students were *doing* science. More than that, they were initiating, experiencing, and loving science. The students were creating, asking, debating, and discovering, but she hadn't taken a moment to stand back and see it. Her classroom wasn't chaotic or messy; it was colorful and dynamic. Carol's students were constructing knowledge. What can you learn from this? Before you think a classroom is loud or unorganized, spend some time observing the students and what they are learning.

Of course, not all classrooms in which children are learning science look or sound the same because there will be differences among teachers and students. Also, just because students are active does not always mean they are engaged in learning. Perhaps, though, there are some common elements in active learning settings. To get around the classroom management wall, you are going to have to take a close look at how you believe students learn. What does learning look like and sound like at different ages and developmental levels? Do students need to have social interactions during learning? How does classroom management affect learning?

In *The Case for Constructivist Classrooms,* Brooks & Brooks (1999) present a list of 11 things that teachers in active learning classrooms do. Think about what these elements look and sound like in the classroom. Which do you already use? Which will you try?

1. Constructivist teachers encourage and accept student autonomy and initiative.

2. Constructivist teachers use raw data and primary sources, along with manipulative, interactive, and physical materials.

3. When framing tasks, constructivist teachers use cognitive terminology such as "classify," "analyze," "predict," and "create."

4. Constructivist teachers allow student responses to drive lessons, shift instructional strategies, and alter content.

5. Constructivist teachers inquire about students' understandings of concepts before sharing their own understandings of those concepts.

6. Constructivist teachers encourage students to engage in dialogue, both with the teacher and with one another.

7. Constructivist teachers encourage student inquiry by asking thoughtful, open-ended questions and encouraging students to ask one another questions.

8. Constructivist teachers seek elaboration of students' initial responses.

9. Constructivist teachers engage students in experiences that might engender contradictions to their initial hypotheses and then encourage discussion.

10. Constructivist teachers allow wait time after posing questions.

11. Constructivist teachers provide time for students to construct relationships and create metaphors. (pp. 103–117)

■ REFLECTING ON YOUR OWN SCIENCE WALLS

The walls we've discussed in this chapter are only a few of those you may be trying to get around. You may have questions and, we hope, at least a few strategies to get around some of the walls. This is just the beginning of your journey, however. Before you continue, reflect on the connections you made in this chapter.

Conversation Starters

- Take some time to think about your science teaching beliefs. What do you think are important concepts in science? How did you learn science in elementary school? What aspects of teaching science make you nervous or worried?

- What is the difference between concept and content knowledge? How do the differences affect what you do with students?

- Make a plan for how you might develop concept knowledge about a topic you are teaching.

- Try to pick out turning points in my teaching of habitats. What resources were instrumental in the changes I made?

- What other questions can you think of that Carla and Tara could have used? What questions would you like to tuck away in your mind to use with students? How can you use questions and activities to help students think about science in new ways?

- In what ways have you planned lessons that perhaps squelched creativity? How could you plan your lessons so that creativity is necessary, encouraged, and appreciated?

- Do you think of classroom management during science as a challenge? Does it keep you from encouraging active student participation? What caused you to think this way? What parts of classroom management are harder during active science than during other subjects?

- Why is making mobiles not science?

- What is your vision of a classroom with teachers and students who utilize the principles of constructivism? Draw a picture of what it might look like.

PART II

Construction Ahead!

Influences on Learning

The winding road through Part I began with the origins of an active learning curriculum and detoured around the walls that may be keeping you from teaching science confidently. The road led you to new places to learn about the nature of science and about the place of science in the elementary classroom. We hope that beginning this adventure in science teaching has been exciting and informative and that you have taken time to reflect on and wonder more about the topics presented. The next part of our journey will take you through a "construction zone" where you will see how students construct knowledge.

Think for a moment about what it means to learn. What is learning? Is it change? Growth? Movement? Understanding? Discovery? Or some combination of these? What happens inside your brain when you learn? What part do emotions play in learning? How about the place of motivation or interaction with others? How do you know when you've learned something? To teach science effectively, you must know what you believe about the way children learn.

Educational and psychological studies, including brain research, tell us a great deal about the way young children learn. In the three chapters of this section, we will investigate some of the research and theories on learning and how they substantiate the need for children to learn *actively*. We will explore several influences on children's intellectual development, namely *maturation, social interaction,* and *physical experiences* (Labinowicz, 1980). In a sense, these three influences are like parts of a diet. If you eat too much, or not enough, of any particular food group, you may not grow and develop as well as you would with a more balanced diet.

Likewise, intellectual development is enhanced in an environment that balances a child's physical and mental capabilities (maturation) with social interaction and active, physical experiences. Therefore, you need to under-stand how children learn and think and interact at different levels of development in order to provide appropriate experiences for them. In the next three chapters, you will begin to see how maturation affects experi-ences and interactions, how physical experiences and social interactions, in turn, promote maturation, and how social interactions enhance physical experiences. Balancing these components is not easy, but we believe our approach enables teachers to provide a wonderful "diet" for children.

4

Maturation and Learning

What do you think of when you hear the word *maturation?* Do you think of learning to walk, losing teeth, or getting pimples? These are all physical signs of maturation that mark different stages in development. We celebrate these important milestones of growing older . . . except maybe the pimples! But maturation is not only physical, it is also cognitive. Understanding how cognitive maturation influences learning is essential in teaching. It affects choice of materials, content, pedagogy, and assessment in all subject areas. Before we examine how maturation affects learning, let's look at how, in general, we construct knowledge.

CONSTRUCTING KNOWLEDGE ■

While earlier we touched on the idea of learning as a process of construction, here we will look at it in more detail. This theory of learning is called *constructivism.* "Constructivism is a view of learning in which learners are actively involved in the knowledge construction process by using their existing knowledge to make sense of their new experiences" (Hewson et al., 1999). A good example of constructivism is the process of learning to teach. How are you learning (or how did you learn) to teach? Is it a matter of having an expert "pour" all the information about teaching into your mind? Freire (1998) used the metaphor of a bank to describe this belief about learning: "This is the banking concept of education, in which the scope of action allowed to the students extends only as far as receiving, filing, and storing the deposits. In the banking concept of education, knowledge is a gift bestowed by those who consider themselves knowledgeable upon those whom they consider to know nothing" (p. 68). If knowledge of teaching could be dispensed this way, you would not need practicum experiences or student teaching, and years of classroom experience would not be of any value. However, we know that learning to teach is much more complicated; it involves learning from reading, listening, discussing, *and* working directly with children. It is a process of constructing new ideas based on past experiences and new knowledge. We hope you are connecting the ideas in this book to your own experiences and beliefs about both teaching and learning.

Photo 4.1   Girls Making Crystals

These young scientists are learning about crystals through experience.

This concept of learning through experience is not new. In fact, John Dewey, starting in the 1890s, advocated learning as constructing knowledge: "Of course intellectual learning includes the amassing and retention of information. But information is an undigested burden unless it is understood. It is knowledge only as its material is comprehended. Education consists of the formation of wide-awake, careful, thorough habits of thinking" (1964, p. 249). The words *wide awake* describe quite well the state of a true learner. Passively receiving information, only to regurgitate it later, is quite different from actively utilizing experience and knowledge to create new ideas and understanding. We can all recall times that we passively (and perhaps *not* very wide awake) listened to information that did not connect to anything we understood or had experienced and therefore did not stay with us. We can also probably recall times when we learned something that did connect to our experiences and that we were able to use to add to our knowledge base. *Wide awake* also implies that learning takes place within the mind; experiences alone do not create learning. Learners must be involved in and reflect on experiences to learn from them.

An experiment conducted by Bruner (1986) illustrated the importance of actively building one's own knowledge. Children were asked to retrieve a piece of brightly colored chalk from under a glass container without leaving their seats. They were given sticks, rubber bands, clasps, and other materials to create a tool to assist them with the task. Children in two different groups were given different types of experiences with the materials before they tried the task. In one group, the children actively explored the materials themselves; in another, the children watched a demonstration about how to tie the sticks together to make a pole to reach the chalk. The children who explored the materials themselves beforehand were more successful at solving the problem and were less likely to abandon the task when they had difficulty. Bruner concluded that constructing their own knowledge about the materials rather than being shown how to use them helped children persist and be successful at their task.

In this way, children and adults are similar as learners—both construct their own knowledge and both need to be active explorers rather than passive receptacles. However, children and adults construct knowledge differently because children *think* differently. It is sometimes difficult for adults to remember this. "Nature seems to have been playing a trick on adults since the beginning of time. We quickly forget what it was like to be a child. Instead we create arbitrary expectations of what children should be like and assume we were that way as children" (Labinowicz, 1980, p. 19). Yet many adults recall childhood incidents that highlight how they created meaning. For example, John remembers as a first grader thinking that every day was 1979. He had recited the date during a daily calendar activity, and "1979" was a part of the date every day. Three-year-old Meghan bounced a ball against the wall and explained that the ball bounced back to her because it was magic. She thought the ball liked her and wanted to be with her. Jerry, at age nine, looked at a drop of water under a microscope and concluded that the moving objects he saw must be rocks pushed by the waves in the water. He wasn't able to imagine animals so small that he couldn't see them in a drop of water with his eyes alone. A teacher might have been tempted to tell John that 1979 was the *year*, all 365 days, or explain to Meghan that the ball came back to her not because of magic but because it hit the wall, or tell Jerry that the moving things he observed were tiny one-celled animals. Would these explanations have been meaningful to the children? Why or why not? These three examples, and probably many of your own, illustrate the importance of understanding how children learn and develop.

In the remainder of this chapter, we'll examine in more detail how children think and how maturation affects the way they construct knowledge. We'll begin with the theories of Jean Piaget, one of the leading experts on child development.

PIAGET: THE INTERACTION OF MATURATION AND EXPERIENCE

Piaget, a Swiss psychologist, closely studied the development of his own children to analyze how children learn. Although he was interested in *what* children know, his main concern was *how they come to know*. By listening carefully to children's reasoning and creating ingenious tasks that uncovered their patterns of erroneous thinking, Piaget was able to reshape common beliefs about children's construction of knowledge. "Piaget was one of the first to put forward forcefully, with extensive supporting evidence, the notion that children construct their own knowledge and that this knowledge is different in kind from an adult's, evolving and changing over the years" (Bliss, 1995, p. 140). Piaget believed that children learn through direct, active experiences with the environment and that maturation interacts with these experiences to help children construct knowledge. Below we will discuss some of the processes by which, Piaget believed, children learn.

Assimilation and Accommodation

Intellectual development—the process of *re*-structuring knowledge—begins with a structure or a way of thinking. Nine-year-old Jerry's structure was that the small organisms in the drop of pond water were rocks being moved by waves. As Jerry observed the organisms, he *assimilated* his observations into his knowledge of pond water. "Assimilation is the activity that permits the gradual incorporation of new ideas and information into a person's mental schemes; that is to say when people tackle new situations they try to incorporate the novelty of the outside world into what they already know and understand" (Bliss, 1995, p. 147). Jerry fit his new knowledge into his existing schemes: He knew from previous experience that pond water has rocks and that, when the water moves, the rocks move. In addition to assimilating, Jerry had to do some *accommodating*. "Accommodation is the adjustment of one's existing mental framework in light of one's perceptions" (Carmody, Hohmann, & Johnston, 2000, p.17). He had to change his existing mental framework, which was that objects exist only when one can see them with the naked eye.

"Some of those who follow Piaget make the mistake of thinking that assimilation and accommodation are different processes used at different times. For Piaget, both are always present—every assimilation involves some accommodation, and every accommodation involves some assimilation" (Bliss, 1995, p. 147). Assimilation without accommodation would mean having to put new experiences and ideas into only a few large structures. Jerry would not be able to think of the drop of water as being a miniature pond with rocks in it if he could not change, or accommodate, his idea of what a pond was based on his new experiences. On the other hand, accommodation without assimilation would mean having to make a new structure for every new experience. If he couldn't assimilate, Jerry would have to create a brand-new category for the drop of water and for the moving organisms, as they would not fit into his existing framework.

Equilibrium/Disequilibrium

During another experience with pond water and microscopes, Jerry noticed small hairs (cilia) on the organisms. This may have caused Jerry to feel *disequilibrium*, "the discomforting inner conflict between opposing interpretations" because this new finding challenged his original idea—after all, rocks don't have hair" (Labinowicz, 1980, p. 36). Disequilibrium creates the desire to question ideas, investigate further, and consider other possibilities. Without disequilibrium, we would not be motivated to learn.

Although it is valuable to go through periods of disequilibrium, in order to reach progressively higher states of intellectual development children must reconcile their observations of the environment with their internal structures. This reconciling or balance is called *equilibrium* and is accomplished by successfully assimilating and accommodating new information (Carmody et al., 2000). This intellectual activity equips children with a more complex thinking pattern and therefore higher levels of equilibration. Jerry's disequilibrium was caused by observation of hairs on organisms he had thought were rocks. He needed to assimilate and accommodate in order to reconcile what he saw with his internal structures. Imagine what you might hear if you could be inside Jerry's brain. You might hear him thinking that rocks don't have hairs (disequilibrium). You might hear him telling himself that the moving objects *might* not be rocks (accommodation), and that they *might* be moss since moss sometimes looks hairy, moves with a current, and exists in pond water (assimilation). Jerry is now in a state of equilibrium because he has reconciled his observations with his thinking. The moving organisms aren't rocks—they are pieces of moss!

You may be wondering if this process could really be considered learning, since Jerry only seemed to add to his misconceptions. However, he did in fact construct knowledge that was closer to the reality, and more important, he created a more comprehensive structure that will help him learn more in the future. Have you ever felt that the more you understood about something, the more questions you had? That also applies here. "The more powerful thinking patterns generate more intellectual activity as they point out gaps and inconsistencies in other existing patterns" (Labinowicz, 1980, p. 91). Jerry was developing more powerful thinking patterns as he worked to construct knowledge about pond water.

Piaget was very interested in how the gradual transformation of children's thinking occurs and the part played by maturation. He proposed four major stages through which individuals progress as they develop cognitively. Let's look at each of these stages.

Stages of Cognitive Development

The four stages of development identified by Piaget are sensorimotor, preoperational, concrete operational, and formal operational. Individuals pass through these developmental stages in the same order; however, the *rate* at which they pass through them varies. This development process is very similar to physical maturation, as mentioned earlier; children walk, lose teeth, and get pimples at different times, and yet children usually walk before they lose teeth and lose teeth before they get pimples. In addition, Piaget's cognitive stages overlap, and development is seen as continuous. This means that moving from one stage to another is not like turning one light off and another one on. Cognitive development is a gradual but continuous process (Labinowicz, 1980). As you read about the cognitive signs of maturation, ask yourself what kinds of physical experiences and social interactions (discussed more fully in the next two chapters) would be appropriate for children at each stage as well as how those experiences and interactions affect maturation. Begin to think about how to use this information to create a supportive science classroom. Although you will have little occasion to work with children at the sensorimotor stage as primary teacher, we have included this stage of development to provide a background for the remaining stages.

The sensorimotor stage of development describes infants from birth to approximately 2 years of age. "During this time, mental development is characterized by considerable progression in the infant's ability to organize and coordinate sensations with physical movements and actions—hence the name sensorimotor" (Santrock, 2000, p. 172). Children in this stage of development make connections by feeling, seeing, smelling, tasting, and hearing new things. For example, when a baby holds a rattle and shakes it, the baby hears a sound. After several random shakes, the baby begins to connect his or her actions with the sound and shakes the rattle purposely to make the sound. Basic reflexes help babies assimilate and accommodate knowledge about the environment. In other words, children in the sensorimotor stage of development are able to use their inborn reflexes to construct knowledge for intelligent action (Moshman, Glover, & Bruning, 1987). Babies at this stage of development also go through a change in their understanding of object permanence. When young infants are shown a toy and then it is hidden under a blanket, they will not look for it. However, as they begin to understand that objects continue to exist even when out of sight, they will actively look for a toy that they saw being hidden.

The preoperational stage of development describes children from approximately 2 to 7 years old. Many children in kindergarten, first, and second grades exhibit signs of operating in this stage. "It is a time when stable concepts are formed, mental reasoning emerges, egocentrism begins strongly and then weakens, and magical beliefs are constructed" (Santrock, 2000, p. 254). Consequently, preoperational learners are able to do things mentally rather than physically. For instance, children are able to imagine turning a book over without actually having to do it. This ability is evident when children watch an action and mimic it later. In order to do this, they must be able to represent the action in the mind. Learners in this stage are also able to play imaginatively, using an object to stand for something else, for instance, pretending that a small box is a spaceship or a car. However, preoperational learners focus on a single dimension of an object or experience and are not able to process changes other than in what they perceive (Small, 1990).

At about the age of 7 or 8, children begin the transition from preoperations to concrete operations. "According to Piaget, concrete operational thought is made up of operations—mental actions that allow children to do mentally what they had done physically before. Concrete operations are also mental actions that are reversible" (Santrock, 2000, p. 358). Learners in this stage are able to organize thoughts more logically and have a more sophisticated understanding of concepts. However, this replacement of intuitive thinking by more logical thought takes place only in concrete situations. In other words, the thinking of concrete learners is restricted to experiences and to objects they can manipulate; they cannot yet wrestle logically with ideas. In addition, children in the concrete operational stage are less egocentric, meaning they are now able to see another's point of view.

The final stage described by Piaget is formal operations, and it often begins between the ages of 11 and 15. However, some adults never become formal operational thinkers, and many go back to concrete operational

Photo 4.2   Students Mixing

Students are excited to see the liquids mixing!

thinking when they encounter a new or difficult situation or idea (Santrock, 2000). "The formal thinker has the capacity to consider verbal statements and propositions rather than just concrete objects" (Labinowicz, 1980. p. 86). In addition, formal operational learners can think metacognitively, in other words, think about their own thinking. "Formal thinking exists as a kind of reasoning operating on symbols and signs, rather than on representations of objects and events" (Bliss, 1995, p. 151).

How does all this affect your science teaching? Understanding children's thinking and reasoning creates a deeper understanding of where they are and how to support them as they move toward more sophisticated ways of thinking. It also provides a starting point for planning science lessons as well as insight into why some ideas may be beyond children's current scope of understanding.

Jerry, the child who was observing pond water, was most likely moving toward the concrete operational stage of development. He didn't think the water was moving because it was magic, and yet he wasn't able to comprehend possibilities that he had no experience with, such as one-celled animals. Although it may have been frustrating for Jerry's teacher to listen to his reasoning, understanding where Jerry was developmentally may have helped the teacher more readily accept his current ways of thinking and assist him in constructing new ideas. Jerry probably wasn't mentally ready to understand one-celled animals, just as young infants generally aren't physically ready to walk. However, with carefully planned, well-timed questions and experiences provided by the teacher, and adequate time to reflect on his observations, Jerry will continue to construct knowledge more effectively.

As you will see in the coming chapters, the present approach to science creates a learning framework for children at all levels of maturation.

Experiencing science both individually and as a community through key experiences, small group workshops, and thinking routines, each child gains a deeper understanding of concepts and progresses to a higher level of development.

As we discussed in Chapter 2, it is valuable to learn the subject of science as a process and as a body of knowledge. However, learning science also helps children develop greater reasoning skills that can be used in all areas of learning. Although teachers cannot necessarily change a child's level of maturation, they *can* help the child build on his or her current level by providing developmentally appropriate experiences and by challenging the child with thought-provoking questions. In the next chapter, we will discuss another vital factor in learning—social interaction.

Conversation Starters

- Why would it be important to understand maturation when teaching science?

- Create your own definition of constructivism.

- If you believe that children construct knowledge, what kinds of activities do you need in your classroom? Think of a time when you assimilated and accommodated. What were you doing? What facilitated the learning?

- Take some time to "think like a child." How did you learn your language, and how did you learn to read? Get a box of crayons and a coloring book; how important is it to color in the lines? To use the "right" colors? Think back to a specific time when you learned that something was really quite different from what you thought. What was the basis for your misconception? Did your explanation make sense at the time? What makes that particular specific experience memorable?

- What should the teacher put in observation notes about Jerry?

5

Social Interaction and Learning

If you were to try to think of all the things you've ever learned in your life, would you be able to remember them all? If you're like most people, probably not. Thinking about all the things you learned in just one year would be daunting. There are probably many things you have learned to do that you aren't even aware of having learned.

Take some time to create a list of 9 or 10 things you have learned in your life—perhaps what you most vividly remember or most value. Your list might include things like learning to read or to ride a bike. It might include things you learned about teaching, or maybe something abstract such as honesty or acceptance of others. After you make your list, rate each item on a scale of 1 to 5 based on social interaction. Assign a 1 to items you learned on your own and a 5 to items you learned with someone or from someone. Rate the remaining items a 2, 3, or 4 based on whether they required more or less social interaction to learn.

How did you decide on a number for each item? Do you see any relationships between the items you gave 5s and the items you gave 1s? Do you see anything that helps you make connections to social interaction? Share your list with another person who has done this exercise. When we did this, we had a long discussion about whether learning through reading was individual or social. Although you are generally alone when you read a book, you are actually interacting with the author. When you learn to see (and there are many types of "seeing"), do you do it alone or do you interact with your environment? And, if someone arranged that environment, are you interacting with that person? What is the difference between learning *with* someone and learning *from* someone? How are these types of learning similar? As you can see, the connection between learning and social interaction is complex, but it is very important.

Look for patterns of social interaction in the list of learning experiences you just made. Are there certain types of social interaction that facilitate learning better for you than others do? Are those interactions also more helpful for other people? For example, can reading an author's work be enough social interaction for children, or do they need to participate in debates with classmates, be questioned by teachers, or write down their thoughts to share with others? How might you, as a science teacher, decide what kinds of interaction work best for your students?

In this chapter, we will look at the role of social interaction in a science classroom and in learning. We want to acquaint you with some of the theories on social interaction as well as with practical ideas to help you facilitate interaction in your classroom. Be sure to discuss these ideas with others, as we believe social interaction is necessary for learning!

■ VYGOTSKY AND SOCIAL INTERACTION

A discussion of social interaction and its importance in the learning process must include the work of Lev Vygotsky, which has stimulated the work of many others. Vygotsky, a lawyer and scholar of philosophy, psychology, and literature, lived in the early 1900s around the same time as Piaget. For political reasons, however, Vygotsky's work was not published until 1956, well after his death from tuberculosis in 1934 (Moll, 1990). Vygotsky brought a unique approach to the study of learning. "It is possible that Vygotsky's creative insights about psychology and child development were partly due to the fresh perspective he brought as an outsider to the field" (Berk & Winsler, 1995, p. 3).

Like Piaget, Vygotsky believed that individuals construct their own knowledge. However, Vygotsky emphasized the social nature of learning much more than Piaget. "Vygotsky's is a social constructivist approach, which emphasizes the social contexts of learning and the fact that knowledge is mutually built and constructed" (Santrock, 2000, p. 262). In other words, Piaget believed that children construct knowledge by transforming, organizing, and reorganizing previous knowledge inside themselves through interaction with the physical environment; Vygotsky felt that children construct knowledge by transforming, organizing, and reorganizing previous knowledge through social interaction with others (Hogan & Tudge, as cited in Santrock, 2000). Vygotsky believed that "we must look not only at the individual and his/her interaction with the external physical world, but also at the immediate social world in which the child is located and at the nature of the interactions that take place within it" (Hodson & Hodson, 1998, p. 36). This "immediate social world" is the context in which children learn, and it includes teachers, peers, and the classroom climate among other factors. In a social constructivist view, this context determines to a large extent the kinds of learning that will take place because it shapes the values children will assimilate and determines the materials needed for learning to take place. Teachers, peers, and climate provide what Vygotsky saw as the necessary tools for learning—language and culture.

Language

Vygotsky saw language as a way to learn rather than simply as a developmental indicator. He believed that children first process their thoughts aloud and then internalize them as they no longer need the auditory feedback for learning. Think back to a difficult class you may have taken or a new skill you were learning. In those situations, did you ever find yourself speaking aloud to get through the steps or the material? For example, you might have talked your way through a difficult statistics problem or your tax form. You might have had to talk through the steps in shifting in a car with a manual transmission. This kind of speech is called private or inner speech (Santrock, 2000). According to Vygotsky, children must use such language to communicate with others and with themselves before they can focus their thoughts inward.

Language, then, is both a way of representing the world and its processes and of communicating that world to others and to oneself. Even as adults, we often talk to others to learn about a topic and later internalize what we have learned. "Most of what humans learn is acquired through discourse and interactions with others" (National Research Council, 2001, p. 88). Unfortunately, children are often discouraged from interacting with others in the classroom. Teachers want quiet rooms with "busy" students who learn material on their own. However, Vygotsky's social constructivism theory suggests that spoken as well as written language should be encouraged, for children need to communicate with others in order to construct knowledge.

Culture

Vygotsky believed that *culture* was as important as biology in learning: "There are two distinct planes on which child development takes place: the natural line and the cultural line. The natural line refers to biological growth and maturation of physical and mental structures. The cultural line refers to learning to use cultural tools and human consciousness, which emerges from engaging in cultural activity" (Berk & Winsler, 1995, p. 5).

Culture, in this sense, refers to both the classroom environment and the larger society. Often, we neglect the effects of culture on learning, forgetting that there are many different cultures even within one society, each culture emphasizing learning differently. While students in one culture are learning to use a computer, students in another culture are learning to hunt for food or to build a home. Culture plays a critical role in what is viewed as important for children to learn and in *how* they learn it.

We also may encounter a multiplicity of student cultures in a single classroom. For example, in most parts of the United States, there are different cultures based on race, ethnicity, and socioeconomic status. The school may have a different culture from children's homes or neighborhoods, one that includes a different language or dialect, even a different value system. In the classroom culture, students are exposed to ideas, language, signs, tools, and people that shape their learning.

The classroom has its own culture and provides an atmosphere in which growth and learning take precedence. A healthy environment enhances children's biological development within a social context; children need to have opportunities to use language, create understanding, and take risks.

Figure 5.1   ZPD Chart

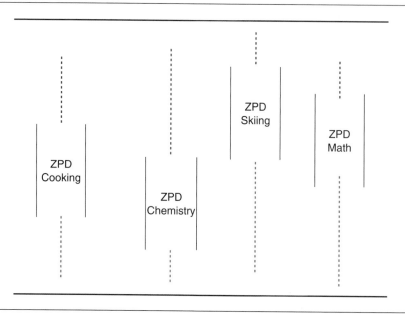

The chart presents one person's zones of proximal development for cooking, chemistry, skiing, and mathematics. Note that each subject area has its own ZPD that depends on the talents, training, and prior learning of the student. Each person has an individual and unique distribution of zones of proximal development.

As with other types of cultures, community interactions within the classroom may be misunderstood. A student teacher once observed a child building a tower with blocks. The child stacked the blocks until they fell and then stacked them a different way in an effort to make the tower taller. At one point, the child stacked the blocks so high that a peer needed to help by getting a stool to stand on in order to add another block. The student teacher was quite worried during this process. What if the blocks fell on the child? Shouldn't the teacher intervene? These thoughts show that the student teacher did not understand the culture of this classroom—that this was a place where children were encouraged to manipulate their environment, to explore, and to try new approaches to tasks and activities. Stacking blocks was an engaging activity in which the child was learning to seriate and arrange materials. The children, being a part of the classroom culture, understood how it operated; as an "outsider," the student teacher looked at events from a different personal perspective.

Of course, teachers must always be aware of safety concerns (see the resource section for a detailed explanation of safety concerns), but they must also be aware of the messages they send children. The experience of the child in the previous paragraph reflects a culture that provided dialogue, support, and autonomy. Eventually, with enough experiences, the child building with blocks will be able to internalize skilled building processes as well as self-support and autonomy; much learning will have taken place. We believe, as did Vygotsky, that learning would not occur without direct experience and social interaction. As you can see, the theories of Piaget and Vygotsky fit together nicely; both biological and cultural factors influence learning. As teachers, we must understand these influences, so we can begin to create an environment that nurtures the development of individual students.

THE TEACHER'S ROLE: PERSONAL EDUCATOR ■

It is clear that teachers are extremely important in the process of constructing knowledge, whether they are parents, more advanced peers, math teachers, or teachers in any subject area. But if teachers and children (students) are *co-constructors* of knowledge, what exactly is the teacher's role in this process? In a sense, the teacher is like a personal trainer, helping educate minds instead of helping train bodies. In this chapter, we will use this analogy to illustrate how teachers weave together biology (maturation) and culture (social interaction) to help individual students learn.

Like getting into shape through exercise, learning is a process that includes high points and low points. You can be filled with adrenaline and excitement one moment and distress, aches, and a desire to give up the next. The key to success in both areas is to stretch your body or mind so that there is stress and tension for a time—but not for too long. In both exercise and learning, there is a zone in which optimum results occur. If you stay beneath that zone, where the exercise or learning is not challenging enough, it is difficult to make any progress and boredom may result. If you try to do too much and go beyond the zone, frustration will prevent you from accomplishing much.

OPTIMUM LEARNING: THE ZONE OF ■ PROXIMAL DEVELOPMENT

Vygotsky referred to this "zone" in which optimum learning takes place as the *zone of proximal development* (ZPD). Vygotsky believed that this optimal zone for learning was unique for every individual. "Each child, in any domain, has an actual developmental level and a potential for development within the domain. The difference between the two levels is what Vygotsky termed the zone of proximal development" (Hausfather, 1996, p. 3). Learning takes place within the ZPD because the material to be learned is challenging yet attainable. However, Vygotsky believed that to operate successfully in the ZPD, learners need to interact socially with peers who have a greater understanding of the subject. "With respect to learning science, Vygotsky's theory suggests that social interaction is essential as learners internalize new or difficult understandings, problems, and processes" (Glasson & Lalik, 1993, p. 189).

Just as different people have different levels of fitness and different exercise zones, different people have different zones of proximal development

Photo 5.1   Building Blocks

Students work to build a high tower of blocks.

for learning in various areas. Look at the ZPD chart in Figure 5.1 showing a hypothetical ZPD for the four subjects. Notice that each subject area is shown in a different place vertically, indicating the relative ease or difficulty this particular individual would experience in learning that subject. The dotted lines above the ZPD represent content that is too difficult for the individual; the dotted lines below the ZPD represent content that is too easy. (Make a ZPD chart for you and the topics you chose. What does your chart look like?)

Learning can take place outside the ZPD, but it is not optimum. In the blue area, learning becomes boring, and one experiences few results. In the red area, learning is frustrating and difficult. Students operating in this area might feel helpless, become resentful, or quit trying. If students remain above their ZPD for an extended time, they may come to believe that they are incapable of learning anything.

The picture of the zone of proximal development provides us with a nice illustration of how individuals progress in their learning. For example, a person might advance more rapidly in physical fitness in the social setting of an aerobics class or with an experienced personal trainer. Similarly, the more social interaction one has with an academic personal trainer (teacher or tutor), the further one can move on the learning continuum. For example, if you are learning chemistry and your only "teacher" is a chemistry book, you may progress more slowly than you would if you also had a chemist as your personal trainer to explain the concepts you were trying to learn. There is no endpoint to the need for social interaction or to a zone; as one learns, the endpoints of the ZPD move so that even experts can learn from other experts. The goal is to keep learners moving forward and to stretch their zone.

IDENTIFYING STUDENTS' ZONES
OF PROXIMAL DEVELOPMENT

Knowing where students are in their understanding of a particular subject is the first step toward helping them move forward in their zones of proximal development. This is not an easy task, particularly in science. It takes time, commitment, and focus; it requires conversations about a topic, assessing students in many different ways, and understanding the content well yourself. Just as you listen to your heart rate to find out if you are exercising within your optimum range, you must listen to students with an authentic interest to determine their zone of proximal development. "During the times when the teacher and children are discussing what they have done, the children will be talking more than the teacher. They will be listening to each other, and responding to each other, and asking each other questions, and giving their opinions" (Duckworth, 1997, p. 26).

Listening to students in a way that facilitates an understanding of their thinking and creates opportunities to genuinely wonder about a topic with them is different from the listening that occurs in many classrooms. In fact, most of the listening that adults do is evaluative, done to find out what facts children know. Fact-gathering questions promote answers that *end* the learning rather than move it forward. "Activity settings in schools need to create and support instructional conversations. To converse involves assuming the learner has something to say beyond answers, engaging learners in the discourse. Too often classroom discourse shuts down students through interrogation instead of dialogue" (Hausfather, 1996, p. 6).

Remember Jerry and the microscope lesson? If I had listened to Jerry only to evaluate what he had learned, my questions might have included

Photo 5.2   Listening to Kids

Mrs. Stiles explores with her students who are growing beanstalks.

these: What do you use a microscope for? What were the things moving in the water? How did you find out what the things were? These are not "bad" questions; as we saw in Chapter 3, there is a place for evaluative questioning and listening. However, promoting active learning within individual zones requires listening to understand *why* a child believes as he or she does. The following questions might have elicited this type of information from Jerry: Describe what you observed. Why do you think there are rocks in the water? What did you notice? "The teacher is compelled to move away from an 'evaluative listening' and toward an 'interpretive listening' in order to open up spaces for re-presentation and revision of ideas—to assess subjective sense rather than to merely assess what has been learned" (Davis, 1996, p. 52). My intent with Jerry was to expand his learning, to help him think in a way that he hadn't before. In other words, I was listening so that I could help stretch his ZPD without pushing him so far beyond what he could understand that he gave up. Listening to his ideas helped me know where he was currently and determine possible directions he could head next.

Note the importance of listening and social interaction in the following experience of a second grade class:

The Great Worm Debate:
The Importance of Listening to Children

Teachers can easily slip into thinking that they know what students understand just by observing them. An incident in my second grade classroom illustrates the importance of questioning students and listening to what they say about what they are observing and learning. One year, we studied mealworms, a type of insect. Near the end of the unit, I heard several children refer to the larvae, soon-to-be beetles, as "worms." I couldn't believe that the students still thought of the mealworms as worms rather than insects. Their thinking was perfectly logical—after all, the insects were called meal*worms*. But I was still flabbergasted that the students were not thinking of them as insects at a different stage in a life cycle. We had completed several activities with the insects, including creating calendars to track their life cycle and experimenting to see what the mealworms would eat. The word *insect* was plastered on bulletin boards all over the room! How could they think these animals were worms?

I concluded that I had focused on the hands-on experiments and observations but hadn't been involved in the students' minds-on work. I wasn't listening; I wasn't questioning the connections they were making. This jolted me into awareness that here was a chance to really help the children learn—to help them move within their zones. The following day we had a debate. I raised the question of whether the mealworms were worms or insects, and students sat on opposite sides of the room according to what they believed. We discussed what a debate was and how to speak kindly to others when challenging their ideas. Everyone had a chance to state reasons for her or his beliefs and then to ask questions to better understand another person's argument. The debate was fascinating. Students on the "insect side" talked about what they had observed during the unit that proved the animals were insects. All asked probing questions and challenged ideas expressed by others.

I had planned the debate for only one science workshop, but several students asked for another debate the next day, so they could have time to collect evidence that supported their ideas. When I agreed, the students scurried to read books, do experiments, and observe the mealworms during free time. Children from different sides of the debate worked together, actively investigating their questions. The unit had come full circle. We started out with hands-on activities, moved to minds-on work, and then came back to more activities as our minds-on work created new questions. "When discrepancies arise between children's thinking and the evidence laid on the table, the teacher assumes a crucial role. Far from being a passive observer, the teacher can actively promote new thinking patterns through a variety of methods" (Watson & Konicek, 1990, p. 684). The debate continued the next day.

Without my listening to their ideas and both questioning and having them question each other, the children would not have discovered as much as they did about mealworms and about pursuing knowledge for themselves. And *I* would not have learned how important it was to listen closely to children rather than assume I understood what they were thinking.

SCAFFOLDING: STRETCHING WITHOUT PULLING

So, once teachers have a feel for where students are in their understanding of a particular topic or concept, how do they get each student moving within his or her ZPD? Going back to our exercise analogy, we see that the personal trainer, knowing the fitness level of the exerciser, must now help the client reach new levels of fitness without pulling any muscles. This "stretching" applied to learners has been termed *scaffolding*. "Scaffolding means changing the level of support over the course of a teaching session, with the more skilled person adjusting guidance to fit the child's current performance level" (Santrock, 2000, p. 261). The more skilled learner—in many cases the teacher—needs to design appropriate experiences, ask guiding questions, and, at times, develop tools for children so that they can learn more effectively. Scaffolding might mean breaking down a task into simpler steps or helping children organize their thoughts and findings in some way. It can also mean building on something the child already knows. Scaffolding requires much planning and knowledge of children's developmental levels, how children learn, and science content.

In exercise, a personal trainer will start with the exerciser's present fitness level and gradually move to higher levels. For example, a person lifting weights might start out with many repetitions of a low weight, gradually adding more and more weight. The trainer might also prescribe specific exercises or regimens for specific muscle groups. Similarly, science teachers start with children's current understandings and provide layered opportunities for them to uncover new ideas about their world. For example, if students do not have a concrete understanding of solids, liquids, and gases, a teacher could begin a study of the stages of matter by providing opportunities for students to observe and manipulate many different familiar solid objects. She might ask them to share their ideas about the properties of the objects (such as hardness, texture, and weight,), then represent and share that knowledge through signs, symbols, and spoken and written language. For instance, students might act out solid molecules stuck together very tightly, draw the concept as an art project, or model it through a modern dance routine. Then, when students have a firmer grasp of what a solid is, the teacher might ask them to connect what they know about solids to a new idea, that of liquids. In a sense, scaffolding is like connecting many different experiences to help learners understand a topic.

Scaffolding children's learning is so important because it provides support rather than merely social interaction. Interaction alone does not guarantee learning: "It cannot be assumed that a child's presence within a stimulating social environment will result in learning. While the presence of others is important, social interaction does not always advance individual learning; particular conditions and forms of interaction are required. Adults need to ensure that the social interactions encouraged by them are of sufficient variety to provide all children with opportunities to interact in ways which suit their learning needs" (Dockett and Perry, 1996, p. 9). Vygotsky's theory of social constructivism isn't only about sharing and learning with others; it is about finding ways to learn through social interactions. Each experience should be connected in some way to what the child knows, enhanced with appropriate language and tools, and planned as a steppingstone to a new level of understanding.

"Another goal of scaffolding is to foster self-regulation by allowing the child to regulate joint activity as much as possible" (Berk & Winsler, 1995, p. 29). Scaffolding is not synonymous with teacher-directed instruction. Students need opportunities to design their own questions and plan their own experiences, and the role of the teacher is to facilitate this, not direct it. "The teacher must collaborate with students to negotiate meaning in ways students can make the knowledge and meaning their own" (Hausfather, 1996, p. 6). An example of this collaboration occurred in a classroom in which students were studying weather. The teacher asked what the students already knew about weather as well as what they wanted to know about it. Many of you will recognize these questions as being based on a great scaffolding tool, an approach called KWL—What we *k*now, what we *w*ant to know, and what we *l*earned. Based on student responses to these questions, the teacher provided a variety of learning opportunities that revolved around students' understanding of weather, their misconceptions about weather, and their interests about the topic. The teacher didn't stop scaffolding there, however. As the students designed projects based on what they wanted to find out about weather, the teacher listened and questioned them. She also provided resources and materials that they might not have thought of using. In this way, the teacher and the students were partners in learning. Students made individual decisions about what they would learn, but collaboration with fellow students and the teacher increased their understanding (moved them forward in their respective ZPD) more than they might have achieved alone.

THE RIGHT AMOUNT OF INTERACTION   ■

Have you ever had a personal trainer who did not give you much direction? How about one who was *so* involved that you never made any decisions about your health or exercise regimen on your own? These two extremes are easy to find in the exercise world. Unfortunately, these two extremes are also found in classroom situations.

The Controlling Guide

When teachers direct students' learning, children may learn skills, facts, and unconnected concepts, but they may not develop dispositions vital to science—including curiosity, continuing interest, initiative, and self-efficacy. Students will not learn to ask questions or dig more deeply into a topic. "Children who are taught what to do, who learn to work within limits and toward fixed objectives determined by adults, and who develop little personal investment in these activities develop a sense of separation from school" (Weikart, 1989, p. 28). In a classroom with adult control rather than adult support, science is often just a collection of facts to be memorized rather than something to discover and wonder about within a community of learners. Science lessons in such a classroom might find students watching and listening as the teacher explains a concept, or learning vocabulary words the teacher believes are important. The result? Often, students become turned off to learning or have difficulty engaging in learning on their own.

Adults also unknowingly contribute to a controlling atmosphere by hurrying students into knowing instead of letting understanding unfold. "As teachers, I think one major role is to undo rapid assumptions of understanding, to slow down closure, in the interests of breadth and depth, which attach our knowledge to the world in which we are called upon to use it" (Duckworth, 1996, p. 78).

The Dispassionate Guide

What does the other extreme look like? Active learning classrooms without enough adult facilitation and interaction are often chaotic and lack direction. Although children in these classrooms have opportunities to create knowledge and try out their ideas, they may fail to reach the understandings they could with a supportive adult or peer questioning their ideas, listening to their reasoning, and helping them find new avenues for learning. "Because of the relative lack of structure and adult involvement inherent in this type of approach, some children may become frustrated. For example, they may have difficulty finding things to do; they may give up in the face of problems; or they may feel anxious, bored, confused, or out of control" (Hohmann & Weikart, 1995, p. 48). This situation can inhibit children from absorbing all they can from their experiences. With too little social support and interaction, children may not be inclined to try a difficult task, to think of alternative ways to do something, or to use all available materials. For example, children looking through a microscope may very well make some interesting observations on their own. However, with even a small amount of adult or peer support, children may achieve a deeper understanding of how microscopes work and of the items being observed. Think about the potential learning involved if a thoughtful adult suggested observing an onionskin, pond water, or words in a newspaper—items a child may not think of investigating with a microscope.

In trying to keep from being too controlling as they implement active learning, some adults fail to offer the support and guidance students need. For example, I once had a two-week period during which I did not start the next science unit because of an upcoming vacation. Instead, I told the students they could study whatever science topic they were interested in. I didn't plan any experiences, I didn't encourage them to build on previous learning, and I didn't help guide their projects in any way. I learned more about the importance of adult support from this experience than the children learned about their chosen topics. With no direction, and without me to wonder with them, the students did not conduct any experiments or inquiries of their own—they simply completed book reports on their subject. Their reports, while not bad, had no life in them. The students chose a topic, looked up some information in an encyclopedia, and wrote down a few sentences. They weren't puzzled, they hadn't struggled, and there was no passion about the topic. Their reports did not reflect the science we could do together as a community; they were not examples of the wonderful ideas and creative insights my students had when I supported them with a variety of materials and opportunities for manipulation, language, and choice.

The Effective Guide

As "personal educators" for students, our job is to foster the appropriate level of challenge with a proper amount of facilitation. "In effect, teaching becomes a matter of orchestrating the learners' experiences rather than of transmitting knowledge, and the teacher is more centrally concerned with attending to emerging understandings than with providing unambiguous explications. The teacher seeks to provide opportunities for learners to make sense in their own way and to derive their own theories, in the process attending, responding, and adapting to student action" (Davis, 1996, p. 232). "Teachers can facilitate learning by conversing with children about their efforts; asking open-ended, thought-provoking questions; making suggestions that help children develop their ideas; and encouraging children to evaluate their own work" (Hohmann & Buckleitner, 1992, p. xii). Social interaction can mean the difference between children excitedly engaging in science ideas, processes, and questioning, on the one hand, and being turned off by science, on the other. Therefore, it is important to listen to children, reflect on actions, and thoroughly understand how different kinds of support affect learning.

Adult facilitation also takes the form of indirect interaction with students, for example,

- Providing resources on topics known to be of student interest
- Carving out time for exploration
- Designing experiences that allow for problem solving and discovery
- Arranging the learning environment for students to learn from one another

In fact, the behind-the-scenes work that effective guides (teachers) do is just as important to the social environment as direct interaction with students.

SOCIAL INTERACTION WITH PEERS ■

So far, we have emphasized the role of the adult in social interaction. There is another important factor in the interaction equation—peers. Peer learning offers many opportunities for cognitive growth. For example, peers often do a wonderful job of helping each other with problems; in fact, students often explain difficult concepts better than adults do.

Students can work together both formally and informally. For instance, you can encourage students with similar interests to work together by providing choices, materials, and opportunities to manipulate objects. During workshops, for example, students choosing to pursue a given type of investigation can be encouraged to work together (i.e., pursue a common interest) and pursue their own approaches, such as presenting their study verbally or through drawings or charts. For more structured learning situations, students can work in cooperative learning groups, specific pairings, or small groups. These groups can be arranged randomly, by the teacher, or by students. Groups should be flexible and heterogeneous, however, and not used as a way of tracking students into ability groups. Students can be grouped according to interest or by differing skills such as reading, drawing, or time keeping. Students can also be grouped so that a different subtopic being studied is covered by each group. For example, one of my

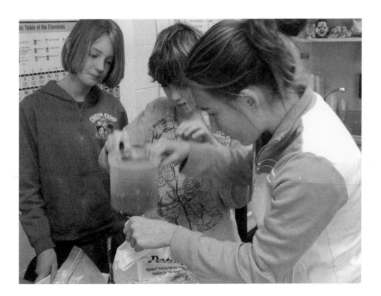

Photo 5.3   Group

Students work together to do an experiment about erosion.

favorite cooperative learning group experiences was with a class of fifth graders making models of mountains. They divided into four groups, and each built a replica in dirt of one of the four kinds of mountains.

Remember that students do not necessarily know how to work with each other. Just like learning to read, ride a bike, or do science, working in a group takes practice and adult guidance and understanding. Two things are being learned—science and how to work in groups. Students need strategies to help them understand what to do when they disagree or when a group member isn't participating or they need help. Children in the younger grade levels may need to spend time practicing the simplest group procedures, such as staying together and speaking respectfully. All of us have had group experiences that were not positive; many people even prefer to work alone on most projects. However, the potential for learning through peer interaction is great if the process is managed well. Sometimes teachers say that they just couldn't let a particular class of students work in groups. Analyze this statement for a moment. Would you not teach reading to a group of children because they had problems at first? Helping students learn to interact in positive ways is a vital part of our educational approach. Rather than look for reasons not to let students work together, structure groups for success by helping students learn how to cooperate and learn from one another and by anticipating potential problems. Working with others is not only a useful tool for learning but also a skill students will need throughout their lives.

Conversation Starters

- Why is social interaction so important for learning? Learning science?

- Social interaction and autonomy seem as though they are opposites. How do they fit together within learning?

- Create your own ZPD chart for teaching. What are some ways you can help yourself "move" within your ZPD?

- Think about teachers who fit into the categories of controlling guide, dispassionate guide, and effective guide. What made you put the teachers into these categories?

- What are some ways to manage students working together? When should students work on their own?

6

Active Learning

As we have seen in the previous two chapters, in order to learn in general and to learn science specifically, children need to develop according to their own maturational timetable and within a social culture that provides them with the tools to construct knowledge. They need to be active participants in their learning both mentally and physically. *Active learning* is our next topic.

ACTIVE LEARNING: HANDS-ON, MINDS-ON ■

When you think of active learning, what do you picture? For many, the term conjures up images of students out of their seats doing a "hands-on" activity. Concrete (physical) experiences are indeed a vital part of active learning. Remember that children at the preoperational and concrete operational stages of development differ in their understanding of representation and relationships. Children who only read about the physics involved in a swinging pendulum do not gain the same depth of understanding as those who are able to observe and manipulate a pendulum. Reading about dinosaurs in a textbook or listening to an "expert" talk about chemical formulas and then repeating what was read or heard does not give children critical thinking skills. Children must *act* upon their environment and *interact* with it. Their writing a play, composing a song, or making models about the material could help turn their minds on and enhance learning.

However, "hands-on" is only a part of active learning. Even being active with one's hands doesn't necessarily mean that conscious learning is taking place. Children must also make mental meaning—that is, construct knowledge—as they experience an event, manipulate an object,

Photo 6.1   Student and Science Log

This student reflects by writing in her science log.

or create something new. Mindless action, such as cutting out premade pictures of the water cycle and hanging them or following specific directions to build a simple machine, does not promote learning. "Action alone is not sufficient for learning. To understand their immediate world, children must interact *thoughtfully* with it" (Hohmann & Weikart, 1995, p. 17). If students are to learn about the water cycle, they need to create the picture of each stage themselves and determine where each belongs in the cycle. If they are to learn about simple machines, they need to experiment with building them, try the machines under different circumstances, look for things that worked and didn't work, and try again. The "active" in active learning is not always something to be seen—it also involves making connections inside the mind about what is happening.

John Dewey (1938) said, "There should be brief intervals of time for quiet reflection provided for even the young. But they are periods of genuine reflection only when they follow after times of more overt action and are used to organize what has been gained in periods of activity in which the hands and other parts of the body beside the brain are used" (p. 63). Experiences that promote thinking, lingering, and mental meandering at the same time as or immediately after the physical activity are keys to learning and to understanding. Providing active learning opportunities means helping children have the richest, most thoughtful experience possible.

> "Active learning is a complex physical and mental process. It is an interaction between the goal-oriented actions of the learner and the environmental realities that affect those actions" (Hohmann & Weikart, 1995, p. 16).

Many concepts in science require formal operational thinking to be truly understood. But this does not mean we should wait to expose children to the *experiences* leading to the concept. It means that we have to design experiences so that children are able to construct the knowledge they are ready for, either on their own or with the assistance of a more knowledgeable peer or adult. For example, most elementary children do not understand changes in matter in the way adults or adolescents do. However, young children in the preoperational and concrete operational stages of development can experiment with different solids, liquids, and gases, describe their properties, and compare them. Building with solid materials or playing with containers and tubes at a water table helps preoperational children form ideas and connections that will be valuable foundations for later learning. The experience of observing bubbles and then drawing a picture of the gas molecules trapped between the liquid molecules helps concrete operational children form a mental picture of the differences among the states of matter. "Piaget intends that teachers provide children with the opportunities to explore to its fullest the range of thought at a given stage and to build the strongest possible foundation for succeeding stages. It is this kind of active exploration which makes children aware of the limitations of a particular kind of thinking and to initiate the construction of more effective ways" (Labinowicz, 1980, p. 158).

"Children's sense-making activities can be seen as efforts to achieve the best understanding they can with the intellectual capacities they possess at a given stage of development" (Katz & Chard, 1989, p. 21).

THE EMOTIONAL SIDE OF ACTIVE LEARNING ■

In addition to physical and mental processes, active learning is also an emotional process. Our prior experiences provide an emotional predisposition to learning, and our moment-by-moment feelings provide a disposition to continue learning or to stop learning. The latest brain research supports this notion as well. Caine and Caine (1991) suggest that "we do not simply learn things. What we learn is influenced and organized by emotions and mind sets based on expectancy, personal biases and prejudices, degree of self-esteem, and the need for social interaction" (p. 90). Emotional events receive preferential treatment in the brain, and emotions themselves help us remember things better and form more explicit memories (Cahill, Prins, Weber, & McGaugh, 1994; Christianson, 1992). Jensen (2005) believes, "Good learning does not avoid emotional states; it embraces them, recognizing emotional states as fast changing, specific neural networks that incorporate multiple areas of the brain" (p. 72).

Children who do not feel safe to explore and try out their ideas will be emotionally hampered in learning. Children who come to believe that learning is for taking tests and going on to the next grade will not feel the need or the ability to take the risks and ask the gnawing questions needed to learn with any depth. For example, at the beginning of the year my students would tell me "You can't do that" when I had them mix salt and water together and spread it on the table to see if the salt would evaporate. Past experience told them it was not okay to spill water on the table. Because of this, they weren't even able to let themselves wonder what might happen in this experiment. Of course, we should not encourage destruction of property for the sake of learning. However, we do need to be aware of how rules, right and wrong answers, the emotional climate of our rooms, and our reactions to exploration affect children's emotions and therefore their learning.

Usually, the students in my room get over their reluctance to suspend the rules quite rapidly. Hillary, for example, after mixing several liquids together in class to discover their properties, went home and proceeded to mix her mother's lotions, shampoos, and so on. Hillary's mom told me

Photo 6.2   Mixing Liquids

Student observes that his mixture turned yellow!

that, although she was really glad Hillary loved science, this was a little much. Our students need to feel safe to explore, but they also need to understand that it is important to ask before exploring! However, in our classrooms we can set up an area that is a "safe" place for exploration.

> Think for a moment about your own feelings and emotions regarding science. How were those feelings formed? How do they affect your learning now? How do they affect the children you work with?

Creating a minds-on, hands-on, emotionally safe place where children can initiate, wonder, take apart, put back together, move, test, and ask is not easy. It takes a new perception of what it means to educate. "Piaget once said: 'The principal goal of education is to create men who are capable of doing new things, not simply of repeating what other generations have done—men who are creative, inventive, and discoverers. The second goal of education is to form minds which can be critical, can verify, and not accept everything they are offered. We need pupils who are active, who learn early to find out by themselves, partly by their own spontaneous activity and partly through materials we set up for them; we learn early to tell what is verifiable and what is simply the first idea to come to them'" (Elkind, 1981, p. 29). The framework we discuss will help you create this kind of classroom—a classroom in which active learning is the foundation for every experience.

Jensen (2005) gives us seven ways we can help engage emotions appropriately to help students learn. They are:

- Ask compelling questions
- Model a love of learning
- Celebrate learning
- Use physical activity
- Engineer controversy
- Use purposeful physical rituals
- Use activities that engage students personally (p. 79)

THE INGREDIENTS FOR ACTIVE LEARNING ■

Although this book is not meant to be a step-by-step cookbook for teaching science, there are some ingredients for active learning that should be included as you prepare your own "recipes." Just as you have a few staples such as sugar and flour in your pantry that can be mixed in different ways for different dishes, the ingredients for active learning can be tailored to individual classrooms, teachers, and students. Each ingredient will help children engage in meaningful, active learning at their maturational level. However, the way in which you put the ingredients together to create a "masterpiece" depends on your situation and your students. Five staple ingredients for learning science are *materials, manipulation, choice, language,* and *adult support.*

Materials

A classroom with a variety of materials that connect to ideas, activities, and exploration promotes and nurtures active learning. What materials come to mind when you picture an active learning science classroom? Manipulatives, books, and computers? Test tubes and safety goggles? Rocks, plants, and live animals? Indeed, materials constitute a wide variety of "things" both inside and outside a classroom. The materials in an interactive classroom do not need to be fancy or expensive, but they do need to be accessible to children, organized, and safe; and we must exchange them from time to time in order to spark children's curiosity and interest. Materials are an active learning ingredient because they

- Provide vital learning connections for students who are not yet able to explore abstract ideas
- Help challenge students' thinking based on their manipulations
- Encourage exploration and interest in learning science
- Provide tactile learning opportunities that affect students' unconscious memory systems

> "Learning grows out of the child's direct actions on the materials" (Hohmann & Weikart, 1992 p. 38).

As we saw in Chapter 4, young children need to observe, physically touch, and manipulate materials because their cognitive structures are not yet developed in such a way that they can think about ideas they have not experienced. Imagine trying to learn about insects if you've never seen one, and how much easier it is when actually presented with ants, beetles, crickets, milkweed bugs, and so on. Topics such as the solar system and the life cycle of stars become more real when children make their own models using pictures, globes, flashlights, paper moons and stars, and other materials that students can manipulate. I often had students create paper costumes with hats depicting different celestial bodies. In small groups, they used flashlights and experimented with the rotation of the earth and its tilt to figure out difficult questions such as how different seasons occur. Students also created moons using plaster of Paris to solve the question of why part of the moon looks dark and part looks light. Keep in mind, these manipulatives correspond to models, and the use of models is a "unifying strand" in science standards (National Research Council, 1996).

Of course, print materials such as books and photographs are valuable resources that can provide great variety and can be changed regularly. There are many wonderful children's books on every science topic! Many of these have multicultural themes. Providing these kinds of books along with photographs and videotapes can create interest in a topic, provide ideas for experiments, and help children better understand a concept. Make sure you offer a variety of books at all levels for students to choose from; even if the reading level of a book seems too difficult for your students, the pictures will be helpful. Check out the list of children's literature in the resource section of this text for suggested books. Your librarian can make recommendations as well.

Materials provide an air of excitement to any science classroom. Children enthusiastically come to science class when they know it is finally the day to make habitats for the milkweed bugs that have just arrived or the day to experiment with the pipes and tubes at the water table. Children feel like the real scientists that they are when they can wear goggles and lab coats and use scientists' tools, such as petri dishes and eyedroppers. Materials make science accessible to students of all levels, enabling them to feel competent.

Manipulation

Classrooms may have a rich supply of materials that are accessible to children and still not be active learning settings. Do you know of classrooms in which students aren't active despite having a lot of materials? The materials themselves cannot cause active learning; they must be manipulated either mentally or physically (preferably both) to facilitate learning. In active learning settings, "the child has opportunities to explore, manipulate, combine, and transform the materials chosen" (Hohmann & Weikart, 2002, p. 38).

Words like *explore, manipulate, combine,* and *transform* are all active verbs. They describe hands-on, minds-on experiences. Compare these words to those often emphasized in science standards and teaching materials, such as *master, comprehend, use,* and *compare.* These are also active verbs, but they do not require students to construct their own understanding. In classrooms emphasizing this second way of learning, teachers dispense knowledge and students are expected to store it and repeat it later.

What does it mean to manipulate an object or idea? What does it look like in a classroom? How can teachers facilitate active learning through manipulation?

Dewey emphasized the importance of active engagement in learning: "Education, in order to accomplish its ends both for the individual learner and for society, must be based upon experience—which is always the actual life experience of some individual" (Dewey, 1938, p. 89). Dewey did not mean "experience" in the way that this word is commonly understood. He described experience as a fully engaging movement in thinking rather than as a passive passage through time. What's the difference? Consider a lesson on electricity. Children might manipulate wires, batteries, and lightbulbs in order to light a miniature house they built. There might be several trials in which something doesn't work and children have to figure out the problem and try a different method. These children are engaged in thinking for themselves, in building their own experience. In contrast, a passive lesson might require children to listen to an instructor describe the necessary procedures for creating a circuit and watch her do so. These children have no experience, in Dewey's sense of the term, upon which to build an understanding of the subject.

Another important component of manipulation is taking something apart and putting it back together to see how it works or to make it do something different. I think of a young boy who once rewired his family's entire phone line in order to gain phone service in his room. When his parents found out about this "manipulation," they made him undo everything he had done. Although this was not a sanctioned activity, it was definitely a learning experience. Think of all of the ideas, problems, and questions this child had to consider as he manipulated the phone wires.

How can you create valid opportunities for children to take things apart and put them back together? This doesn't have to be a physical activity; manipulation can be done mentally as well. In fact, active learning can be thought of as the tie between physically and mentally manipulating an idea or a problem. A science problem could be "taken apart" and then "put back together" through conversation, debate, or questioning. When students are allowed to manipulate materials and develop and discuss ideas, learning doesn't end. Manipulation and reflection generate new questions and new possibilities.

Think of a time when you were really engaged in manipulating an idea or an object. What did you learn? What feelings did you have? Many people describe becoming engaged in a project or an idea as "getting lost" in their work. Have you ever been so engaged in something that you lost track of time or didn't hear someone talking to you? Sadly, science in school is often a time of getting the right answer rather than getting lost in the process of learning. "Of all of the virtues related to intellectual functioning, the most passive is the virtue of knowing the right answer. Knowing the right answer requires no decisions, carries no risks, and makes no demands. It is automatic. It is thoughtless" (Duckworth, 1996, p. 64). In contrast, asking questions, wondering aloud, and listening to children's ideas as they manipulate objects create opportunities for them to learn actively.

Choice

The word *choice* may be frightening to you. Thinking about letting go of some of the decision making often creates images of students out of control in the classroom, or at least not actively engaged. However, giving students choices and the freedom to make some of their own decisions actually helps them become responsible for their actions and more interested in their work. It also gives them a sense of accomplishment when they finish. "Since learning results from the child's attempts to pursue personal interests and goals, the opportunity to choose activities and materials is essential" (Hohmann & Weikart, 1992, p. 38).

The choices you provide in a science workshop setting will depend on the level of children's maturation and the type and purpose of the activity. Think about the different kinds of choices involved in the examples below.

- At the beginning of the year, a class of students was learning to observe from different perspectives. I asked them to *choose* one object from the room and draw it. Then I had them *choose* a different position (standing up, lying on the floor, moving to a spot across the room) to observe that same object and draw it. Later we discussed what happens to our perspective when we change our position.

- When we studied plants, I brought in many kinds of seeds and asked groups of students to *choose* ways to categorize them. The groups shared their categories and how they had come up with them.

- At the end of a two-month unit on solids, liquids, and gases, we made taffy to study the different states of matter of one substance. The students got to *choose* the color of food coloring and a flavoring to add to the taffy, and a role for each participant in the group.

- During another lesson on solids, liquids, and gases, students built towers as tall as they could. Later, they evaluated the properties of solids and discussed reasons that it was impossible to build a tower with liquids or gases. Students got to *choose* materials from an assortment of solids, how to build their towers, and how to display the finished towers.

- When we studied the human body, students *chose* the system (respiratory, circulatory, and so on) they were most interested in studying. They *chose* a project to make and share, as well as the materials they would use. One group formed each bone out of boiled spaghetti to show the skeletal system. One group created a pumping heart, arteries, and veins out of pop bottles, plastic tubing, and red or blue water, which they pumped by squeezing the bottle.

> Think about lessons you have planned. How could you add elements of choice into those experiences?

As you can see, letting children choose takes a lot of trust and a different kind of planning. Sometimes, children make choices that adults wouldn't make. If, however, we want our students to learn actively and develop socially, emotionally, and cognitively, we need to let them make decisions and help them understand the consequences of those decisions. As Kamii (2000) said, "Children learn to make decisions by making decisions" (p. 65). However, it is clear from these examples that children are not left entirely on their own when making choices. The teacher is actively involved in structuring the choices. When an activity could be dangerous (as with the taffy experiment), choices are restricted. When the lesson is very broad and has room for more depth (for example, studying the body systems), more choices can be given.

Why is choice so important for learning? Giving students a variety of choices empowers them to wonder, explore, and become "experts" on a topic. It gives them autonomy, enabling children to think for themselves and believe in their answers. Having to decide about materials, the next steps in a project, and ways to share with others requires deeper thinking than simply following a recipe. In making decisions, students access their prior experiences and knowledge and build from there. In addition, having some control over their learning is a powerful motivator. If children choose to study the human brain because it interests them, learning is more meaningful and engaging. Aren't you more eager to read a book or engage in a task that you find interesting rather than do something that is required? Finally, making decisions, choosing paths, is important because this skill will serve children well throughout their lives. Connecting to past experiences, predicting the consequences of their decisions and actions, and reflecting on their choices will help children be successful and independent in all their endeavors. In short, choice:

- Empowers students
- Makes connections with past experiences
- Motivates learning
- Develops decision-making skills

Materials, manipulation, and *choice* are vital, interrelated active learning ingredients. Making decisions about what materials to use and then physically and mentally manipulating them requires a great deal from children. However, there are two other important ingredients: language and adult support. Language and adult support are necessary because they challenge children to think more deeply. Perhaps it is useful to think of materials, manipulation, and choice as the batter of a learning cake. It tastes good on its own, but it isn't quite finished. An oven is needed to transform the batter into a delicious cake. Language and adult support provide the "heat" necessary to activate the first three ingredients.

Language

As you saw in Chapter 5, language is a tool—for communication, representing ideas and specific vocabulary, and connecting thoughts. We often think of language as involving words, but, more broadly, language is also present in music, art, poetry, and movement. However you define language, it is important to understand that language transforms learning and needs to support materials, manipulation, and choice. "Language plays a crucial role in a socially formed mind because it is our primary avenue of communication and mental contact with others, serves as the major means by which social experience is represented psychologically, and is an indispensable tool for thought" (Berk & Winsler, 1995, p. 9).

We usually view language as a final learning product that shows us what students have learned: a summary paper, artwork, or an oral report. Language is a valuable assessment tool; however, it is also a *transformational* tool for learning. Language can be used, then, not just to show that learning has occurred, but as a way to learn. In other words, language isn't just a way to represent thoughts and ideas. It is a way to create meaning.

To illustrate, learning is taking place as students collect and manipulate different liquids. However, the transformation in *thinking* about liquids takes place as the students use words to describe them, such as *sticky, thin, bubbly,* and *opaque,* or as they draw the liquids, categorize them, and explain to classmates why they chose the categories they did. They form new mental structures as they organize information and use language to describe it. In other words, language gives order to students' thinking. It is a tool that helps them create knowledge.

Language can be used at different levels of thinking as well. Memorization and organization are two examples. Many of the ways you memorize items likely use language; for instance, you might memorize a list in alphabetical order or create an acronym out of the items. Memorization is a very basic connection between cognitive development and language. A deeper level of thinking provided by language is organization. Language organizes the insights students gain while manipulating materials. Once I brought in several kinds of seeds for my students to observe and manipulate, everything from apple seeds to acorns to peanuts. As they observed, they discussed the differences in the seeds, categorized them, debated which they thought were seeds and which weren't, and shared with the class their rationales. Although some children believed that not all of the items they were observing were seeds, by the end of class they better understood what made something a seed. The tool of language helped them organize their ideas about seeds, challenge those ideas, and reorder them into a different scheme. Not only did students learn about seeds, but also, through language, they created different mental structures that would later help them learn other ideas.

Language can also create disequilibrium for children, which, as we saw in Chapter 5, leads to greater depth of understanding. Therefore, language creates a cycle of learning: language provokes learning, which provokes more language, and so on. For instance, Yair and Andrew created a wall-sized mural during a study of the ocean. They exercised choice, used a variety of materials, and manipulated their ideas within the languages of art, research, and conversation. Yair drew all kinds of ocean animals that he had read about, but then was thrown into disequilibrium by Andrew's questions about what those animals ate and what their shelter was. The two boys scoured the library to find the answers, and then added these details to their mural. Without these conversations, Yair and Andrew might have experienced this topic just on the surface level. They may not have discovered the relationships between animals and plants or the consequences of human actions on the ocean. Their learning about the ocean would have ended where it began instead of cycling through many different questions, ideas, and insights.

"The notion that language shapes mental functioning is not unique to Vygotsky's approach. Many contemporary theories emphasize that cognitive development involves increasingly sophisticated forms of representation, each advance permitting the child to engage in more complex cognitive operations" (Berk & Winsler, 1995, p. 21).

Language is also used to create mental representations of actions and ideas. Piaget called this "reflective abstraction—or the chance to reflect on one's thinking, without which development does not occur" (Watson & Konicek, 1990, p. 684). Pondering an action, observation, or idea—through mental or written language—is something we don't often give children time to do. Instead, we scurry from topic to topic, never really letting concepts sink in or develop. All of us have been puzzled by something in our lives that we wanted more time to think through. Have you ever said, "Give me a minute to think about it"? Children need those "minutes" as well. "Teachers are often, and understandably, impatient for their students to develop clear and adequate ideas. But putting ideas in relation to each other is not a simple job. It *is* confusing; and that confusion *does* take time" (Duckworth, 1996, p. 82). Have you ever learned more about a topic through writing about it? We are definitely learning as we write this book. Using language to reflect on actions or ideas allows us to think about what we are learning, develop a deeper understanding of the learning that has already taken place, and forge a pathway for new learning.

Although language is an integral part of subjects like reading, writing, and language arts, it is also vital to science, as Yair's and Andrew's experience illustrates. "Because of its crucial role in transforming cognitive development and its importance for effective communication and participation in cultural activities, language and literacy should receive the utmost attention" (Berk & Winsler, 1995, p. 151). Students need opportunities to define their ideas, debate disagreements, and share findings. They need time to reflect silently or in writing about their materials, manipulations, and choices. They also need to be asked questions, listened to, and given new ideas to contemplate. Conversation is often treated more as a leisurely endeavor than a serious mental action. However, having conversations around meaningful topics and explorations can be highly engaging and thoughtful. "Conversation has a spirit of its own, and the language in which it is conducted bears its own truth within it—it allows something to emerge which henceforth exists" (Gadamer, 1964, p. 383). Through language, children wonder together, imagine together, and question together. This language bond should be facilitated through group work, peer mentoring, and the provision of time for conversations.

Meaningful conversations between teacher and student are particularly rare. Limited time, multiple objectives, and the number of students all reduce opportunities for these conversations. However, they are perhaps one of the most valuable learning tools of all. Language from an adult is different and usually more complex than that from another child, and adults often have background knowledge of subjects or topics that help them ask more probing questions or clarify a point better than a peer. Read on to discover more reasons that adult support is a vital ingredient of active learning.

Adult Support

In some ways, adult support is really what this book is all about. It is the teaching adult who will obtain materials, provide choices, encourage manipulation, and probe for representation in the form of language. It is the adult who recognizes the uniqueness of each child and assesses what will best help the child construct knowledge.

Beyond these forms of support, what else do children need from adults? What types of support are we talking about? When should they be given? This highly depends on the particular student and situation. Each is unique; each needs an individual approach and the teacher's discernment.

I often enabled students in my classroom to work on different projects based on the same topic. For example, they created representations of different systems of the body. I supported them in different ways and to varying degrees as necessary. Some students only needed someone to challenge their ideas and push them to new levels of learning with questions and conversations. Others needed specific learning tools, like word webs or other organizers. Still others needed step-by-step guidance, help with reading, and immediate feedback on their projects.

Some of your support doesn't even occur during class time. It involves assessing individual children's maturational level and science interests,

Figure 6.1   Mountain Climbing Guides

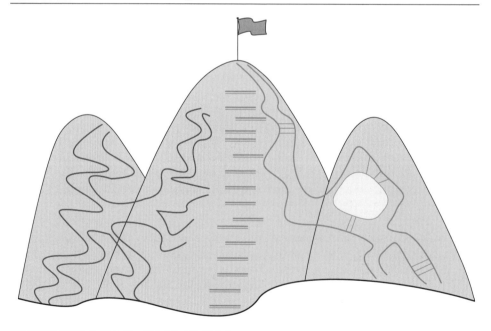

Supporting students is like helping them climb a mountain. You can be a dispassionate guide (left trail) who leaves students on their own to "get lost" and go slowly towards the summit. You can be the controlling guide (middle trail) who gets students to the summit quickly but does not allow any choice in their learning. We recommend being an effective guide (right trail) who enables student choice but also provides guidance as students make their way to the summit.

gathering and organizing materials, and planning and developing science experiences that are both physically and mentally active and that are scaffolded from experience to experience in order to provide appropriate activities. In the classroom, your support might include asking questions, listening to children's ideas and challenging them, providing both cultural and language tools for individuals, and learning with the students.

Language and adult support can also help students develop metacognition. For example, when a student chooses the next step in a project, or a particular type of material to use, or a method of representation, the teacher and student can consider why the student made these choices. Together, they can explore the student's unique learning style, capabilities, interests, attitudes toward science, and problem areas. They can then devise strategies for learning that take these into account. Learning is complex, and these aspects of the learning experience are not readily developed without language and adult support.

Adult support is vital to active learning, but it must be the *right kind* of support. As we saw in Chapter 5, offering your support to students does not mean telling and demonstrating, and it doesn't mean sitting back and letting students stumble their way through activities. True support is the art of helping students get to the place where they don't need support any longer. After all, they won't always be in your classroom!

Ask yourself if your classroom (or one you have observed) is an active learning setting. Are the students engaged mentally and physically with science problems and ideas? Are they emotionally engaged in science? Does the classroom utilize the ingredients of materials, manipulation, choice, language, and adult support? Active learning will give students wonderful opportunities not only to learn science but also to become lifelong learners!

Photo 6.3   Adult Support

Students have a conversation with their teacher who provides adult support for their experiences and ideas.

In this chapter, we've looked at the ingredients necessary for students to flourish—ingredients that take into account individual maturational and social needs. Children construct knowledge by choosing materials, manipulating them physically, constructing representations of them mentally, and being "stretched" in this process through interactions with adults. As you think about ways to support children's active learning experiences, keep in mind the *whole* child. We don't teach English or history or biology or physics—we teach André and Chen and James and Elena!

Conversation Starters

- Is there really a difference between active learning and learning? Is one able to learn without being actively engaged in the topic?

- Since emotions are so closely connected to learning, what changes might you make to the physical aspects of your classroom to capitalize on this fact?

- Of the five ingredients for active learning, which do you believe is the most important? Why?

- Are we missing any ingredients for active learning?

- Why do you think this book on teaching science has three chapters about learning in it?

PART III

Classroom Experiences

You have made it through the construction of Part II! Next, we move into the nuts and bolts of teaching science at the elementary level—the classroom structure and experiences that foster children's intellectual and social development, their independence, and their understanding of science. John Dewey said, "The belief that all genuine education comes about through experience does not mean that all experiences are genuinely or equally educative" (1938, p. 25). What kinds of science experiences are "genuinely educative" for elementary children? What structures best enable students to participate in those experiences? How do teachers utilize their knowledge of individual students?

Several classroom concepts and components—key science experiences, thinking routines, and workshops, all of which you will learn about in this section—will help you create meaningful, educative experiences for all children within a supportive environment of teachers and peers. We have identified a cycle of six *key science experiences* that are an important part of any science activity: observing, representing, organizing, patterning/questioning, experimenting, and sharing. Although these experiences generally follow the order listed here, each may occur at any point during a particular activity or unit of study. Each may also occur at different levels of learning depending on the needs and maturity of individual students. We discuss this cycle in greater depth and provide some examples of each part of the cycle in Chapter 7.

Chapter 8 examines *thinking routines*. Although the key science experiences frame much of what must happen within science lessons, thinking routines create a framework for individuals to create their own pathways toward learning new ideas. Although adults use thinking routines almost constantly while planning vacations, solving problems, and working with others, young children do not automatically have these structures. This chapter examines what thinking routines are and helps you embed them in your lessons, so students can begin to use them automatically as a part of their learning.

The final chapter describes the lesson planning structure of a workshop. *Workshops* are small-group or individual experiences centered on a particular content topic. (For the purposes of this book, we will consider only workshops dealing with science activities.) Workshops bring together the aspects of active learning, maturation, social interaction, the nature of science, the key science experiences, and thinking routines to create learning opportunities for students. In Chapter 9, we describe workshops in general, give examples of workshops we have created, and present some tips for developing your own.

The information in this section will build on your knowledge of active learning, the nature of science, maturation, and social interaction to help you develop a sense of how to implement an integrated educational approach within your classroom. We want you to be able to teach science in a way that helps children develop their problem-solving abilities, their scientific knowledge, their metacognitive (learning about their own learning) knowledge, and their disposition toward science.

7

Key Science Experiences

Because we are interested in an educational approach that addresses the *whole* child, not simply the part that will learn science, our key science experiences reflect more than just what children learn in science. We are interested in more than educating young scientists; we want to develop self-reliant young people who know they can (and who do) achieve what they are capable of achieving. We want to help children reach their full potential as individuals, as citizens of our democracy. Therefore, as we consider the key science experiences, we will examine them from at least two perspectives: how they relate to science itself (and how the ability to learn science develops) and how they relate to the development of the whole child (how these experiences develop children's learning potential).

THE KEY SCIENCE EXPERIENCES ■

The individual words in *key science experiences* are a clue to the meaning of the whole phrase. Each of us knows the "key" to something. For example, I called my mother about making pies at Thanksgiving one year, and she told me "the key to good pie crust is cold water." What she meant, of course, was that using cold water produces satisfactory or better results more frequently than using water of other temperatures. The adjective *key*, then, means that an item plays a central role in a process—it is something either essential or at least more important than other factors for success.

An *experience* is an interaction, an event in which one participates. The experience may be passive, in which case the environment acts upon the individual, or the experience may be active (as the key science experiences are), in which case the individual acts upon the environment or interacts with others. Thus, the key science experiences describe interactions children have with their environment that are important for their development. Although we present the key science experiences in a general sequence, students themselves will exhibit them in different ways and at different times. With time and experience, they will use these capacities in different and more sophisticated contexts. As you plan opportunities for these experiences in your classroom, you will note children's strengths and weaknesses and can provide activities supporting their individual needs.

■ A WHEEL OF KEY SCIENCE EXPERIENCES

As we discussed earlier, science is a way of knowing as well as a set of tentative conclusions about how the world is organized and how it works. The elementary key science experiences are the means by which students learn this "way of knowing." We have used parts of the key science experiences discussed by Blackwell & Hohmann (1991), ideas from Gardner's multiple intelligences and from the *National Science Education Standards* (1996), and our own ideas to create *key science experiences* that follow a typical pattern of scientific investigations. We have organized these processes in a cycle or wheel, as shown in Figure 7.1. *Observing, representing, organizing, detecting patterns/questioning,* and *experimenting* form the ring or rim of the wheel. The hub—about which all the other processes revolve—is *sharing.* "Doing science" involves using all of these processes, although not necessarily all at one time. For example, a person can do one or two of these activities in any given session and still be doing science. However, for a complete science study on a particular topic, students will participate in all of the processes.

Note that each process involves several different subprocesses. Many of these activities also help students learn skills that can be used in other life areas. For example, when Ellie makes a drawing of a tree in science, she is also developing her spatial intelligence and artistic and motor skills. When Henry imitates a grasshopper, he is developing his bodily/kinesthetic intelligence. Let's examine each of the key science experiences and how to incorporate them into the classroom.

Observing

Observation probably starts several months before birth, as soon as the nervous system begins to mature, and it continues throughout life. Infants take in information about their world through their senses—touch, sight, sound, taste, smell—as well as through proprioceptors (receptors that tell them, for instance, where their body and its parts are in space). This sensory data is processed by the brain to construct knowledge about the environment. From the most basic ways of observing—handling a material, looking at it from different perspectives, tapping it, listening to its natural sounds (if any) and those made when it is tapped, struck, stroked, and so on—to the most advanced techniques that are being developed today, observation is a central skill.

Therefore, children should be given every opportunity to develop their observational skills. This begins with handling materials that are safe

Figure 7.1 Wheel of Key Science Experiences

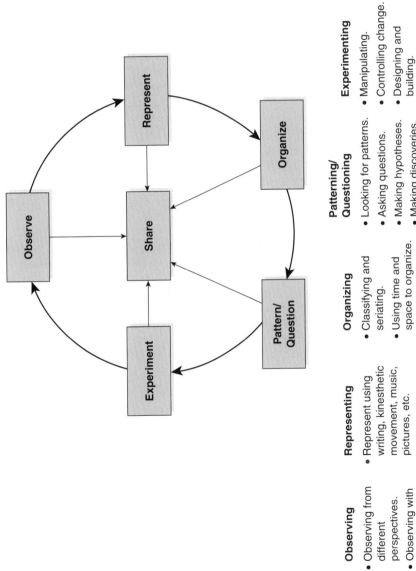

Observing
• Observing from different perspectives.
• Observing with different tools.
• Observing with different senses.
• Designing chances to observe.

Representing
• Represent using writing, kinesthetic movement, music, pictures, etc.
• Represent in groups, or alone.
• Represent using many media.

Organizing
• Classifying and seriating.
• Using time and space to organize.
• Graphing charting.

Patterning/Questioning
• Looking for patterns.
• Asking questions.
• Making hypotheses.
• Making discoveries.
• Relationships.

Experimenting
• Manipulating.
• Controlling change.
• Designing and building.
• Problem solving.

Sharing
• Debating, reflecting, reporting, using interpersonal and intrapersonal skills.

for them to touch, such as leaves, rocks, sticks, organisms like mealworms and earthworms, electrical wires, batteries, and various kinds of wood. In short, so long as the material will not harm the child—and the child will not harm the material!—every effort should be made to let the child handle it and observe it with as many senses as possible. We are hesitant to recommend that young students "taste" or even smell unknown materials, however, because of the danger of their trying this on their own.

Although simply handling materials is a way of learning about them, children will more efficiently use their powers of observation when they have a purpose for observing. For example, they will more closely observe and gain more information about mealworms (larvae of certain beetles) if they are looking for specific parts or ways to distinguish these organisms from the larvae of other insects. Hence, teachers should provide a purpose to observation and not simply direct children to "observe" an object or event.

After giving children plenty of opportunities to use their senses to observe, introduce simple and then more complex instruments to help them observe. Extension of the senses enables children to make finer distinctions in their observations and quantitative assessments as well. Children can learn to measure in nonstandard units (the number of steps from their seat to the door, the number of pipe cleaners equaling the length of the room), move on to standard measurements (inches, pounds, gallons), and then to scientific measurements (centimeters, kilograms, liters). From determining with their bodies whether something is hot, warm, comfortable, cool, or cold, students can graduate to measuring temperatures in Fahrenheit or Celsius with a thermometer. And so on.

You might be hesitant to use more complex observational instruments with young students. Of course, your knowledge of your students is always a powerful decision-making tool. However, do not underestimate how much young scientists can do. Magnifying glasses and even microscopes are appropriate in most cases.

Remember that children need to *actively* observe. In addition to providing materials, give them choices. They could choose

- The order of observation
- The angle of observation
- The senses they will use
- The tools they will use

Choices such as these will enable students at all levels to challenge themselves and make the observations their own. For example, if a class of kindergarteners is asked to observe materials and determine which will float or sink, allow them to choose the materials. Encourage the kindergarteners to observe the materials with different tools to help them make predictions. Suggest materials that are more difficult to categorize for students who have had experience with sinking and floating while suggesting more basic materials for those who have not. Choices such as these will also help young students learn to think about their actions, plan ahead, and make decisions—all important life skills.

Observing is a vital action in any science lesson. However, observation and the word "observe" can be incorporated into many lessons. Students in math can "observe" patterns in their answers or manipulatives and pictures to help them solve problems. They can make observations about characters in stories and changes in their own work over time.

Observation is closely tied to both representation and sharing. Students can describe what they observe in words, pictures, or actions. After representing and sharing their observations, they can organize their findings and perhaps notice some patterns. Although some learning will occur simply from observation itself, encouraging students to extend those observations in some way will help them make links among all the data they collect.

Representing

Representation allows us to communicate ideas and observations to others. In fact, it is even how we consciously communicate with ourselves. Representation is key to learning because it allows us to be accountable for what we understand or have observed. Have you ever thought you understood something until you had to represent it? I often remind myself that I didn't really know what a decimal was until I had to cut a piece of paper into ten pieces. Representing something that we have observed requires a different level of understanding than merely observing it.

Part of your role as a facilitator of learning is to encourage children to use multiple ways of representing. You can do this by making a variety of media available: pencils, paper (lined for writing and unlined for drawing), coloring tools (crayons and markers), media for molding and sculpting (for example, clay), and cameras to take pictures of things they have observed.

Photo 7.1   Picture of Magnet Lesson

This is a first grader's rendition of working with magnets at three different stations. He discovered that he could move paper clips on top of his table with a magnet under his table. He discovered that he could attract more than one paper clip to his magnet (notice the numbers 1, 2, 3 as he counted how many he could attract).

Sometimes you might indicate the way you want children to symbolize their observations:

- "Draw a picture of what you saw"
- "Write a description of what happened when the little girl turned the spinning wheel sideways"
- "Show me how the monkey walked"

In other instances, you can leave the choice up to them: "Choose some way—a story or a picture, maybe—to share what you noticed." Remember that younger students, especially, may need some initial assistance in making and carrying out this choice. In time, they will become more independent. As the skills and tools of observation increase, making measurements and representing observations in numerical form become more important. Remember, too, that some representations will take place over time. A study of insects or plants might require several representations after observing each day or each week.

When you ask children to represent, take into account their individual strengths and learning styles. When you were in elementary school, how many of you could have represented your understanding of a topic very well in a drawing but wouldn't have done so well on a written test? Some children may represent what they know by putting material to music. The water cycle, for example, is summarized nicely in a nursery song: "The itsy bitsy spider crawled up the water spout. / Down came the rain and washed the spider out. / Out came the sun and dried up all the rain. . . ." Putting new vocabulary to a rap beat can make it easier to recall for some students. Some students may represent the water cycle in a picture and others by acting out the process. Some of my favorite memories of teaching science include creating "body models" of scientific phenomena. Students represented the earth's rotation by making hats and then actually moving the way they believed the earth does. During a unit on solids, liquids, and gases, students made body models of each state of matter by huddling closely as solids and then progressively getting further apart for gases. Varying the method of representing creates opportunities for all learners to be successful.

This brings up the issue of whether all students should be required to represent in each type of medium. For instance, what if a student simply can't draw? Students should be encouraged to try all types of representation, but they should not be required to put the results on display or have them shown indiscriminately. Skills and talents often develop at different rates in different children; not being able to draw today does not necessarily mean being unable to draw later in the school year.

The way a child represents observations, collections, ideas, and so on is often a very good assessment tool and indication of how the child is developing in general. For example, a picture drawn by a child shows not only the way the child understands the content but also the level of motor skill development and understanding of spatial relationships and spatial organization. Written descriptions reveal development in the linguistic-verbal area. Because linguistic-verbal proficiency is so critical to school progress, monitoring this area is important. During the earliest years, oral sharing will be useful in monitoring student progress. As children progress into second and third grades and use printing and writing more often in their representations, you will get an idea of their neuromuscular development (well-shaped letters), spatial organization (appropriate space between the letters and words), and a variety of literacy skills. The ability of a child to master the language and vocabulary of science, in other words, is an indication of growing fluency with linguistics in general and with associated skills.

As with observation, the representation piece of the wheel of key science experiences is easily integrated with other subjects. Students can represent math problems with pictures, create plays representative of stories, and take pictures of different shapes with cameras. In addition, students will be using many skills from other subjects while using the "representing" key science experience. Writing, art, music, mathematics, and physical movement are just a few examples.

Once students have represented their observations, they may need to go back and do more observing. They may find that something is missing in their representation, or another student may ask a question that moves them to need to go back and observe. However, they may also be ready to organize their representations in order to make more sense of their ideas. Organizing is the next key science experience.

Organizing

An organization is a grouping or arrangement of materials, information, and so on that serves some useful purpose. In the classroom, organizing can be a directed activity—"Put all the smooth stones in one pile and the rough stones in another"—or one that the child does spontaneously—"I want to show you my baseball card collection." (You can be sure that the cards are not arranged haphazardly!)

Organization of numerical and geometrical material reflects growth in logico-mathematical intelligence. Organizing measurements into tables and graphs, for example, reflects increasing levels of numerical understanding. Facility in making, reading, and using tables reflects growth in mathematical skills, and reading maps reflects growth in spatial skills.

Organization does not always have to be in terms of tables or graphs, however. Young students may make piles of things that all look the same, such as leaves, or they may create pictures showing how things are different, such as pictures of various breeds of dogs. Organizing may take place only in the mind of young children and may need to be shared aloud several times as they are working.

Utilizing space is another organizational skill. For example, has a student organized her or his representation spatially in any way? There are also more general spatial organizational skills to monitor, among them the ability of the child to organize the workspace, maintain the organization of the science area (or other area), and organize resources for a science activity.

Actively organizing something requires students to have choices and numerous "right" answers. It is easy, as a teacher, to have in mind an answer that you want students to develop within their organization. For example, you may want students to organize food into the five food groups, and they may organize them into foods of similar color. Although you may not get to your objective quickly, you should emphasize that, as long as the students have rationales for their organizational strategies, their organization is "right." Remember that we want students to become

Photo 7.2   Organizing Shells

This student is organizing shells into categories she has created. She uses the yellow dish as a tool to help her sort.

proficient in the processes of science as well as the content. How might you get the students to move toward the content in this case? Perhaps, it might be necessary to put some parameters on the organization. For example, have the students reorganize the material again in a different way or do some organizing yourself and share along with the students.

Organizing information into tables, graphs, and other formats often helps students come up with ideas or answers to problems. These visually represented organizations create pictures for students to analyze. Creating a class graph enumerating different animals seen on the playground gives students much more information about animals than merely talking about the animals on the playground.

This kind of organization stimulates the search for patterns and may raise questions or problems for further examination: "Why might there be more bugs than birds on the playground?" "What might happen if we did the same thing tomorrow?" You as the teacher may need to facilitate these wonderings at first and then begin to listen as students come up with their own.

Detecting Patterns and Questioning

Detecting patterns and questioning involve several subprocesses: (a) asking questions, (b) detecting (observing) changes, (c) correlating one change with another (i.e., linking changes together in the form of "causality"), (d) linking sequences of changes, and (e) noting patterns from the observations. In addition to making these links consciously about the external world, the child will also be making links unconsciously about himself or herself and the outside world—valuable links such as "I can ask a question and then act to answer it."

Providing certain kinds of recording materials can facilitate finding patterns. For example, when children observe the stages of the moon, you may provide paper with multiple circles on it so that students can track on one piece of paper the changing appearance of the moon. That way, they can see and begin to note any patterns. Sometimes, it may be important to keep class observations rather than individual observations. You may want to keep a class tally of the number of cold days compared to the number of hot days, for example, so that students can look for patterns. Remember the purpose of the activity is to learn about weather, but students can also look for patterns. It can be easy to record data about weather yet forget to look for patterns.

One of the main characteristics of young children is their curiosity, their desire to know about the world around them. This curiosity is reflected by the questions they ask—lots and lots of them! Although sometimes a child's incessant questioning annoys adults, asking questions should be encouraged, not discouraged. We want children to maintain their curiosity throughout life, so they continue to wonder and learn and grow. Start forming a list of questions asked by each student. Although you won't be able to answer all their questions, you can use the list for a number of purposes. Knowing children's interests can help you when creating science workshops (see Chapter 9) and even when selecting books for children to read. You can also use students' questions to scaffold learning. For example, answering some questions requires answering more fundamental questions first: Understanding how planets move requires knowing a little about gravity, and understanding insect metamorphosis requires knowing a little about life cycles. In fact, letting students know that answers sometimes come in a sequence and helping them identify what can be answered now and what can't is a very valuable science lesson in itself! One teacher of third and fourth graders uses a science question of the week to help students learn the process of framing and answering scientific questions. She and her students select a question each Friday, sometimes casually and sometimes by vote, from among student questions. Interested students do research throughout the week and work as a class to answer the question by the next Friday. Usually, she would start science by asking if anyone had data that might help students understand the question, and students had to say where they got information. This process taught students a great deal about the "reliability" of information as well as about the sorts of questions that are not answerable (or not easily answerable). Since students (and we ourselves) often find it difficult to identify particular questions, the ability to generate many questions and ideas needs to be nurtured. At first, their questions may be haphazard, that is, they may not seem to be related to each other. Part of this stems from young children's inability to link concepts or to organize thoughts and ideas well. With maturation and additional practice in those key science experiences, children will more easily identify questions and patterns. Helping students arrange observations (data) into ways that suggest patterns is one way we can help facilitate this. Practice in seeing patterns and identifying questions is a lifelong process.

Another part of the patterning/questioning process involves engaging students in using their imagination by using "what if" questions: "What if I altered the height of the ramp? What if I oiled the wheels? What if the car is moving when I put it on the ramp?" Some questions raised by "what if" thinking can be tested directly through experimentation (the next science process, discussed below). As children ask "what if . . ." they should be encouraged to respond with "I think that . . . because . . .": "What if I oiled the wheels? . . . I think that the car will go faster because Joey's did when he oiled his."

Experimenting

How do you picture experimenting? To many, it is the hands-on manipulation of physical materials. By this definition, however, any "hands-on activity" could be experimenting; therefore we suggest that experimenting is manipulating materials for a specific purpose—*to discover something you did not know before.* The discovery might be observing an object's characteristics, observing what happens when the material is acted upon or altered, and so on. Thus, the manipulation does not have to be complex or out of the ordinary. The material being manipulated need not even be physical; one can also manipulate ideas and concepts to discover something new. This is true of most mathematical experiments as well as Einstein's famous thought ("gedanken") experiments.

Experiments at the elementary level will vary from manipulating materials in order to observe and describe them more completely to planning multi-step processes in order to solve a problem or obtain information (data) about a question. Experiments in the former category involve collections and sorting and classifying based on one characteristic. For instance, students may observe a result—what happens if I mix liquid soap and oil?—and repeat the activity to see if it happens again (with liquid soap and water or with other liquids, such as food coloring and water). When students become proficient at classifying and sorting based on one characteristic, they can be encouraged to classify based on two or more.

When students construct and build objects—toys, bridges, paper airplanes, and so on—they are also involved in experimenting. Their goal, generally, is to improve one or more characteristics of whatever it is they are building. Often, they do this through trial and error, making a modification, keeping it if it makes the material work better, making another modification if it does not. Trial-and-error methods are often used at this age because devising specific plans and keeping them in an organized array requires more short-term and active memory space than young children typically have. You may be familiar with a similar problem if you have ever tried to run an advanced computer program on a computer with very limited memory: it either doesn't work at all or it takes an extremely long time. Or perhaps you've reached the limits of your memory when trying to do a complex Sudoku puzzle: some adults can hold five to six "necessary" consequences in their minds, but need to "test out"

Photo 7.3   Experiment About Erosion

These students have developed an experiment to help them answer their questions about erosion.

a number in pencil rather than mentally when more steps are required. So it is with children at this stage of development. As more and more information and techniques become automatic for them, they can begin to use more systematic approaches. As students become more adept at manipulating materials and making modifications, planning and patterning should be encouraged.

Remember that we are encouraging active science and thus active experimentation. In other words, students should be the ones experimenting! Although there are times when a demonstration is more appropriate for safety reasons, students should be doing the experimenting the majority of the time. Choices should also be incorporated based on students' questions and hypotheses. For example, students in my second grade classroom created experiments with mealworms based on their own questions. Some wanted to know if mealworms liked jellybeans. Others wanted to know if mealworms could swim. (We discouraged this question for the sake of being humane to the mealworms!!) And still others wanted to know what kind of bed the mealworms like. The students then came up with ways they could answer their questions as well as ways they could prove their answers to others. I don't know if mealworms *really* like jellybeans, but they sure spent a lot of time on the jellybean!

Experimenting is not just a key science experience. Real experimentation allows students to take risks in learning and helps them understand their role in learning. Those "what if" questions work well in all subjects, not merely in science class. We hope that young people who begin to experiment will always be compelled to try novel ideas and think outside the box!

Sharing

Recall that the hub of the wheel of science is sharing. Sharing entails exchanging one's experiences with the teacher, other students, parents, and other individuals. Sharing can follow any of the activities on the rim of the wheel—observing, representing, organizing, and so on. Moreover, the very act of sharing can lead to one of the other activities. Sharing may uncover patterns that were not obvious before or further questions to be investigated.

Most sharing employs a symbolic system of one type or another. The only exception occurs when one individual involves another in the actual experience, for example, when I show you something so that you can observe it yourself or I repeat an action so that you can see the effect yourself. Students can share in a variety of ways. They can make oral or written reports, pictures, or models to share observations, data, observed patterns, experimental results, and so on. They can even share information through debates or role playing ("You're trying to convince your parents to recycle tin cans. What would you tell them?").

In the earliest primary years, sharing will probably be in the form of oral reports or of drawings accompanied by oral reports, reflecting the normal developmental sequence of first speaking and subsequently writing. Children can also make models, using such materials as Tinkertoy or Lego pieces, blocks, or modeling clay. Later, children can start producing written reports and booklets or pamphlets on specific topics. Incorporated into these works would be diagrams, tables, charts, and other means of organizing information.

Photo 7.4   Kids Sharing

Students have the opportunity to share their observations with the class.

Role playing and debates foster dialog and interaction among students, simulating what occurs in the real scientific world. Students might role-play a controversial science issue highlighted in the popular press. For example, a student could play a member of the city council trying to convince the rest of the council to limit the types of auto emissions in the city. Gathering and organizing scientific data on the content and effects of auto emissions could lead to thoughtful discussions and deeper learning.

Like role playing, debates can engender informed discussions, further learning of a topic, and a better understanding of another's point of view. Recall our description earlier about a class debate on whether mealworms were worms or insects. This debate led to an active gathering of evidence, heated discussions, and in-depth learning experiences that challenged the students to organize their evidence and present persuasive arguments.

Social interactions such as these, and sharing in larger groups, also foster development of interpersonal intelligence. Students come to understand that an issue usually has more than one side; that while they have strong ideas, so do their classmates; and that democratic practices mean providing all with a chance to share ideas. Sharing puts a "face" on such social graces and provides a forum for learning them.

■ PUTTING IT ALL TOGETHER

We've looked at all the key science experiences individually, examining some of their characteristics and some of the ways children develop in these areas. Putting them together in a complete cycle constitutes a science study or a science experience. Students should participate in the entire sequence frequently; this is the way they learn science as a way of knowing.

One can enter a science experience from any point on the wheel of science. For example, an investigation may start with a specific observation and then move on to the stages of representing, organizing, patterning/ questioning, and experimenting. This sequence is illustrated by Wilhelm Roentgen's discovery of x-rays.

Notice how his scientific study progressed. First, he made a chance observation—a shielded platinum-barium screen glowed when he ran electricity through a nearby Crookes tube. He then conducted systematic trials—experimentation—to see which materials would prevent the screen from fluorescing. He organized the data to make sense of the results. And continued progressing around the wheel.

Another way to enter the science wheel is through organizing and representing data, as illustrated by the search for a way to organize the chemical elements into a periodic table that would make sense of the data. That tentative organization would have to be tested and the wheel completed. No matter where one is on the wheel, the results give a tentative view of the world, a view that can be altered with another turn of the wheel. This continuous process is how we investigate the world. Repetition is key to this process; students do not learn science by turning the wheel of science once a year! Each time they participate in science, they should complete the trip around the wheel, engaging in each step.

As you begin to think about the key science experiences, remember that they fit together within any science topic. Although you may not do all of them for every topic, they will flow naturally together in many topics. Check out Table 7.1, and begin to put some of your ideas about the key experiences on paper! Although the chart has only one experience under each key science experience, there may be many opportunities for observation, representation, and so on. Remember also that, although they are written in a specific order, that order may not represent the best order of events for that topic! If you were to scaffold these experiences, what order would work best? Why? What might you need to add based on the maturation and experiences of your students?

The Key Science Experiences and Maturation

As children experience these processes and move from the preoperational to the concrete operational stage, each child's unique characteristics will become apparent. We have developed a table addressing the relationship between students' actions within the key science experiences and Piaget's stages (Table 7.2). Teachers can use this list to assess the unique developmental profile of each child and to plan appropriate activities.

SCAFFOLDING FOR THE TEACHER   ■

Implementing the key science experiences from the wheel may seem daunting for both prospective and experienced teachers, although for different reasons. Prospective teachers may be overwhelmed by the thought of having to not only learn and implement the experiences on the wheel but also apply all the other aspects of our proposed approach to science (workshops, plan-do-review, assessment, etc.). Experienced teachers, who have developed lesson plans and a teaching style they are comfortable

(Text continues on page 109)

Table 7.1   If You're Studying . . .

If You're Studying . . .	States of Matter	Sinking/ Floating	Insects	Sounds
Observing	Ask students to observe solid objects such as rice, hard candy, chalk, aluminum foil, or beans.	Ask students to pick five different objects from around the room and put them in water to see if they sink or float.	Ask students to observe how many insects they find inside the boundaries of a hula hoop that they have placed at one spot on school grounds.	Ask students to listen to different sounds for differences in pitch and loudness.
Representing	Ask students to represent the molecules in solid materials with a group of students. Are they close together or far apart?	Ask students to draw a picture of what happened to the five objects.	Ask students to tally the numbers of insects they observed within the circumference of the hula hoop.	Ask students to draw their own sound waves according to what they hear.
Organizing	Ask students to organize the objects in piles of solids and non-solids.	Ask the students to organize their objects in two groups: sinks or floats.	Ask students to organize the insects they saw into different categories.	Ask students to organize the pictures of the sound waves into some kind of order.
Patterning/ Questioning	Ask students to come up with questions they have about the solid objects. What makes something solid?	Ask students to come up with any reasons that they put the objects in the two piles.	Ask students to keep track of an insect such as a mealworm on a calendar over time. Is there a pattern?	Ask students to look for patterns in their pictures and write three questions about those patterns.
Experimenting	What happens when you try to build with solid objects? Have students build the tallest tower they can with the solid objects.	Ask students to pick two more objects that they think will float and two that they think will sink and try them.	Ask students to determine whether mealworms prefer light or dark by experimenting.	Ask the students to experiment with different objects to make sounds. Which pictures of sound waves might fit with those sounds?
Sharing	Share the tower they made and describe which materials worked better for building.	Share the results of their experiments with the class.	Share the results of each of the activities listed above.	Have students write or tell someone everything they know about sounds so far.

Table 7.2   The Key Science Experiences and Piagetian Characteristics

---

OBSERVING

Preoperational stage:

- Uses all the senses to investigate, explore, and observe the world
- Collects materials of many kinds
- Observes color, shape, form, or pattern (one at a time)
- Initiates an observation to solve a problem or answer a question
- Compares the properties of materials (one at a time)
- Observes the attributes of objects
- Observes similarities and differences between two objects, including differences on a singe dimension
- Measures by producing a length to match another length
- Counts events over time
- Observes and identifies a change

Early Concrete Operational Stage:

- Looks at something familiar in a new way: observes closely, systematically, and objectively
- Takes something apart to observe it more closely
- Observes changes over time
- Observes the quantity of a material or the frequency of an event
- Uses instruments (magnifiers, binoculars, slow-motion camera, tape recorder, etc.) to assist observations
- Uses standard measuring tools (ruler, thermometer, calipers, scales, timers, etc.)
- Measures properties and changes using standard or nonstandard units
- Observes multiple similarities and differences
- Observes similarities and differences in structural patterns

Late Concrete Operational Stage:

- Uses audiovisual media for planned and systematic observations (e.g., photographing a tree once a week for a year)
- Observes an object from different perspectives
- Observes the subsystems of an environment or structure to see how they interact. ("We've noticed that the fish die if we don't add enough food, but too much makes the fish tank dirty.")
- Measures using both whole units and fractions of a unit
- Estimates measurements ("It looks like it's about 2 feet tall.")

REPRESENTING

Preoperational stage:

- Discusses observations in simple terms—one term at a time
- Draws simple pictures, perhaps requiring discussion of what each represents
- Begins to use scientific terms and comparative vocabulary in reporting observations (but terms not entirely correct)
- Represents observations using real objects (models as symbols)

Early Concrete Operational Stage:

- Discusses observations in more complex terms and complete sentences
- Records and displays numerical data
- Models more detailed

(Continued)

Table 7.2 (Continued)

Late Concrete Operational:

- Discusses observations in more complex terms, with good descriptive language, and using complete, often complex, sentences
- Records and displays numerical data often using graphs and formal equations to describe results
- Produces even more detailed models, drawings, etc., and uses these to illustrate specific items and properties
- Makes models of objects and systems to show how they work (making a model of a stream bed using sand and buckets of water)
- Uses a scale model to study the features of a larger or smaller object (model of a bicycle gear made from spools and rubber bands)

ORGANIZING

Preoperational Stage:

- Classifies materials into small groups based on one common attribute
- Reports sequence of events
- Draws sequence of events
- Uses real objects mounted on material to form charts and record events

Early Concrete Operational:

- Orders objects according to variation along a single dimension
- Groups objects according to structural patterns
- Classifies material into two groups based on the presence or absence of one attribute
- Organizes information into simple charts and tables
- Records and organizes numerical data
- Arranges collections and displays
- Separates and measures the parts of a mixture or material to describe its composition (for example, separates and measures the wheat flakes and raisins in a box of cereal)

Late Concrete Operational:

- Uses an identification guide to look up organisms or nonliving materials (e.g., uses books to identify trees or wildflowers)
- Classifies or orders using two-dimensional matrices (for example, orders screws by length and diameter)
- Classifies hierarchically: groups into categories and subcategories (birds, birds of prey, birds of prey that live in Michigan, etc.)
- Uses bar graphs, line graphs, and tables to present data
- Uses time and space appropriately in presenting oral and written reports

PATTERNING/QUESTIONING

Preoperational Stage:

- Asks questions
- Observes and identifies a change
- Observes similarities and differences
- Repeats an activity that produces a change to gain awareness of possible causes
- Counts events over time; reports sequence of events
- Identifies the cause of a change

Early Concrete Operational Stage:

- Uses testing: assesses properties by comparing effects of standardized procedures (test the strength of several fibers by tying them to a standard weight and observing which ones break)
- Compares the effects produced by increasing or decreasing a causal factor (compares the effect on the color of water of adding a larger quantity of food coloring)
- Observes and describes a pattern of change in events and movements (life cycles, cycles of motion, weather changes)
- Predicts a change in a situation from observation of change in other similar situations ("The sky is gray and the wind is blowing. I think it's going to rain.")
- Identifies more than one possible cause of a change ("The lawn mower won't start. Maybe it's out of gas or needs a tune-up. We have the most trouble on chilly days.")
- Tries to rank and sequence data

Late Concrete Operational Stage:

- Recognizes that a sequence of change (winding up a toy car to make it go) involves a sequence of causes and effects ("Winding the key of the car makes the gears move, which turns the car's wheels and makes the car go.")
- Relates the magnitude of the effect to the magnitude of a cause ("A strong wind will cause many more leaves to fall off the tree than a gentle wind.")
- Begins to recognize that explaining a change may require keeping some variables (possible causes) constant ("I think this toy car goes faster than the other one because it's built differently, but it might be because I oiled it before the race. Let's oil the other car, too, and then try racing them again.")
- Measures the increase or decrease in a causal factor in order to relate it to the change in an effect ("Let's see how much farther the car goes if we raise the height of the track 3 inches.")
- Prioritizes ideas—identifying what is important and pertinent in observations

EXPERIMENTING

Preoperational Stage:

- Manipulates physical objects to produce an effect or change (blows out a candle)
- Repeats an activity that produces a change to gain awareness of possible causes (repeatedly pushes an empty bottle under water and watches as bubbles are released)
- Designs and builds simple structures (makes a garage for toy cars out of blocks and boards)
- Changes a structure to solve a problem in its design ("Maybe the tower won't fall over if I use the flat blocks instead.")
- Compares the performance of similar structures or materials ("The ramp works better this way.")
- Uses plans supplied by others to make a simple structure or material (a paper teepee, flour paste)

Early Concrete Operational:

- Designs and builds more complex structures (realistic objects constructed with conventional building materials, tools, and fasteners)
- Builds simple containers or environments for living things (an insect box, a window box garden)

(Continued)

Table 7.2 (Continued)

- Improves a structure or material through trial-and-error modifications (varying the height and length of a ramp to increase the speed of a toy car, adding sugar or water to icing to change the consistency)
- Uses plans supplied by others to make a more complex and functional structure or material (making dog biscuits, making pinwheels)

Late Concrete Operational:

- Builds structures with moving parts (latches, hinges, wheels, and axles)
- Builds with simple electrical circuits
- Analyzes and solves problems in a structure by taking it apart, modifying parts, and rebuilding it (troubleshoots a problem in a windup car by separately examining the wheels and axles, the spring mechanism, and the gears)
- Identifies more than one factor affecting the operation or effectiveness of a structure or material (recognizing that the problem of fastening two materials together may be affected by the type of fastener—e.g., tape, screws, nails—the size of the fastener, the smoothness of the surfaces being joined and the weight of the pieces to be joined)

SHARING

Preoperational Stage:

- Discusses observations with simple terms—often incomplete sentences
- Shows drawings, collages, and artwork
- Sharing times are "egocentric"
- Begins to use scientific terms and comparative vocabulary in reporting observations
- Oral reporting with everyday language is much better than with expressive language
- Reports and represents observations using drawings, tape recordings, photos, or real objects mounted on charts

Early Concrete Operational Stage:

- Discusses observations and ideas with complete sentences
- Discusses several aspects of drawings, collages, and artwork, and all visual representations are more realistic
- Uses books, pictures, charts, and computers to gain further information
- Aware of time and space issues in presenting oral and written reports

Late Concrete Operational:

- Discusses observations and ideas with complete sentences in expressive language, for example, defines technical terms and uses more than "street" language
- Uses bar graphs, line graphs, and tables to present data that support the discussion
- Recognizes the importance of the views of others and allows alternative opinions and views
- Uses time well for oral reports and space well for written reports, spending more time/space on issues of greater priority

with, may feel oppressed with requests to learn new ways of interacting and planning. The good news is that one can implement the key science experiences gradually. In fact, by making several changes all at once, you may have difficulty implementing and assessing the program carefully. Implement first those changes you feel most comfortable with. Gradually modify lesson plans and activities that you already have or that your school system has already established.

The 80:20 Rule

If you are a veteran teacher with several developed science lessons, consider applying the 80:20 rule (also known as the Pareto principle) to your science program. Pareto, an economist who examined the pattern of wealth in eighteenth-century Italy, found that 80% of the wealth was concentrated in 20% of the population. Since his original description, the 80:20 distribution pattern (at least approximately) has been applied to many different phenomena. For example, 80% of complaints come from 20% of customers; 80% of company sales are made by 20% of the sales force, and so on. Try applying this principle to your science program by improving just 20% of your lessons. Even small improvements applied judiciously can have a tremendous effect on your science program!

As you begin to feel more comfortable with the key science experiences, stretch your wings and try some things that may be moderately uncomfortable until you fully incorporate all these key experiences into your routine.

Conversation Starters

- Which of the key science experiences did you encounter as a young learner? In school? Outside of school? Why do you think you experienced these?

- Think of a science lesson that you have experienced or taught. Which key science experiences did the lesson use?

- Are there any experiences that you think should be added to our wheel of key science experiences? Why?

- How does the developmental level of the students in your classroom affect how the key science experiences will be used?

- How do the key science experiences connect to active learning and social interaction?

8

Thinking Routines

For a moment, imagine a diver ready to dive into the ocean, hoping to get as deep as possible to see the spectacular sights waiting under the water. What would the diver need? Well, first the diver would need a way in to the ocean, a boat perhaps or a spot from which to wade toward the deep water. Then the diver would need something to help him or her stay in the water, such as a wetsuit or a snorkel. Finally, something to help the diver go down further—a weight belt, flippers, or an oxygen mask—would be needed. Diving into the ocean is a great analogy of what we want for learners in our classrooms. We want them to have a way "in to" the learning, we want them to participate actively in order to "stay in" the learning, and we want them to go as "deep" as possible within their learning. This chapter is about helping students develop their own tools that promote deep thinking within science as well as in other subjects and in life.

Thinking routines are one tool helpful in providing young students opportunities to learn how to think deeply (Ritchhart, 2002). Thinking routines are like most other routines in that they consist of a few steps, they are easy to teach and learn, they are easy to support, and they get used repeatedly. Thinking routines, however, guide mental actions rather than behavior and create opportunities for deeper understanding. They facilitate making connections, generating new ideas and possibilities, and activating prior knowledge (Ritchhart, 2002). Thinking routines are like other routines in that they are accessible to all learners, yet they are different in that they provide a structure for thinking rather than facilitating only a specific task or problem. In other words, thinking routines help students get the most out of using the key science experiences and participating in workshops.

Not all routines develop this kind of deep thinking. For example, in some classrooms, students participate in routines that include bringing the class to order, discussing homework, listening to a lesson on a new topic, and finally doing homework individually.

Routines like round-robin reading or the class routine described previously are not thinking routines because they do not serve to encourage or actively support students' thinking, or mental engagement. While purposeful, thinking routines are more instrumental than other routines. That is, thinking routines act as a means for achieving broader goals rather than as goals themselves, and they continue to be applicable outside of the classroom. Through thinking routines, students develop abilities within the topic they are studying, sensitivities to know when there might be an issue or problem, and inclinations to learn more (Ritchhart, 2002).

Many routines developed throughout the years could be labeled thinking routines, even though they are not necessarily labeled in that way. If you think about it, you may have experienced one or more of these as a student or just as a person trying to solve a problem. For example, in the early nineteen hundreds a philosopher named Kilpatrick proposed a problem-solving routine that included, "purposing, planning, executing, and judging" (Kliebard, 1995, p. 141). Kolb (1984) developed a learning cycle that includes engaging, exploring, explaining, extending, and evaluating. The learning cycle developed by the Science Curriculum Improvement Study project in the 1970s contains three phases: the exploration phase, concept introduction phase, and the application phase (Beisenherz, Dantonio, & Richardson, 2001). Wasserman (1988) created a routine for young children involving playing, debriefing, and replaying. A thinking routine that has become very successful for both young and adult learners is the plan-do-review routine developed by the High/Scope Educational Foundation (Hohmann & Weikart, 1995; Williams, 2004).

What do you notice about the thinking routines listed above? Are there similarities? Any differences? Although they may seem different, in some sense, thinking routines all help students develop a way in to learning (for example, purposing or planning), a way to become actively involved in the learning (for example, explaining or playing), and a way to stay deeply within the learning (for example, reflecting or replaying). "For students to be successful as independent learners, they must be aware of their own cognitive processes and be able to identify purposes of tasks, determine what is important to learn, acquire information, and monitor the success of their learning" (Bruning, Schraw, & Ronning, 1999, p. 214). We must not forget that the children we teach need to be able to learn independently and to apply their knowledge.

Although thinking routines may sound simple, they are in fact quite complex. Adults can go through this process purposefully or unconsciously, making adjustments, learning, and relearning, because we have the cognitive skills necessary to do so. For young children, however, this is not so easy. Students between kindergarten and sixth grade have shown an inability to monitor their comprehension accurately, and they have difficulty with metacognition—describing their own cognition (Bruning, Schraw, & Ronning, 1999). So, they need strategies and a structure to help them become metacognitively aware. They need opportunities to think ahead of time about tasks and processes. They need reasons to think about what they are doing and why they are doing it while they are doing it, and they need time afterwards to reflect on what happened. In classrooms, we should see "students who are learning about learning while they are learning" (Levine, 2002, p. 334). Thinking routines make it possible for students to not only construct knowledge but also learn *how* to construct it.

GETTING "IN TO" THE LEARNING IN THE CLASSROOM ■

Too often, we rush students through the school day and their assignments, anxious to have them learn a certain "quota" of material. We tell them what they will study and, often, how they will study it. We gather resources for them and design experiences for them. We give them feedback on how they "performed." We rarely give them the opportunity to plan their solutions on their own. Yet the ability to set goals and decide on a course of action to meet those goals is critical to the kinds of learning we want students to experience. In science, and in all aspects of life, we need deliberate, creative, and efficacious thinkers.

What does getting "in to" learning look like? It may be as simple as providing some time for students to think about a problem that they are solving before they begin. It may be the "*K*" (*K*now) part of a KWL (*K*now, *W*ant to learn, *L*earned) chart. What do we already know about the topic? It may be a specific assignment to write a plan to solve a specific problem. The important idea within this piece of a thinking routine is that the student not the teacher does the "getting in to." We often tell students how to proceed without asking what they already know or how they might proceed themselves.

Students in my classroom were learning about the relationship between the earth, sun, and moon. We had conversations about what they knew and read some related nonfiction children's literature. Then, instead of telling them to create models of the three celestial bodies, I asked them to get into groups and write a plan to represent the relationship between the earth, sun, and moon. One group of students proposed to use clay and make models of the three; others planned to make hats and use body models to represent the rotation of the earth and moon. Still others drew a picture. The students in this example learned not only about the topic of study but also about how to develop a solution to a problem.

This kind of thinking ahead of learning doesn't always have to be a formal writing time. Sometimes, it might just be time to think. For example, students in my classroom were given the problem of determining whether toothpaste was a solid, liquid, or gas. We had been studying the three states of matter, and students needed to put their prior knowledge to work. In groups, they came up with ways to test the toothpaste, and then we shared their ideas. Then students put their ideas to work.

One of your jobs during this initial stage of a thinking routine is that of listener and questioner.

Some things you might say are

- Tell me about your ideas for solving this problem.
- What made you decide to solve it this way?
- How much time do you think you will need?
- What materials will you need?
- What do you think will happen?
- How can I help you?

As always, your role is also that of safety expert and guide. If students plan something inappropriate or potentially harmful to themselves or to materials, you need to help them come up with another idea.

Not all projects promote students doing all of the thinking ahead. At times, you will need to do all of the planning or at least help them with ideas. When we were learning about the different seasons and how they affect habitats, I planned to have the students go on a walk to see the changes in the habitats during winter. However, students and I talked together about what they might collect as evidence. Getting into the learning within thinking routines does not mean that you do not plan! You still need to develop activities for students to experience. It does mean that you give them opportunities to think ahead about what they might do.

■ STAYING ACTIVE IN THE LEARNING

As important as getting in to the learning is, meaningful learning requires students to have actual experiences as well—with materials, ideas, and other people. Without the experience of putting their ideas into action, students won't advance beyond the "what if" stage. Teaching is a great example of the importance of carrying out your plans. As a preservice teacher, you probably planned many sample lessons that you never actually taught. Although you thought through the process, content, and expectations—all important steps—you probably didn't learn as much as you could have if you had actually taught the lesson.

Exploring, executing, or playing lets students put their plans into action—investigating, experimenting, pondering, discussing, reading, representing, trying new ideas, and, yes, sometimes failing and trying again. Remember that the ingredients for active learning—choice, materials, manipulation, language, and adult support—are important pieces of thinking routines.

The students who worked on the problem of representing the earth, sun, and moon actually carried out their ideas. They physically made clay models; they created earth, sun, and moon hats for each person and rotated around each other. They drew poster-sized pictures showing where each celestial body was in relation to the others. The students who made plans to test the toothpaste actually did the tests they created. Based on their past experience with other solids, liquids, and gases, some decided to put the toothpaste in water to see what would happen. Some tried to build with the toothpaste, and others tested to see if the toothpaste would take the shape of a bowl or keep its own shape.

Once again, your role during this part of a thinking routine is to listen, wonder aloud, and help students make sense of what they are doing. You might say

- What happened?
- I wonder why that happened. Any ideas?
- Do you need to change your plan?
- What might you do next?
- What would you tell others about what you learned?

GOING DEEPER WITHIN THE LEARNING ■

Another hugely important aspect of thinking routines is that they take learners to a deeper level through reviewing, replaying, evaluating, or judging. Indeed, reflecting on one's actions is valuable in any kind of learning. Schön (1983) identifies two types of reflection: *reflection in action* (thinking on your feet) and *reflection on action* (retrospective thinking). Thinking routines provide both kinds of reflection. Reflection in action takes place while students carry out their plans, revising them as necessary to complete their projects. For example, a group of students creating an archeological dig area in the classroom ran into a problem when the dirt they were using wasn't as hard as they had envisioned. They wanted to be able to use archeological tools to scrape away the plaster of Paris bones they had made. Right then and there, they reflected on their plan and made decisions about how to improve it. Reflection on action takes place after students have completed their actions. Students write, draw, and share their ideas about what happened and what they thought, felt, and learned as they worked on their projects.

These two kinds of reflection provide layers of learning, giving students numerous reflective entry points and different perspectives. Students make more connections and learn material at a deeper level. For example, the students who created the archeological dig area were able to think on their feet when a problem occurred. The reflective entry point was immediate. The students didn't have time to sit and ponder the problem but instead used their collective past experiences and knowledge to solve the problem quickly. Afterward, the students wrote about the experience, which allowed them to think more deliberately about the problem and how they solved it. This reflective entry point occurred in a quiet place as students took time to slow down and think deeply about what had happened, what they had learned, and what they might do differently next time.

The final layer is sharing. Students share their ideas and their creations in a safe atmosphere, with their peers asking questions and providing feedback. The reflective entry point is once again different as students talk and answer questions about their experiences. Thinking on their feet, writing their thoughts and feelings, and then sharing and answering questions all require different thinking processes and develop different types of metacognitive knowledge. This kind of comprehensive thinking is vital to learning because it causes students to rethink ideas and experiences from many different angles and perspectives.

The students who planned projects about the moon, sun, and earth had a chance to write about what they had done, as well as about other students' projects. For another unit of study, our reflective piece included a debate about whether students considered toothpaste a solid, liquid, or gas. Students defended their ideas, listened to others' thoughts, and had a chance to reflect on their ideas verbally.

Photo 8.1   Student With Magnets

A student is excited to share his understandings of magnets.

Getting deep into the learning requires a teacher who is willing to give time and energy to this important piece of a thinking routine. It is much easier to move on to the next topic rather than take the time to have students reflect. However, leaving reflection out of a thinking routine promotes actions without making connections. Your job, then, during this phase of the thinking routine is to provide time to reflect, provide thoughtful questions, and provide a safe environment for sharing. You might

- Ask students to write, draw, or talk about their experiences.
- Ask students to tell you what happened and how they felt about the project.
- Ask students what they found out.
- If students are writing their reflections, help them get started with sentence starters such as "I found out . . ." or "I did it that way because . . ." or "If I had it to do over again, I would. . . ." As students get better at reflecting, they will automatically ask themselves these questions and others. The goal is for them to think through their work on their own and make decisions based on those thoughts.

■ WHY USE THINKING ROUTINES?

Students become more purposeful in their pursuits. Thinking routines help children work, think, and communicate deliberately rather than impulsively. Dewey differentiated between acting with a purpose and acting impulsively when he wrote, "A purpose differs from an original impulse and desire through its translation into a plan and method of action based upon foresight of the consequences of acting under given observed conditions in a certain way" (1938, p. 69). Children often engage in whatever first comes to mind rather than thinking through several ideas and possibilities. Although trial and error is a useful strategy at times, children need to learn to use their prior experiences to help them learn more efficiently. Thinking routines help children organize the knowledge they already have about a topic and use it to guide them. In other words, planning, purposing or engaging launches learning!

Students are more motivated to learn. Thinking routines allow children to work on issues that really matter to them, something we talked about in Chapter 6 as being central to active learning. This is highly motivational for students. Students who ask their own questions and plan their own strategies are also motivated to work persistently on difficult problems. Because they take ownership of these questions, they are much more likely to accomplish their goals.

Students gain self-efficacy. As they take responsibility for their own learning, students learn that their ideas are valuable. They can independently propose goals and a plan of action and carry out their plan, giving them a sense of achievement. They learn to evaluate their efforts and adjust their goals themselves rather than relying on the feedback of others.

Students learn important life skills. For example, thinking routines allow students to gain

- Initiative and a proactive approach to learning and to life
- The "capacity to express their intentions" verbally and in writing
- A habit of thinking before acting, of deliberately considering various alternatives
- Creativity through building on what others have done using their own ideas, for "one cannot be creative without learning what others know, but then one cannot be creative without becoming dissatisfied with that knowledge and rejecting it (or some of it) for a better way" (Csikszentmihalyi, 1996, p. 90)
- Organizational skills by working out not only the ideas themselves but also the timing and sequencing of steps

Students make sense of their experiences and evaluate their understanding. Thinking routines allow children to discover what it is they know and to increase their metacognitive knowledge by providing different ways to think about experiences. Boud, Keogh, and Walker (1985) called this a "recapturing of experience."

Students challenge what they know and seek out new ways to understand an issue. Within thinking routines, learning is often challenged by the reality of experience. That is, these routines cause disequilibrium for students as they find that their previous understanding of something does not agree with new findings. This disequilibrium may cause them to make further investigations to try to sort things out. Thus, thinking routines lead to active, conscious deliberation and to further exploration.

Teachers can assess children's understanding. As students articulate their knowledge in a more meaningful way through the process of a thinking routine, teachers get a window into the deeper knowledge children have acquired from their experiences. In addition, thinking routines help teachers to get at misconceptions that students have about science topics. For example, students might write that the moon and the sun revolve around the earth in the K (what you think you know) portion of a KWL chart. This would allow you as a teacher to come up with some activities to help students understand that the moon revolves around the earth, but the earth revolves around the sun in the L (what we learned) portion of the chart.

■ MATURATION AND THINKING ROUTINES

You may be wondering whether young children are capable of utilizing thinking routines to help them learn. In some sense, it depends on the thinking routine and the adult support within the classroom. High/Scope's plan-do-review routine (Hohmann & Weikart, 1995), for example, is used with children as young as three years old. Three-year-olds are able to plan where they want to learn and what they will do there, actually go and learn there, and then talk to an adult about what they did.

Older children may be able to engage in a more sophisticated thinking routine such as a problem-solving routine. There are many other problem-solving plans. (For some references, see http://www.mapnp.org/library/prsn_prd/prob_slv.htm.) For example, Mel Levine in *A Mind at a Time* (2002) presents a 10-step model, which is complex and provides detailed instructions for each step. One important step in this model is what Levine calls "previewing the outcome." That is, before embarking on a solution, one should know what a satisfactory solution would look like. For example, if the problem is to measure something, what would the measure look like? Once students understand the goal and what an answer might look like, then they can seek solutions.

We have developed the problem-solving plan shown below. It is meant to have the fewest number of steps without making the process too simple. Check out the steps in Table 8.1.

The problem-solving process can be implemented gradually as children move from the preoperational to the concrete operational stage. Many mental processes will become automatic with practice, and children's working memory bank will increase in size. Both developments will enhance their ability to hold several concepts in mind at any given time—a prerequisite for true problem solving.

■ SCAFFOLDING WITHIN THINKING ROUTINES

Students of any maturational level may not be able to use each of the pieces of a thinking routine successfully at first. They may not understand the purpose of each step or what they are supposed to do during this time. It is crucial that you help them by scaffolding with language, tools, and the physical environment until they no longer need your assistance.

Table 8.1   Williams's & Veomett's Seven Step Problem-Solving Plan

Identify Problem	Preview Solution	Assemble Resources	Analyze Resources and Plans	Select Plan and Begin Doing It	Monitor the Process	Assess the "Solution"
Help child recognize "problems" Help define and state Encourage resolve to solve	What would good solutions look like? Is there more than one solution?	What child has learned Offer new techniques, materials, facts	Are present resources enough? Where can one get additional resources? What plans will give solutions?	Encourage child to risk a solution Choose a solution with a "reason"	Is one making progress toward the solution? Are there sub-problems that must be tackled?	Does the solution look like that "previewed?" Is it solved? Should steps 2–7 be repeated?

Scaffolding With Language

At first, students may need to talk to you or their peers about their ideas for getting in to the learning, staying in the learning, and going deeper within the learning. They may need help in the form of questions on the board, individual questions and suggestions, or different choices. For example, imagine that you and children who have had little experience with thinking routines are studying what makes a plant grow. First, you might ask the whole class for several different plans to investigate what would be important for plant growth. Then you might let small groups choose which plan they will use rather than having them come up with a plan themselves. With very small children, their way in to the learning may be just telling you where they will go. For example, you may ask them to plan whether they will observe the seeds, the roots, the stems, or the flowers. Reflection with children who have not experienced thinking routines may be having them tell you something they learned or drawing a picture of what they did. For example, after students observed the seeds, roots, stems, or flowers, you might have them get in a circle and tell one thing they noticed.

As students get more accustomed to using thinking routines, they may only need a problem telling them what they need to plan; for example, "What things does a plant need to grow? How could we find out?" They may only need questions written on the board to help them with the reflection, and they may be able to write it instead of tell you.

In my classroom, students often shared their reflections with the class. To get them to think deeply about their activities and get ready for sharing, I would tell them to think of all the questions I might ask them about their project and try to answer them on paper before I ask. This language scaffold challenged students to stump me and got them thinking beyond the basics of what they had done. What language scaffolds can you come up with?

Scaffolding With Tools

An example of a tool that might help students is a story map (see Figure 8.1). As the students become proficient at recording what they want to do and what they did, you might ask them to talk to a partner about their story map, making sure they add some details about what they found out or what they might do the next day.

As students gain confidence, ask them to write their own ideas and reflections. Be sure to pull these prompting tools away slowly, so students develop their own ways to review. If you always provide students with a story map, they may never go beyond the mapping questions. Remember that scaffolding is meant to be a launching point, not a crutch.

Another tool that may help students utilize thinking routines is posting the actual routine in the classroom. This works especially well with thinking routines like a KWL chart or the problem-solving chart described previously. Charts such as these help students keep track of their thinking as well as help them go through the process of a thinking routine with ease. Large charts in the room can remind students of steps, help students generate writing ideas, or be written on directly. They can be used with a whole group at first, then in small groups, and, finally, individually. Check out Table 8.2 and 8.3 for examples.

Figure 8.1   Story Map

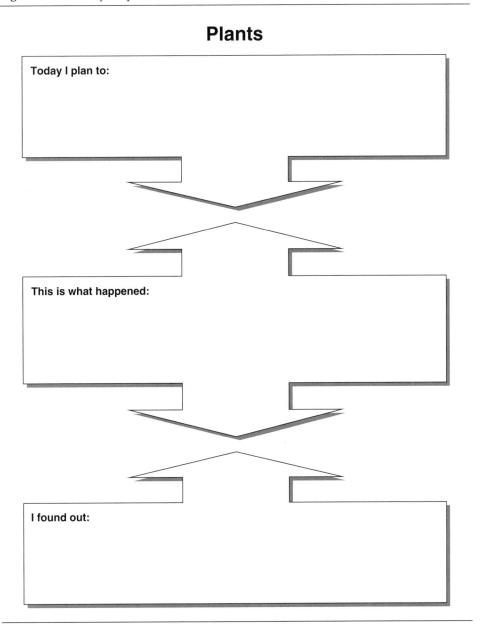

Plants

Today I plan to:

This is what happened:

I found out:

Scaffolding With the Environment

Create an environment in which it is safe for students to take risks and think deeply by encouraging them to choose their own writing places or by providing help with spelling. Students may wish to write or draw with markers or pens that they don't usually get to use on assignments, or maybe they can create a science log by using special paper or a notebook.

Be sure that materials are accessible and that the students know what is available. At first, you might provide the materials that they will need.

Table 8.2 An Example of How the Problem-Solving Chart Might Be Used

Identify Problem	Preview Solution	Assemble Resources	Analyze Resources and Plans	Select Plan and Begin Doing It	Monitor the Process
What kind of soil will a bean seed grow in: soil from outside our classroom, humus, sand, water, rocks, or clay?	We think that a bean seed will grow best in humus because it has nutrients in it.	We need soil from outside our classroom, humus, sand, water, rocks, clay, see-through cups, beans, and a well-lit place in our classroom.	We need to make sure each cup gets the same amount of light. We need to make sure we use the same amount of planting material.	Each group of four students needs to plan the experiment and do it.	What is happening to the seeds? After 4 days? After 8 days? Why is this happening?

Table 8.3   An Example of How the KWL Chart Might Be Used

K	W	L
What Students Know	*What Students Want to Know*	*What Students Learned*
We know that • Plants need sun. • Plants need water. • Plants need soil. • Plants give us carbon dioxide.	We want to know • How much water do plants need? • Why are plants green?	We learned that • Plants really give us oxygen. • The amount of water depends on the plant. • Plants are green because they have chlorophyll in them that helps them make food.

However, as time goes on, you may encourage them to come up with creative ideas about what materials to use. For example, when your class studies magnets, it may be important to have certain materials that students test for magnetism. The next step might be to have the students choose materials they want to test.

Create an environment that is full of time to share. Having students share their ideas provides them with one more layer of understanding of their experiences. Sharing offers a setting for safe social interaction, with questions, clarifications, debates, and celebrations. "Piaget contended that

Photo 8.2   Wow a Magnet!

This student chooses to work with two magnets at his table.

clash of peer opinion, combined with cognitive maturity, leads to a decline in the egocentrism believed to underlie the illogical thinking of children. As a result, children begin to reflect on their own cognitions and adapt to the perspectives of others" (Tudge & Rogoff, as quoted in Berk & Winsler, 1995, p. 18). In other words, sharing is another way for children to reflect and make connections. Have you ever been very sure that you understood something until you talked to someone who had a different perspective? Did this make you rethink your position? As important as it is for children to review quietly on their own, it is equally important for them to be able to share their ideas with others so that they can begin to see that there are many different ways to think and solve problems. Sharing also develops pride, motivation, and excitement for past, present, and future projects. When students share their activities and thoughts, it is a celebration of learning!

■ GATHERING YOUR BALLOONS

Thinking about putting all of the ideas discussed in the past eight chapters into practice may seem a bit like trying to gather balloons with no strings and hold them together. You may feel you have captured the idea of active learning but still have questions about how to tie it to the key science experiences. Meanwhile, principles from the nature of science may have floated away and need reviewing! Indeed, putting all of the ingredients into practice is an *active process* and requires creating some strings to tie all of those balloons together. Once you can see the ties, it will be easier to gather the balloons and create one bunch so that all the ideas are linked. Take a moment to try to make some ties among the concepts discussed up to this point—active learning, social interaction, maturation, the nature of science, the key science experiences, and thinking routines. How can you tie them together and incorporate them into your classroom?

One tie, or relationship, might be among maturational issues, key science experiences, the nature of science, and active learning. Active learning experiences must be developed based on each of these other aspects of learning. Without taking into account maturational issues, you may develop active learning activities that are inappropriate for your students. Without planning activities around the key science experiences, you might not give students the kind of tools they need for learning science as well as other subjects. Without thinking about the nature of science, you might plan activities that do not help students do "real" science.

Another tie is between social interaction and the nature of science. Social interaction enhances the nature of science through the communication of ideas. Scientists communicate their ideas to others in papers and oral presentations. Without this social interaction, discoveries would go unnoticed and unchallenged. As social interaction is a vital part of the science community, so it should be of the classroom.

Social interaction and active learning make strong connections with thinking routines. Social interaction is necessary to help young learners scaffold toward their own thinking about learning. And, thinking routines help students to construct knowledge about a subject such as science in an active way.

Figure 8.2   Gathering Balloons

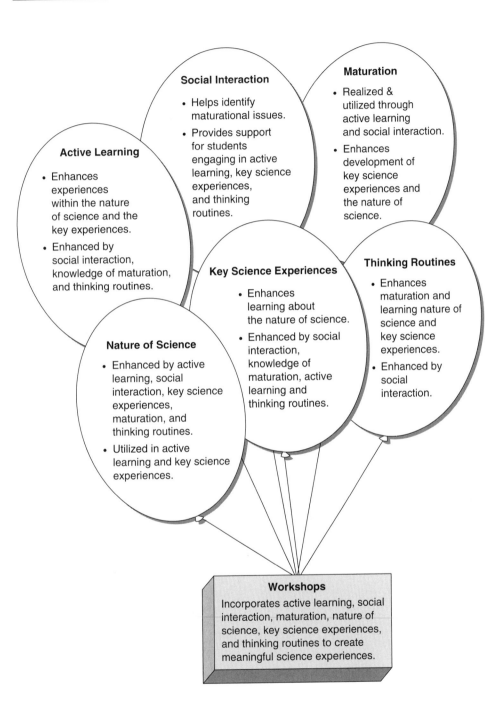

To further understand the importance of all five balloons and their connections to one another, try undoing the connections and see what results. First, imagine a classroom in which students are actively learning science (if you need to, review Chapter 6). What are the students doing? What is the teacher doing? What social interaction is taking place? How are the key science experiences being used? Are the students *doing* science? How are their maturational needs being met? Are they beginning to be able to utilize thinking routines to help them construct meaning? Now take social interaction out of the picture. How does that affect active learning? How does it affect the key science experiences and the nature of science? Maturational needs? Next, take out the key science experiences, the nature of science, thinking routines, and maturational needs. How does each of these pieces affect the whole? As you can see, taking away any one of the six drastically changes the whole picture.

There is a string that binds all of these balloons into one bunch, yet allows them to be arranged flexibly according to individual classroom needs. That string is called workshops, and is the subject of the next chapter.

Conversation Starters

- What thinking routines do you use when you
  - Read?
  - Write?
  - Go on vacation?
  - Do your taxes?
  - Run errands?

- How do thinking routines support the theory that people construct their own knowledge?

- Develop or change a lesson so that it incorporates a thinking routine. Share it with someone.

- What thinking routines do you think Einstein used?

- Think of a specific child you know who could benefit from using thinking routines. How would a thinking routine help?

- How might thinking routines support differentiation in classrooms?

9

Planning Science Workshops

Constructivism is often thought of as an approach or a group of activities. However, constructivism is really a way of thinking about learning. It is the belief that, in order to learn, people must construct knowledge. The approach we advocate in this book is not constructivism itself but rather components that will help you facilitate the construction of knowledge about science in yourself and in your students. We believe that, in order to help students construct knowledge, teachers need to understand active learning, the topic being studied (in this case science), maturation, social interaction, themselves as learners, key experiences, and thinking routines. Teachers also need to understand structures that will help them integrate all of these components into classroom activities promoting the construction of knowledge. This chapter is dedicated to helping you do just that within a structure called science workshops.

Science workshops provide teachers with a framework to plan opportunities for students to learn actively, interact and mature in accordance with their own skills and timetable, and to engage in the key science experiences as they learn science content. Science workshops promote the use of thinking routines to help young students develop the ability to solve problems, think deeply, and become aware of their own learning. The workshop planning structure is very flexible and provides for the individuality and creativity of both teachers and students.

■ WHAT IS A SCIENCE WORKSHOP?

So what is a workshop? How do you plan one? What does the classroom look like during workshops? Before we begin to answer some of these questions, we have a few for you to answer. What are your own thoughts about workshops? What does the word imply to you? What are some ways a workshop might be structured so that it incorporates all of the important elements discussed in earlier chapters and nurtures children's understanding of science? How might a workshop differ from regular science instruction? Thinking through these issues will help you create the best workshops for your students. Let's add to your picture of workshops now.

Workshops are small-group or individual instructional experiences. Workshops are blocks of time for introducing, developing, experiencing, and reviewing specific content. In this sense, workshops aren't all that different from a traditional science class; in both cases, content is learned along with the processes and vocabulary of science. What makes a workshop unique is the way the content is learned and how students are grouped for instructional activities. In a traditional science class, much of the instruction is presented in a whole group, through lecture, reading, or demonstration, and is generally driven by a textbook. In a workshop format, however, students form small groups or work individually and actively participate, plan, and reflect on activities that are initially created by the teacher but that also allow students considerable choice. Activities are developed based not only on textbook and district requirements but also on student interests and needs.

Workshops are flexible. Another difference between traditional science instruction and science workshops is that, during workshops, students may not all be doing the same activity at the same time. Periodically, small groups may be engaged in the same workshop activity but carry it out differently according to group interests or preferences.

Workshops allow teachers to develop activities based on the content they need to teach, students' maturational levels, and students' interests. Workshops can be set up so that the students need to complete all of the activities at a station or so that they can choose from several. The size of the group can also be varied based on maturation and activity requirements. Students might work together or alone at different stations.

Workshops are teacher facilitated. Workshops can be designed so the teacher moves from station to station or so the teacher stays at one specific station for safety, assessment, or explanation purposes while students rotate through other stations. Teachers provide flexible structures such as the key science experiences and thinking routines to help students learn in accordance to their needs.

Workshops may be short or ongoing. Generally, students will rotate through a few stations during one workshop period. However, when workshop activities are more complicated and will take a lot of time, children might do only one or two per day. For example, if students were creating their own machines to lift a book from the floor to the desk using less work than lifting it by hand, they would need quite a bit of time and many resources. It would be difficult to accomplish both this and another activity in the same period. Workshops can be set up so that there are one, two, or three different activities for students to complete, or there may be as many as six or seven, which can be completed over several days.

Workshops provide opportunities for differentiation in a single classroom. Workshops provide opportunities for students who are more experienced as well as for those who need a lot of experience. For example, you may notice that there are students in your classroom who do not know anything about rocks and students who know quite a bit. The workshops you plan might include a station where students are able to observe and feel rocks as well as a station where students have the opportunity to use a rock tumbler. Through workshops, all kinds of students can participate in activities that suit their needs without being pulled out or given a different assignment.

As you can see, there are many ways to structure an effective workshop. Science workshops often look different each day depending on the activities and goals of the teacher and students.

WHOLE-GROUP INSTRUCTION ■

Should students *always* work in small groups? Not necessarily. Is there a place for whole-group instruction? Yes. Teachers can gather the whole class together at the beginning of a unit of study to introduce students to the important concepts they are going to explore and to give a brief explanation of workshop activities. Together, the class might develop questions or discuss what students already know about the topic. This allows for the sharing of ideas and for the teacher to get a sense of what students understand and where they might need to explore further. Teachers might also hold a whole-group discussion when a workshop activity is dangerous. For example, during a unit on the states of matter, a teacher should discuss the importance of being careful around steam.

Whole-group instructional time should *not* be used to lecture students or to have students read aloud to one another from a textbook. The teacher's role should continue to be one of questioner and facilitator. Even though teachers may be tempted to get through material (science as a noun) quickly (and with less mess!) by explaining it to the whole class at once, students won't be doing science (as a verb) if whole-group instruction is used exclusively.

Whole-group time is also a valuable opportunity to add children's literature to science instruction. During a study of rocks, you might use books such as *Iktomi and the Boulder* or *Sylvester and the Magic Pebble* to begin a workshop in which students measure and categorize different sizes of rocks. Whole-group story reading can spur students' interest, ideas, and plans for observation, organization, and experimentation. However, adding literature to science does not mean having literature *be* the science. Reading a story about rocks and then having students draw pictures of boulders is not science. When you use children's books during a lesson, ask yourself whether they will enhance any of the key science experiences or help students become excited about a topic. Will students be doing "real" science in the activity that follows the book reading?

Whole-group instruction is also vital at the end of a unit, when students share projects or the ideas they discovered. Recall from Chapter 7 that sharing is an important piece of learning science. Whole-group sharing can help students learn new ideas, appreciate other perspectives, and gain self-confidence and listening skills. Students should know ahead of time that they have the opportunity to share in front of the whole group, and, most of the time, sharing should be optional. At the end of large units or big projects, you might invite parents or other classes to be a part of the sharing. Remember that your role here, as during other times, is not to lead but to listen and wonder with your students. Take some time to think about ways to structure whole-group time so that students lead the conversation.

■ THINKING ABOUT CREATING WORKSHOPS

Now that you have an idea of what workshops are all about, spend some time thinking about how to incorporate them into your classroom.

- Pick a topic and a key science experience.
- Ask yourself *WHY* students need to learn these things. No fair answering that they need to know because this is one of your objectives!
  - Why are you teaching the topic?
  - Why do elementary scientists need to know this?

- Now think about the concepts (both content and skills).
  - What activities would be valuable for students to complete?
  - What order might work the best? (In other words, how is each activity connected?)
  - What key science experiences will children use?
  - Should the children complete all of the workshop activities or select a few?
  - What do the students already know about the topic?

- Think about a good configuration for students to learn this content.
  - Would small groups of two or three work best?
  - Would two or three groups of 7 to 10 children be better?
  - What are the benefits and limitations of each type of grouping?
  - Should individuals work on this by themselves?
  - How might preoperational children react in larger groups? Concrete operational children?

- Think about materials.
  - Are there enough for each group?
  - Will all the children be meaningfully engaged?

- Are there objectives from other subjects that could be covered within this workshop?

A SAMPLE WORKSHOP UNIT ■

An example of a unit of workshops might help you get a sense of how to put into practice the theoretical ideas we've discussed. Keep in mind that this unit was developed for a specific classroom of children and that you need to design workshops that work for *you* and *your students!* It is tempting to use prescribed activities in the same way for every group; however, it is important that your students have choices and that their ideas are valued in practice. This doesn't mean that you can't use others' ideas, but be sure to make them fit your classroom as well. Often, teachers take activities from a colleague or book and implement them exactly as described. Remember that teaching is an art—create an original piece, don't paint by the numbers!

The example below is based on a study of rocks in a second grade classroom. Workshops were created based on the school district's curriculum objectives, on what the teacher knew about the maturational levels of the students, and on what students added to the KWL chart during the first day of the unit. As you read through these examples, note the variation in the workshops based on specific answers to the questions we posed earlier. Note that sometimes students work on the same problem and sometimes students work on several different problems.

Photo 9.1   Looking at Rocks

Max observes two different rocks and compares them.

ROCKS ■

Beginning day

Problem: How are rocks in our world different? The same?

- Class has whole-group conversation using a KWL chart, discussing what students know about rocks and what they want to know. Next, they are introduced to the stations, and they plan which three they would like to visit. After students complete three of the workshop stations (which may take more than one day), students are asked to write or draw pictures about their ideas in a logbook.

Station A: Students observe a pile of rocks, noting in their science logbooks what they observe with their eyes, what they observe with a hand lens, and how the rocks feel.

Key science experiences: observing, representing

Station B: Each student observes a pile of rocks and puts them into different groups. Students name their groups and record the information in their science logbooks using pictures and written descriptions.

Key science experiences: observing, representing, organizing

Station C: Students hypothesize about what might happen to rocks if they are submerged in water. After dipping them in water, they record what happened to both the rock and the water. Students discuss what might happen if the rocks were left in the water overnight and for a year.

Key science experiences: observing, representing, patterning/questioning, experimenting, sharing

Station D: Students choose a rock from a pile and observe it, noting their observations in their logbook. Students write a story (writing) about what might have happened to the rock to cause its characteristics.

Key science experiences: observing, representing, questioning

Station E: Each student chooses a rock from a pile and observes it carefully without a partner seeing the chosen rock. After putting the rock back in the pile, the student tries to describe it to the partner so that the partner can identify it.

Key science experiences: observing, representing, sharing

Station F: Students use a rock tumbler to polish several rocks, then write answers to such questions as "What happens in the tumbler? Is there a similar process that occurs naturally in the world?"

Key science experiences: observing, patterning/questioning, experimenting, sharing

Next workshop day (This may not be the very next day depending on your schedule)

- Students form triads and share findings about the observation workshops from their logbooks. Students pick two findings to share with the entire class. Each triad shares something for the *L* part of the KWL chart.

Key science experiences: patterning/questioning, sharing

Next workshop day

Problem: To sort rocks by size

- Teacher reads *Iktomi and the Boulder* (reading) and asks students to come up with a definition for a boulder, a pebble, a cobble, gravel, and sand. How is this language categorizing the differences? (Size)

- Teacher gives students the different measurements (math) that classify rocks as boulders, pebbles, and so on, along with rulers. In pairs, students go on a scavenger hunt to find rocks of each size. Students plan a way to share the different sizes and names of the rocks. Students share their projects with the whole class.

Key science experiences: observing, representing, organizing, patterning/questioning, sharing

Next workshop day

Problem: What are the differences between igneous, sedimentary, and metamorphic rocks?

Stations: Students observe a different type of rock at three stations. Students move from station to station as needed; a discussion about how many students can comfortably observe at one station takes place before the workshop starts. Students use hand lenses, water, brushes, and sandpaper to test the rocks' characteristics. Students compare all three types of rocks and explore ideas about the way they were formed.

Key science experiences: observing, representing, organizing, patterning/questioning, sharing

Next workshop day

Problem: How can we test rocks to determine how hard they are?

- At the beginning of the workshop period, the teacher asks the students how they might test rocks for hardness. They offer ideas such as throwing the rocks on the ground or putting a lot of weight on them. If no one comes up with the idea of rubbing two of the rocks together, the teacher could suggest this as a way to test for hardness without hurting anyone or anything in the classroom.
- Students work in groups to determine which of the rocks given to them are the hardest. Rocks might include those from the surrounding environment as well as igneous, sedimentary, metamorphic, and river rocks.

Key science experiences: observing, organizing, patterning/questioning, experimenting, sharing

Next workshop day

Problem: What are the differences between sand, dirt, potting soil, and clay?

Stations: Students go to four workshops this day, so managing time should be discussed before beginning. At each station (sand, dirt, potting soil, clay), they observe one of the materials, using their senses and tools such as a magnifying glass, a microscope, water, and white and/or black paper.

Key science experiences: observing

Next workshop day

Problem: How can we share the differences and similarities we found between sand, dirt, potting soil, and clay?

- Teacher does a mini-lesson on making a chart to share information.
- In groups of three, students use their observation notes from the previous day to make their own charts showing the differences and similarities between sand, dirt, clay, and potting soil.
- Students are encouraged to create charts that suit the information they collected rather than to make one exactly like the teacher's.
- Charts are shared at the end of the workshop period.

Next workshop day

Problem: How are sand and soil made?

- Two stations have the same materials available, including rocks, sticks, clay, dirt, and grass or weeds. Students may add other items as they need them. Switch stations after half the class period.

Station A: Students plan and implement experiments to make sand.

Key science experiences: observing, representing, organizing, patterning/ questioning

Station B: Students plan and implement experiments to make potting soil.

Key science experiences: observing, representing, organizing, patterning/ questioning

Next workshop day

Problem: What influences rocks, sand, and soil outside? (Water, heat, cold, wind, animals, and so on; some answers connect to social studies)

- Teacher asks students how sand and soil are made outside. Students pair up to go outside to look for evidence of influences, and they share their findings after returning to the classroom.

Key science experiences: observing, organizing, patterning/questioning, sharing

Next workshop day

Problem: How are rocks, sand, clay, and soil used in our lives?

- Students choose to go to as many of these six workshops as they want. This set of workshops may span several days, and parent assistance would be helpful.

  Station A: Students use a lump of pottery clay to make pottery, beads, sculptures, or whatever they would like.

Key science experiences: observing, representing, patterning/questioning, experimenting

  Station B: Students sand pieces of wood with sandpaper of varying coarseness. Pencils also work well in place of wood pieces; students can sand the pencils and then paint them.

Key science experiences: observing, patterning/questioning, experimenting

  Station C: Students use a variety of rocks—including river rocks and igneous, metamorphic, and sedimentary rocks—to make something that uses the strengths of each rock.

Key science experiences: observing, patterning/questioning, experimenting

  Station D: Students use a variety of soils to create a miniature bean garden in an aluminum foil dish. They experiment to determine which soil is the best for the beans.

Key science experiences: observing, organizing, patterning/questioning, experimenting

  Station E: Students create miniature "bricks" of sand, clay, soil, and rocks using cookie cutters. They determine which are the sturdiest.

Key science experiences: observing, organizing, patterning/questioning, experimenting

  Station F: Students use plaster of paris and "playing clay" to make fossils of objects around the room.

Key science experiences: observing, organizing, patterning/questioning, experimenting

◆

Although these examples give you an idea of what science workshops look like, remember that yours will be different depending on your students' needs and interests and your curriculum goals. In this particular example, students continued their study of rocks by learning about volcanoes, earthquakes, mountains, ecology, and fossils. Note also that each activity included one or more key science experiences. When you create science workshops, ask yourself if any key science experiences are included. If there aren't any, the activity might not be science! It is important to offer students as much choice as possible in workshops, to provide sharing time, and to help children make connections between workshops as well as within workshops. Thinking routines really help children make these connections and enable them to make educated choices. Can you see the thinking routines embedded within the sample workshops?

Workshops allow for individualized instruction and provide students with opportunities to direct their own learning, supported by a structured format. Because of this, workshops require increased flexibility in planning. You may not be able to plan a whole unit ahead of time within this framework. The workshops presented here, for example, were not planned all at once but evolved as it became apparent what students needed and wanted to know about the topic. You can, however, begin to gather resources, predict what students might be interested in studying, and make sure that objectives are covered. Planning like this requires patience and an understanding of how to scaffold learning.

■ SCAFFOLDING WITHIN WORKSHOPS

As you read in Chapter 5, one way to think about scaffolding is as a way to build on what students already know. The workshops in the previous example began with a discussion of what students already knew about rocks and with opportunities for them to explore rocks from their surrounding environment—objects they were probably familiar with. If the unit had started with content about unfamiliar types of rocks and their technical names, or with a particular science process such as patterning or experimenting, students would not have had much to connect to. Remember that any unit of study, and for that matter an entire year of learning science, is a process—a back and forth between what is understood and what is not, what is misunderstood, and what can be scaffolded. The content in the example workshops was scaffolded to meet the students' needs as well as the district objectives and the *National Science Education Standards*. However, the order of the workshops presented is definitely not "the" right order, nor is this the only way a study of rocks can be scaffolded. There are many connections to make when presenting any content, and finding ways to help students make those connections requires only that you take the time and effort to scaffold well. As you think about the workshops in the example above, what connections do you see from workshop to workshop? How is the content from one workshop connected to the content of the next? How are the key science experiences tied together? Can you see places where there are gaps? What workshop experiences might you add to close those gaps?

There are three main areas to think about when designing scaffolded workshops: (1) the content and how it fits together, (2) the students—what they know and think they know, and (3) the key science experiences.

SCAFFOLDING CONTENT   ■

To create connected workshops, you must have a deep understanding of the content. This does not mean that you have to be a geologist to design workshops about rocks. However, it does mean that you need to take some time to read through resources on rocks and even ask experts what activities are important for children (think of this as your own scaffolding experience). This needs to be done at the beginning of the unit, but also as it continues. Your district objectives and the *National Science Education Standards* are good sources to start with, but remember that those objectives have large gaps. For example, an objective might be for students to learn the differences between sedimentary, igneous, and metamorphic rocks. If your initial workshop centers on that objective, students will not be able to connect the new information and experiences to ideas they already understand. Even if you design a workshop primarily around student interests—say, volcanoes—you need to begin where they are, with some ideas that they can connect to the subject. Note that in the sample workshops above, we started with all kinds of rocks and took the time to observe them in many different ways. We made our way toward examining specific rocks in detail and classifying them, but we didn't start there. Was that an objective? Maybe, but most likely we needed a good place to begin. Scaffolding content provides students a place to start assimilating and accommodating new information.

SCAFFOLDING FOR STUDENT NEEDS: ■
DIFFERENTIATION

You may be wondering how to find a beginning place for workshop activities when you have students with different background knowledge and different maturational levels. This is probably one of the hardest parts of teaching, but it is also one of the reasons this approach works so well. Again, let's use an example from the sample unit on rocks. The unit began with a conversation about what students knew. They then did some basic observation of real rocks from their neighborhood. (Remember that you want to create *experiences*. Learning about rocks requires actually having some for students to observe!) Students who needed the very basic experience of feeling the rocks had a chance to do that. Students who had already played with rocks had the opportunity to observe rocks in other ways (for example, with magnifying glasses) and to begin to manipulate them (for instance, "painting" them with water). *Each level of experience was valued and accommodated in the initial workshop.* The flexibility and open-endedness of workshops, along with teacher and peer interaction, make each experience fit individual children. Think about some options in a workshop for students who have had many experiences with a particular topic or material. What if they haven't had any?

Managing workshops so that they are scaffolded for each child probably seems difficult. However, because workshops offer students choices, all kinds of learners can be accommodated. Choices can range from letting students choose the workshops they want to participate in to encouraging them to go in directions that aren't necessarily mapped out at a particular station. Once students start to really wonder about a topic and feel that their ideas are valued, they will expand on workshop activities based on their individual preferences and intelligences. I recall a student named Amanda who was a very gifted artist. During a workshop session on sand, students sanded pieces of wood with different grades of sandpaper to learn the difference between coarse and fine. Amanda, however, planned to make her own sandpaper by gluing sand to some cardboard in different ways. She siphoned the sand with screens, creating "designer" sandpaper with coarse and fine sections. Amanda demonstrated her understanding of texture and grade—the objective of the workshop—but in a way that stretched her further than the workshop required. She started at a workshop and made it her own. This kind of flexibility in planning and in what students are permitted to actually do in a workshop creates a classroom in which each child is able to start where necessary and reach a place of understanding that he or she might not otherwise. Workshops can be created for all kinds of learners because the learners help develop them as they go along.

Scaffolding for each student begins with a great deal of listening and observing on the teacher's part. It also requires trusting students. You will not be able to create workshops that connect to children's existing schema without getting to know them, and students will not proceed in the directions that are right for them if you don't trust them. I could have felt frustrated that Amanda was not doing what she was "supposed" to be doing at the station. It would have been easy to tell her to get back "on task." However, allowing Amanda to chart her own course for learning about grades of sandpaper benefited her learning greatly. Workshops are opportunities not only for students to learn and meet objectives but also for you to understand them as learners and push them to new levels of learning—to stretch their zones of proximal development.

Scaffolding for individual students might be as simple as sitting next to a child and wondering aloud what might happen if ____. It might be as difficult as creating an entire station around the interests and needs of an individual child. As we mentioned earlier, depending on the activities, you might spend the workshop period at one station or move from station to station to support students. Spending time at one station allows you to concentrate on one aspect of content or the key science experiences; moving from station to station lets you concentrate more on certain children or groups of children and get an entire picture of the workshops for that day. It is also helpful to take notes about individual students as they work and to stand back and just watch for a minute or two. All of this listening and observing will help you better understand your students and create opportunities for them to grow.

■ SCAFFOLDING THE KEY SCIENCE EXPERIENCES

The key science experiences discussed in Chapter 7 also need to be scaffolded for students—connected in such a way that they are meaningful to them. Although many students have had experiences observing their world and manipulating variables informally, in order to learn content, they must learn formal science processes, and these need to be scaffolded. It would be difficult for children to create experiments with multiple variables before they have even experienced observing with a purpose. Very young students can start out observing with all of their senses, then move into observing with tools, and finally observe for the purpose of finding a pattern or identifying a question. If students have limited experience using tools for observation, let them explore the tools and fully understand the procedures for using them before you expect them to use the tools to learn content. When students are learning to use a microscope, have them start with everyday objects such as salt, string, or newspaper before materials like pond water.

Other science processes may not need to be scaffolded apart from content. Instead, they can be combined *with* a study of content. A lesson in patterning or questioning, for instance, is not needed outside of a content area. However, sometimes you may conduct a mini-lesson to help students learn about certain science processes. An example of this is a whole-group mini-lesson on categorizing, conducted before students categorize their rocks. Note that it is a *mini*-lesson. Telling students *how* to categorize rocks is not the goal—helping them understand the general process of categorizing is. Mini-lessons should be short (say, 10 minutes or so) and used only to give students enough background to complete a workshop activity successfully. Remember that there is no "right" way to scaffold the key science experiences. However, it is vital that students develop the ability to build on previous processes.

This progressive learning of science processes may be scaffolded over an entire year, particularly for younger students. Content can be specifically planned over the year to help with this scaffolding. For instance, a study of insects might work nicely at the beginning of the year because students would have many opportunities to make observations. A study of rocks following this would give students opportunities to observe as well as organize data and ask questions. Depending on the content and objectives, specific science processes can be highlighted. This does not mean that, in a study of insects, students wouldn't be asking questions and making hypotheses. However, it does mean that the *focus* might be on observing. Scaffolding the science processes throughout the year allows children not only to learn content but also to use the tools of science with increasing skill and understanding.

Scaffolding provides both the necessary structure and flexibility students need to pursue their own learning. Considering science concepts, the individual children you are teaching, and the key science experiences will require a great deal of planning and thinking ahead of time yet allow you to adapt activities to follow where students lead.

Photo 9.2   Pile of Rocks

Creating workshops may seem like climbing a mountain of rocks. Take it one step at a time!

■ TIPS FOR GETTING STARTED WITH WORKSHOPS

Remember at the beginning of the book when we said that this would not be a book of recipes for you to follow? We hope that you are seeing now that helping students learn science requires you to think critically and keep learning rather than to just follow someone else's directions. In a sense, creating workshops is a problem solving experience! Perhaps, in order to get started, it would help to use a thinking routine discussed in Chapter 8. The first step is to *define the problem:* students with differing maturational levels and background experiences, a wide variety and depth of science topics to teach them, and a certain amount of time to do it. (You may have additional or more specific problems.) Next, *examine the problem* and *collect information* to solve it. What content do the students need? What do they already know? Where are they developmentally? The third step is to *structure the information into a solution.* What workshops can you develop to assist students in learning the content? How can the workshops help meet their social needs? Fourth, select the plan that will work best for you and your students, and do it! Finally, assess the outcome and think through some modifications for next time.

In addition to our suggestion that you use the problem-solving process to get started with workshops, we have several others. Consider these suggestions with your own needs and those of your students in mind, and make sure you are true to what you believe. Do what works for you and your students within this structure!

Make Collections. Because workshops are based largely on the particular needs and interests of a class of students, you need not and should not plan every detail of every unit before the school year begins. However, you *can* start collecting materials for the topics you know you will be teaching. For example, if you're going to teach a unit on spiders, get a folder or box and start collecting photographs; ideas for lessons, activities, and experiments; resources for ordering spiders; materials for making webs; supporting literature and magazine articles; and so on.

Making collections will help you not only plan workshops when the time comes but also learn more about the content before you begin. Add to your collections as the year progresses, and you can easily pull out ideas and organize them when you begin a unit. When you start a new unit, make sure to talk to your students about what they want to know and what they already know about the topic. This will let students know that their ideas are valuable and accepted, get them excited about learning and exploring, and help you scaffold your workshops. If, based on your conversation with students, you find that you need additional activities or lessons in your collection, find or develop some!

Start simple. As you begin to develop your own workshops, start out simple. Rather than set up six stations with six different activities, set up one or two workshop stations at which everyone is doing the same activity. As you and your students become comfortable with the workshop routine, gradually add more stations. Keep the workshops themselves simple, too. The best workshop activities are often the ones that students can expand on their own. Having students observe many different kinds of rocks, for example, is a simple activity but one that offers many jumping-off points. Students have ownership in a simple workshop such as this, which does not have step-by-step instructions. If there are some stations that require step-by-step instructions, make sure students understand the difference between the two types of station before they start. Remember that the more open the workshop, the more individualized it is. Also, workshops don't have to be pretty. In other words, at first you might not have time to make signs for each station that tell the students what to do. That's okay. Although fancy signs and decorations look nice, they don't necessarily enhance learning. Spend time learning content and thinking of higher level questions instead. As you have more time, you can make the stations more attractive if you want to.

Help children understand the social aspects of workshops. Students who are not used to taking responsibility for their own learning may have a hard time initiating, making choices, and thinking for themselves. Talk to them about what is expected during workshops and when working with others. If you don't want 25 students at one station at the same time, discuss the reason. Have them help you make the guidelines for workshops, such as what the signal will be for too much noise or how to help someone who is having difficulty during an activity. After a workshop period, discuss what went well and what they might need to work on the next time. Social goals might be as important as academic goals for a while, and that is okay.

Understand that classroom management will be different in an active learning classroom. Classroom management might seem a challenge as you begin to use science workshops in your classroom. A class in which students do various activities at the same time is going to look and sound different from a traditional classroom in which students are working quietly in their seats. It may look chaotic and sound noisy at first. Stand back and really observe for a few minutes of every workshop period. Listen to what students are talking about and watch to see what they are doing. If they are not engaged in the activity, help get them back on track with questions and support. However, if they are excited and engaged in the workshop, don't worry so much about the noise. Before they visit, prepare principals and parents for what they might see and hear in your classroom, and encourage them to talk to students and find out what they are learning. Ask parent volunteers to come during your workshop period, so they can really engage in the activities.

Others might suggest that your classroom is unstructured, but, in reality, it is more structured than a traditional classroom. It has to be—it takes a great deal of organization to get a class of students to successfully carry on several different activities at the same time. Students who are passive recipients of knowledge and who are encouraged to speak only when called on do not learn how to make decisions, help one another, or solve problems. If there are conflicts or difficulties that arise during workshops, think of them as opportunities for learning important lifelong skills!

Try out activities ahead of time. It is important that you try experiments yourself, with the exact materials you will be using, before having students try them. Many things can go wrong with activities. For example, during a unit on teeth, I wanted the students to make models of teeth. Having used plaster of paris before with fossils, I decided to use it again. However, I needed something the students could put in their mouths that would make imprints of their teeth. I decided that bubble gum would work, and I even tried it out ahead of time. However, I didn't anticipate the amount of time it would take second graders to chew several pieces of bubble gum until it was soft enough to model! It was quite humorous to watch 25 children desperately trying to chew the gum all wadded up in their mouths. We all laughed and decided to chalk that one up to experience. Don't forget that the students you are working with may not have the skills you do (or the chewing power!). The unexpected isn't always negative, but when you are getting started with workshops, it helps to know what will probably happen with an activity.

Recruit helpers during workshops. If a workshop requires a lot of adult supervision or outside time, ask for parent volunteers or recruit some older students. Invite business people or university scientists to help with workshops one day. Often, people in the community have valuable resources and expertise that can be translated into an exciting activity for students. I had a parent who regularly volunteered in my classroom. She saw an activity in a book once and asked if she could do it with the students. During an animal unit, she used lard and plastic to make gloves that simulated blubber and had the students dip their hands in ice water with and without the gloves on. It was a wonderful activity, and it meant one less station for me to develop for that day. Of course, not all parents will be that resourceful, but many have hidden talents and expertise that you can tap into if you take the time and energy to get to know them and invite them to be a part of your classroom!

Develop authentic and challenging questions for workshop activities. Questioning is vital to children's construction of knowledge during workshops; questions help students think critically and stretch their understanding. Before a workshop, develop two or three questions for students to answer either in writing or in a discussion. Make sure they are higher level questions (see Chapter 3 for a review of questions). You might also carry a pad of paper during workshops so that, if you think of more questions you want to ask at the end of the period, you can write them down.

Review what happened during the workshop period. You can do this through journal writing or during reflection time, or you can talk with others about what went well during the workshops and what you would like to change. Reviewing will help you improve your workshops and your interactions with students and also give you a chance to vent or celebrate! Over the long term, you will be able to look back on how you and your students have improved.

Another resource that will help you get started is the list of questions in this chapter. Use them to help you think through all of the many issues surrounding workshops—including those associated with each of the five balloons we talked about earlier—and to ward off potential problems. As you get started planning and implementing workshops with your students, remember that learning to teach in this way is a process, just as learning science is a process for students. At first, the work might be frustrating and show few results, but, if you stick with it and learn from your efforts, it will get easier—and you and your students will really take hold of those balloons and fly!

WHY WORKSHOPS?   ■

Perhaps after reading this chapter you are wondering why you should change your current practice to incorporate workshops, or maybe you are excited about the possibilities you see in workshops. Perhaps you are wondering whether they will be more work than you can manage. You may be concerned that students won't be exposed to the required science material if they are allowed to follow their own learning path. You might be worried about how you will manage workshops with all the other content you have to teach, and how you will incorporate standards and benchmarks into your workshop activities. You might be wondering, why workshops?

We can offer a partial answer to this question, but you will also need to answer it for yourself as you reflect on what you have learned and then try implementing workshop activities. It's important that you believe in the value of workshops and not simply because someone else says you should. We encourage you to ponder the questions you may still have about workshops and to try to answer them using the information presented in previous chapters. Discover for yourself some reasons workshops will help you teach science more effectively. Here are some to get you started.

Workshops provide both the structure and freedom students need to actively learn science. Students are able to make decisions, manipulate materials, use language, and stretch their thinking, supported by adults in a safe environment. Workshops not only make learning science a positive, engaging experience but also help students discover that they can accomplish tasks, come up with creative ideas, and be successful learners.

Workshops provide social as well as academic goals. Through small groups, student involvement in planning, and the hands-on nature of the activities, workshops encourage high levels of student participation and decision making. All children can discuss, debate, and question rather than simply listen to lessons or instructions.

No matter their level or pace of learning, all students can successfully participate and grow within the workshop structure. Individual maturation and interests are accommodated through materials, peer and teacher support, and a variety of open-ended, engaging, challenging activities. This is possible because teachers design workshops with the help of their students rather than relying solely on curriculum guides and textbooks. Students feel successful during workshops because they have the power to make choices and are able to use their strengths as well as address their weaknesses in a safe environment. Since students are engaged in many varied activities at the same time, no one has to be pulled aside or made to feel different when needing extra assistance or an extra challenge. During workshops, each student can receive attention according to his or her unique needs.

Workshops provide a laboratory for young scientists to develop their skills, knowledge, and curiosity. The nature of science involves thinking and participation, not passively taking in information and memorizing facts. During science workshops, students actively question, hypothesize about cause and effect, problem solve, work toward individual and group goals, and manipulate materials to find answers.

Workshops allow students to engage in the key science experiences. This is because students are asked to use what they know to solve problems. When planning a workshop, teachers can focus on particular processes yet also leave room for students to experience others. Which setting would teach more of the science processes—a classroom in which the teacher demonstrated which rocks were the hardest or a workshop in which students tested the rocks to determine which were the hardest?

Perhaps it is not possible to entirely answer the question of why workshops are worth pursuing without actually trying them in your classroom. The reasons we have given here only scratch the surface and do not begin to describe the enormous *emotional* benefits of workshops—the excitement and pride students display as they discover something fascinating, the changes in their attitude toward learning, the renewal and challenge that teachers feel as they design successful, engaging activities. These benefits are as valuable as the benefits to learning. Our mission as teachers should be to teach children not only about science but also about learning and life. Creating workshops geared specifically for the children in your classroom is one way to accomplish this mission.

■ CREATING YOUR OWN WORKSHOPS—A CHECKLIST

The following questions will help you create workshops that benefit your students' learning of science. Use them to start planning a unit of study, keeping in mind that you will modify your plan as you learn more about your students and their needs. In other words, these questions can help you predict and plan, but they provide only a guide as you listen and question to find out what your students need.

At the Beginning of the Year

- What content objectives am I required to teach? Do any objectives from other subjects fit with these?
- How do the content objectives from my district fit with the *National Science Education Standards?* Are there any standards that could be combined with district objectives?
- What information must students know at the end of each unit?

- How can I scaffold across topics the content I am required to teach? What unit of study would work well at the beginning of the year? How might the content connect to later units? (For example, you might study insects first and then scaffold to the human body, looking at the differences and similarities between insects and humans, such as life cycle differences.)
- What key science experiences seem best suited to each unit of study? Students will likely use multiple processes in each study, but you may want them to focus on one or two for each unit. For example, students might focus on experimenting when studying machines. A decision like this affects the order of a study. Where in a unit might it work best to focus on experimenting?
- Should any units be studied at a particular time of year? Consider such factors as weather, holidays, and testing. If you are doing a unit on seeds and plants, will it be difficult to find some in the winter in your area? Will you have enough time for a certain unit? Are there concepts you must cover before a certain testing date?
- How can science topics be integrated with other subjects? For example, a social studies unit on houses and homes might coincide with a science unit on rocks and minerals.

Before a Unit

- What do I know about the individual students I teach? What are their interests, strengths, and areas to continue to develop?
- What specific content do the students need to know? Are there gaps in the content? What content might fill those gaps?
- What background might students have on the content?
- What key science experiences would fit with the content?
- What experiences would move students toward the content and science process goals?
- How can those experiences be scaffolded?
- What literature can complement the unit?

Before a Workshop

- What is the content or problem children will work with in this workshop?
- How can this content or problem be scaffolded from what students have done previously?
- What experiences might help them move toward understanding the content or problem?
- What key science experiences will help children understand the content or problem?
- How can this workshop be tailored to the individuals in my classroom?
- What choices will I give students in the workshop? What things will be required?
- How will I structure the workshop? How many stations will I create? Will the students work as a group or as individuals?
- What materials will I need for each station?
- How will students know what to do?

- What will my role be at each station?
- What questions do I want to be sure to ask?
- How will the room be set up?
- Which students will work together?
- How many children should be at each station?
- Are there safety issues?
- How will I review how the workshop went?

Remember . . .

Effective science workshops offer students choices and opportunities to use language, manipulate materials, and interact with adults and peers. They require that teachers understand individual children and their development so that appropriate experiences can be planned. Science workshops incorporate the tenets of the nature of science and key science experiences so that students can experience "real" science.

Remember our balloon analogy in Chapter 8? Although the six balloons—active learning, the nature of science, maturation, social interaction, the key science experiences, and thinking routines—are tied together within workshops, they are still separate. When you start planning workshops, ask yourself if each balloon has been covered. Is this experience an active learning one? Are there opportunities for social interaction? What key science experiences are being utilized? How does this activity reflect the nature of science? Are individual maturational needs being met? Do students have the opportunity to utilize thinking routines? In asking yourself these questions, you will ensure that the workshops you develop are complete learning experiences for students. As you become more familiar with this approach, you may not need to review each balloon individually. However, as you get started, remember that each one is vital and that it is connected to all of the others.

Conversation Starters

- What are some advantages of using science workshops? Any limitations?
- What differences do you see between workshops and traditional science instruction?
- What will be the most difficult part about creating workshops for you?
- What are your impressions of the sample workshop? Which aspects of the workshop process seem easy? Which seem difficult?
- What is the difference between an activity and a workshop?

PART IV

Science Is a Community Affair

This final section of the book actually brings us back to the beginning, back to using science to help children become accomplished, self-confident, self-reliant, long-term learners. As we complete this cycle, we are reminded that education—including science education—is a community affair. The importance and role of the community in science education is seen in the three chapters in this section: "Assessment" (Chapter 10), "Access to Science in a Classroom" (Chapter 11), and "Connections to Curriculum" (Chapter 12).

The term *community* originates from several different Latin words with similar meanings: *communis,* meaning "shared by all or many," and *communitas* ("fellowship"), which itself comes from two words meaning "together" (*com*) and "oneness" (*unitas*). We like to think of community in this last sense—a "together in oneness" with students and others in our lives. It is in community that we grow and develop, live and work.

But being "together in oneness" does not mean we are actually one, or all the same. Howard Gardner points out that, though we all share the same intelligences, we are very diverse with respect to them. He also notes that we often deny or ignore that diversity, although we have the opportunity to revel in it. The classroom, especially, should be a place that fosters oneness even while allowing us to be different, a place to rejoice in our differences and yet remain "together."

One way to do this is by monitoring students' progress and knowledge through assessment. Chapter 10 ("Assessment") is devoted to the ways we can join ourselves to students to learn more about how they understand the world and how they are growing in knowledge. We'll discuss using the skills of questioning and listening and rubrics, portfolios, and other tools to accomplish this.

In Chapter 11 ("Access to Science in a Classroom"), we discuss the science community in several different forms: the physical and social community of the classroom; the psychological "safe home" where students can think, reflect, explore, and express themselves without judgments, tasks, or evaluations; and the broader communities of the family, schools, museums, and nature itself. Each of these communities should support curiosity, creativity, and growth by providing stimulation, scaffolding, and security.

In Chapter 12 ("Connections to Curriculum"), we discuss ways to make connections among your school district community, this approach to teaching science, and yourself as both a teacher and learner. Your experiences with and understanding of curriculum, including district objectives, provide a firm foundation on which you can rely. As you begin to connect those objectives to teaching science, make the approach your own as you continue to help students learn science objectives from the community where you teach. In other words, expand the community in which you live and work to include new learning, the students' interests, and your own ideas!

10

Assessment

You might be wondering why a chapter on assessment would be placed in a section labeled "Science Is a Community Affair." Shouldn't it go with the nuts and bolts of Part III? Assessment of science definitely requires practical tools, and we will present some in this chapter; but we also hope to help you consider assessment as a way to get to know students and their understandings, just as you would get to know a neighbor in your community! Just as it is important to ask yourself why you might want to meet new members of a community and how you might go about doing so, it is important to *know why you are assessing* and *what tools might meet those needs.* Take some time to think about why we assess our students. What does the assessment do for the students? Parents? Teachers? School districts and communities?

The Latin root of the word *assess* is *assidere,* meaning "to sit beside, to sit alongside a judge" (*Merriam-Webster's New Collegiate Dictionary*). Although it may be difficult to distinguish assessment from evaluation, this root helps us do so. Assessment means to *work beside* students, facilitate their learning, and plan the next step in the learning process. In other words, it means to tell them what is right, what is wrong, and how to fix it (Lockett, 2006). In contrast, to *evaluate* means to *judge* how well a student (or teacher, school, or school system) performs relative to a standard or to others' performance. Most of the discussion in this chapter will deal with assessment *for* learning, which is carried out for improving student-teacher interactions and increasing student learning. However, since evaluation *of* learning has become a major goal on the educational and political fronts, we'll discuss this as well.

Assessment and evaluation are often used interchangeably when in fact they are quite different. In the education world, they are known as formative and summative assessment. In the first, data are collected and used to modify practice as the process is going on. This information is not used as a judgment regarding progress toward a specific goal, and it is not as useful to someone removed from the situation as to those immediately involved in the process or activity. Nevertheless, it provides helpful information. For instance, if we ask a kindergartner to tell us about her favorite (or least favorite) animal, we can gain insight into what types of organisms the child thinks are animals, what she likes (or dislikes) about them, what stories might interest her, what pictures she might like to draw, and so on. Although none of this tells us whether the child is meeting particular expectations, we do get information that can be used for various purposes—what to read at story time, for example.

Summative assessment, in contrast, is generally used at the completion of a project or task. Data are collected for judgmental purposes—to summarize what has occurred and measure progress toward a goal. We frequently assign a value to this progress. Familiar types of summative assessment are end-of-unit tests and achievement tests. These assessments can, of course, be used to determine what will take place next, but they are not really used to modify activities during the short term. Both types of assessment are necessary, and both have a place in education, although they serve somewhat different purposes.

Let's apply these two types of assessment to the task of taking a trip. First, we'll fly to Chicago, where we'll catch an international flight to the European continent. As the plane takes off from our home airport, it will not head directly to O'Hare airport. In fact, the plane will generally gain altitude and circle (or at least change direction) before heading in the direction of Chicago. En route, the crew of the aircraft will make a number of measurements of direction, wind speed, altitude, and so on, and make several corrections to the course of the plane as necessary. These measurements are formative assessments: they let us know what changes are necessary to stay on course, and they must be made frequently to ensure a smooth, efficient flight. These assessments are seldom given a value such as *good, excellent,* or *superior.* They are used simply to make corrections and accomplish our goal.

When we get to Chicago, we will use summative assessments. Are we actually in Chicago or somewhere else? Are we on time? Early? Late? What terminal and gate are we at? Can we make the next flight? Did our baggage arrive? And so on.

Although this summating information is important, it has not helped us reach Chicago from our home airport. It merely tells us whether the goal was met. We may also use this type of information to make qualitative ratings: For instance, we may say that the airline was excellent, meaning, generally, that we took off on schedule and landed on schedule, the ride was smooth, luggage arrived on time, and so on.

Note that these two types of assessment are independent but related. There may be instances in which we reach opposite conclusions from the same data. For example, if the plane hit a terrible storm on the way to Chicago and for safety reasons made corrections around the turbulence, we might get into Chicago 30 minutes late, but we would land safely. A summative assessment of *good job* might be given. On another day, with no in-flight corrections for safety, a 30-minute late arrival might be given a *poor job* rating.

This scenario demonstrates the different purposes of formative and summative assessments: One assists us in reaching our goal, and the other allows us to evaluate whether the goal was met and helps us rate our experience. It may be helpful to consider your role as formative assessor in the classroom as that of a coach helping students to find their way, making suggestions, giving feedback. Your role as summative assessor might be thought of as that of a referee, who gives judgments concerning how the game is going but does not really help the players to get better.

FORMATIVE ASSESSMENT ■

The goal of all educators is to enhance students' learning. As educators, we want our students to realize their full potential, understand their world, take an active role in society, and love and appreciate learning so much that they continue the process actively throughout their lives. We consider assessment that enhances the learning process and helps students attain these goals—that is, formative assessment—to be the most important assessment we can do. Let's look at some of the features of formative assessment and then how to use it in the classroom.

Features of Formative Assessment

Learning is a journey of the mind, comparable in many ways to the physical airline journey that we discussed earlier. And just as the flight crew needed to make frequent assessments to keep on course, so we—teachers and learners—need to make assessments to remain on the learning course. Formative assessments are therefore central to the learning process. Summative assessments have much less effect on the learning process because they don't influence the process—they only place a value on the results.

Results of much research support these conclusions. Black and Wiliam (1998) conclude from their analyses of over 250 papers dealing with formative assessment that formative assessment produces the greatest, most consistent improvement in learning. Here are several of their conclusions:

- In more than 250 studies reviewed, formative assessment always led to increased performance on learning objectives. In other words, formative assessment had no negative effects on learning in any of the studies. "Although there is no guarantee that it will do so irrespective of the context and the particular approach adopted, we have not come across any report of negative effects following on an enhancement of formative practice" (p.18).

- The 250 research studies were very heterogeneous in nature. Many were done by teachers in their own classroom, some were done by researchers under atypical conditions, some were part of other studies emphasizing student motivation or constructivism, and so on. In some studies, great emphasis was placed on teacher-student interaction; in others, the emphasis was on other aspects of pedagogy. Since effects held through all these diverse situations, we would expect formative assessments to have the same positive effects in your classroom or ours.

- The positive effects on learning were particularly strong for "weaker" students, although enhancements were found for all students. Black and Wiliam (1998) described the results of one study (by Bergan, Sladecezek, Schwarz, & Smith, 1991):

The criterion tests used, which were traditional multiple-choice, were not adapted to match the open child-centred style of the experimental group's work. Furthermore, of the control group, on average 1 child in 3.7, was referred as having particular learning needs and 1 in 5 was placed in special education; the corresponding figures for the experimental group were 1 in 17 and 1 in 71. (p. 13)

Formative assessment had the potential to be life transforming for many of the students in this last study. For example, about 80% of children labeled as having particular learning needs would not have had that label had formative assessment been used regularly in their classroom.

■ FORMATIVE ASSESSMENT AND MOTIVATION

Formative assessment often involves giving feedback to students with the intention of motivating them to try harder, think deeper, stretch themselves further, and, in some cases, arrive at a "correct" answer. When this type of feedback is focused on the task the student is engaged in (called *task orientation* in some studies) the feedback can be very effective in enhancing students' performance and motivating them to continue. However, when we seek to motivate students either by comparing their performance to others' or to a standard—known as *ego-involved* feedback—or by offering some type of a reward—*extrinsic motivation*—we actually hinder students from doing their best. Let's look at these three types of motivation and how they are often used, deliberately or unknowingly, in formative assessment.

■ TASK ORIENTATION AND EGO INVOLVEMENT

Sometimes, mastering a task itself provides the reward for students; they want to design the winning go-kart, bowl the 300 game, or learn their lines for a play. Feedback assessments that deal directly with the task enhance students' performance, keep them on task longer, and increase their desire to practice and engage in the activity.

Another type of motivation taps into students' innate ability and talent. Because it involves the ego, it is referred to as ego-involved feedback. Students motivated by ego want to demonstrate their competence and their ability to perform in comparison to some set of norms—either established norms ("All competent students can do . . .") or generally norms established by peer performance ("The most talented students will do . . ."). This type of feedback from teachers can virtually obliterate the beneficial gains of formative assessment.

Let's use our example of the plane again to illustrate the difference between task-oriented and ego-involved motivation. En route to Chicago, an assessor is working with the pilots. An assessor oriented to task might say, "Do you think we're making corrections for wind speed frequently enough? Does this wind speed fall in the normal range for this route?" A different assessor might say, "I don't think you work well with strong winds. You might talk with Harry about how he handles winds like these." In this last case, the assessor is involving the ego of the navigator.

In the classroom, task-oriented feedback involves statements reflecting what the student has done toward reaching a goal on a particular piece of work or task. If the student was learning about magnetism, the teacher might comment on the student's application (or nonapplication) of the principle that magnets affect only some metals (a characteristic important in the recycling industry, for example). The comments are directed toward the task and its completion rather than toward any assessment of the student's ability, which would involve ego. An ego-involved assessment would include placing some value on performance—either specifically made ("That was a good comment you made in . . .") or implicitly made ("That was a C answer.") It is very difficult to make pure, task-oriented statements without invoking some kind of value. For example, a comment such as "You didn't think about what metals are affected by magnets" carries a negative connotation regarding the student's ability. However, a comment like "How would the fact that aluminum is not affected by magnets impact this process?" is less value laden. Phrasing feedback in the form of questions may make it easier to remove the ego factor.

Why is it preferable to use task-oriented feedback rather than ego-involved feedback? Butler (1987) conducted studies in which she used task-oriented feedback (only comments pertaining to the task), ego-involved feedback (only letter grades and praise, no comments), and a combination (letter grades and praise plus the task-oriented comments). Student performance after the task-oriented feedback was superior to performance in either of the other conditions (which were indistinguishable from each other). Ego-involved (summative) assessments actually changed student response to task-oriented (formative) assessments and reduced the benefits associated with formative assessment.

Black and Wiliam (1998) had a very telling observation about these two types of feedback: "In particular, feedback which is directed to the objective needs revealed, with the assumption that each student can and will succeed, has a very different effect from that feedback which is subjective in mentioning comparison with peers, with the assumption—albeit covert—that some students are not as able as others and so cannot expect full success" (p. 17). The implication is that students need not be told specifically what is valued in order to detect it; they pick up on what the teacher wants or thinks is important, and this perception changes students' responses.

Yet another type of motivation is extrinsic—learning or doing something for a goal that does not reside within the individual. Common forms of extrinsic motivation are doing something for parental or teacher praise, for resume enhancement for college or graduate school, and for appearances in a political race. If one of our goals is to produce lifelong learners who are motivated to pursue their own development and excellence, then such extrinsic motivations can be counterproductive (Kohn, 1993).

Keep in mind that these three types of motivation are really more complicated than described here. There is usually an element of each type present, although one form or another may predominate in any given situation.

You may wonder whether formative assessment of this type truly does increase students' learning. Research has repeatedly found this to be the case, regardless of how well (or how poorly!) the assessment has been done. What is of primary importance is that you, the teacher, use the information you gain to alter what and how you teach. You are the critical link in improving the learning process. You may rest assured that, if you use formative assessments, you and your students will learn more than you would have without using them.

■ TOOLS OF FORMATIVE ASSESSMENT

Helping Students Self-Assess

One element of formative assessment that needs to be stressed is involving students in making self-assessments. Unlike other skills, this skill is infrequently taught or modeled for children. Students do, however, make assessments based on their personal experiences; for example, they often sense when their effort has been productive based on the results of their activity or the responses of their parents and teachers. But we should also explicitly teach them how to assess themselves and their own progress—particularly if we do not want them to rely on summative assessments.

Periodically, model self-assessment for students. As students learn the process, use their self-assessments to check your own assessment of a situation. They will need repetition and many opportunities to self-assess, just as they do for any other process they learn. It may be important to help students assess their work using sentence starters or cognitive maps. Check out Figures 10.1, 10.2 and 10.3 for ideas. You can use these or create your own based on the students' maturational needs. For example, kindergarteners may need tools that require less writing than third graders. Quick self-assessments are also very helpful for students and teachers. Having students determine whether they understand a concept and then having them hold up fingers to show you can be an easy, quick way to self assess and develop metacognitive skills.

- One finger: I don't get it at all and need help.
- Two fingers: I kind of get it but may need some help.
- Three fingers: I just need to make sure I get it.
- Four fingers: I really understand.
- Five fingers: I understand and could teach someone else.

Self-assessments not only help students become aware of their learning but also help you as a teacher know how they are feeling and thinking about their studies. Knowing how students are feeling about their work will help you plan and utilize information to improve instruction. It is easy to develop self-assessment tools that give you the information you want. Just change the questions!

Questioning as a Type of Formative Assessment

One of the easiest and most informative ways to learn what students know is to ask questions as they are engaged in an activity and to encourage them to ask *you* questions.

Figure 10.1   Sample Post-Workshop Self-Assessment Tool for
Students That Write

Name _____

We are studying _____

Here are some things I think I did well:

Here are some things I think I need to keep working on or have questions about:

Figure 10.2   Sample Post-Workshop Self-Assessment Tool for
Students That Struggle With Writing

Name _____

Studying animals is

I understand a lot of ideas
about animals

Friends could come to me
and ask me about animals

I understand what animals need

I understand where animals live

I am a good science student

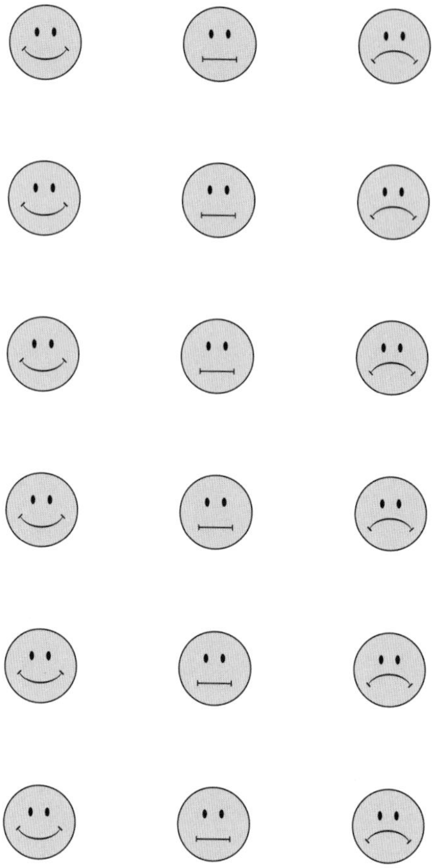

Figure 10.3   Sample Post-Unit Self-Assessment Tool for Students That Write

Name _____   Date_____

Here are some things I learned during our study of animals:

1.

2.

3.

4.

5.

I understand these things because I

1.

2.

3.

The technique of questioning has been used in the learning process since time immemorial. For example, most of us associate Socrates with questioning. Actually, questioning can be used for many purposes, not all of which are relevant for teaching and learning. For instance, a question can be a way of asking a student to guess what you are thinking. The question "What do magnets do to each other?" can really mean, "I know the answer, and I think you do, too—so guess what point I'm getting at." This is a common way of questioning students. Many textbooks include a list of questions (with the appropriate answers in parentheses) for teachers to use in their lessons.

Yet this is only one way to question students. You can also use questions as a way of trying to understand how the student thinks. That same question—"What do magnets do to each other?"—can yield an answer that will help you in this. (You will probably need to ask follow-up questions to get deeper insight into the student's reasoning). A question can also be an invitation to a student to explore a topic with you—to learn together. For example, "What do magnets do to each other?" can invite students to see what happens when you place a bar magnet near a ring magnet suspended by a string.

Questions that are used as gateways to thinking are important components of formative assessment. Students' answers tell us what they're thinking and how their minds are organizing and working with the material, which provides us with information for determining the next steps in the learning process. Since what is important is the way the answers are used, all types of questions, even those generally asked for "summative" purposes, can be employed. For example, true-false test questions can be very effective if students are directed to change a false statement so that it is correct, that is, to indicate why the statement is incorrect. This allows a glimpse into students' thinking, reveals patterns of thought that indicate misconceptions, and suggests the next stages in the learning process. Multiple-choice questions, another common type of summative assessment, can similarly be adapted for formative use. Though there is usually a single correct or best answer to such questions, any response can be probed in order to enter the child's thinking pattern—*if* we follow the path of the student's answer. (Sometimes doing this leads to a different way of viewing the original question and reveals a different "correct" answer!)

As you can see, effective questioning involves not only asking the right questions but also *listening* carefully to students' answers. Listening involves extracting the meaning from communication—not only what is said but what is unsaid as well. Great artists, for example, often stress the importance of the "missing" as defining their work; for example, Michelangelo is quoted as saying "I saw the angel in the marble and carved until I set him free." In other words, it was the missing rock that defined the angel! Similarly, it is often the missing information that defines how a student is thinking, and seeing or hearing that gap helps us scaffold the next stage. Both the art of asking questions and the art of hearing answers are needed—and both require practice on a continual basis.

As noted, any form of questioning can be the beginning of formative assessment. However, some method is needed for recording and analyzing students' answers and for gathering more information than is available from simple one-word responses or one-letter answers on multiple-choice tests. Two methods that are especially powerful and useful are note taking and student journals. These methods help the mind express itself by having students describe and explain how they think something works, how certain things are related to each other or to a third item, what they think will happen "when" or "if," how something appears to someone (or something) else, and so on.

Anecdotal Note Taking

To help in the formative assessment process and to keep a record of students' development, you might use index cards, sticky notes, a computer file, or some other form of data storage. Index cards are handy for making short notes during a period of observation. After an initial assessment to determine the stage each child is in and the proficiency of skills—that is, a preliminary determination of where each is in the core science processes—you can construct an index card with notations about what to look for. For instance, jot down a couple of the key science experiences on each card and concentrate on those during any given period of observation. Also, because you will be looking closely at each student, concentrate on a few students each day rather than trying to observe all the students at once. However, if you see a student doing something that should be recorded, do so even if it is not that student's day! District science objectives can also be used to collect information about student progress. Sample index cards used to record both student participation in key science experiences and student progress toward district science objectives are shown in Figure 10.4. You can put the cards on a clipboard for the students you're monitoring and take notes throughout the science period you're focusing on. You can also monitor students' understanding of the material by appropriately questioning them and recording notes on what they say. You might note other characteristics, such as particular interests displayed.

After the day is over or at any appropriate later time, enter your notes onto a master record sheet for each student. In addition to helping you monitor students' overall development, these notes can be of great use in planning lessons. As you've probably realized, keeping records of this type requires a great deal of organization. Implement this system slowly so that you don't lose sight of the forest (the child's learning) by concentrating on the trees (the use of the cards and sheets)! Take a moment now to think about the question at the beginning of this chapter. Why do this kind of assessing? How will it help you? Your students? Parents? The school district?

Student Journals

Journals are another excellent, almost unbeatable source of information for understanding students and knowing where they need to go next. Journals can be adapted for all grade levels. In kindergarten and first grade, the journals might be sketch pads in which children draw their ideas and communicate with you by pictures. As children learn to write, they can print stories along with their illustrations. And by using computers, even very young children can create sophisticated journals.

Figure 10.4   Sample Index Cards for Recording Student Participation and Progress

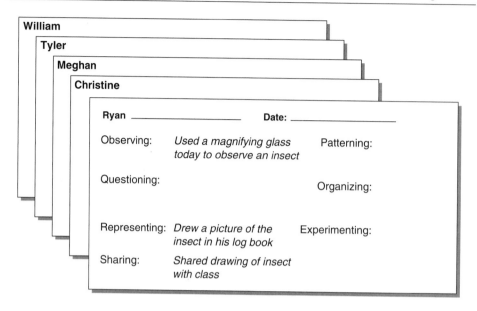

- Cards such as these can be copied and put on a clipboard. When the teacher observes a student doing one of the key science experiences, the observation can be written. This kind of note taking could also be used for documenting how individual students complete district objectives.

<u>**Ryan**</u>

1.4.1 The learner will be able to explain how roots, stems, and leaves have different roles in plants.

11/5 Ryan collected and observed different plants. He said, "Some plants have long roots and some have short." We talked about why that might be the case. He said, "They need to get water."

11/7 Ryan participated in a demonstration of what roots, stems, and leaves do. He was the leaf in his plant and acted out collecting sunrays and making food.

Allot some time after (and occasionally during) each lesson for students to reflect on some aspect of the experiment, activity, or reading. If you have been observing them, questioning them, and taking notes, you are in an excellent position to know what to have students reflect on. You can further personalize the process by knowing what type of scaffolding might help a particular child. For example, you might have Charles, a child with a passionate interest in sharks, describe what type of food web he would have if he were a shark.

Journal responses, of course, will vary depending on the grade level and maturational level of each child. Young children should be able to tell you what they think or know when asked for explanations. Sometimes, they can draw pictures or demonstrate something to show you what they under-stand. For example, after an exploration of magnets, children can tell you what happens when two north-seeking poles are brought near each other.

You could also ask them to identify materials that would be attracted by a magnet or to pretend they are magnets and act out what a magnet would do with certain items in the room or with another "magnet."

Students' responses will become more complex as they enter and move through the concrete operational stage of development. Note how they communicate, represent, organize, recognize patterns and analyze them, experiment, and observe—that is, how they use the key science experiences. For example, note how students use scientific terminology, spontaneously include the reasons behind their conclusions, and organize evidence in the form of graphs, tables, or pictures.

One benefit of journaling is that it helps students make associations. But what if those associations aren't "correct"? To the child, of course, they are correct, and they are useful to you because they reveal how the child is thinking. If they are not correct, you have an opportunity to do some scaffolding—lay the structural framework—to help the student see that his or her present idea does not work in certain ways or areas. That is, you can try to place the child in some form of disequilibrium that will lead to growth, as we mentioned in Chapter 3. It will be interesting then, to go back through a journal and see growth!

Both journaling and informal record keeping and note taking are par-ticularly useful types of formative assessment. None is graded or used to evaluate a student's standing with respect to a standard or to other students. The goal is to find out what the student knows and thinks about the particular material being studied and to try to decipher how the student is thinking.

Photo 10.1   Girl Journals About Magnets

As she records what happened at her station, this child traces along the magnet.

Rubrics

Rubrics are a form of assessment that contains very specific criteria for students and teachers to observe at a number of different levels. For example, if you were developing criteria for how well students organize (a key science experience), what would students do at a mastery level? What would they do at a potential level? How about at a beginning level? Rubrics are not as open-ended as anecdotal note taking or journaling and thus provide more specific feedback about certain skills and processes. The following example shows a possible rubric for organization skills within science. How is it different from other rubrics you have used? Are there similarities?

Although rubrics are often used as summative assessments, they were originally developed as a way to give tips to improve performance or products rather than to assign a judgment. Used carefully and created thoughtfully, rubrics can become both a tool to help students improve as well as a way to collect summative evaluations of students.

When creating a rubric consider the following:

- Not all assignments lend themselves to using rubrics. Long-term projects and processes (such as the key science experiences) work best with this tool.
- Students need to be an integral part of creating the rubric and need to be aware of its contents before its use.
- When writing a rubric, use verbs in order to promote growth. For example, instead of saying a student is able to . . . (a more summative use of rubrics) use a verb so that a student reading his or her rubric knows what to do to move to the next level. If I want to move from beginning to great potential, what do I need to do?
- Use language that describes the benefits of getting to the highest level and that makes sense to students. For example, the rubric in Table 10.1 uses the word *groups* instead of *categories,* so young children will understand. Avoid language that is arbitrary like "appropriate" or "quality." Who gets to decide what appropriate means?
- Use "skinny" + columns so that, if a student is between levels but has made progress, that can be shown.
- Use positive language. Keep telling yourself that the language needs to convey a message of help rather than of judgment.

Portfolios

Portfolios have often been used as a place to put work when it is finished, as a kind of storage facility. As with many things in this book, portfolios can be used in many different ways depending on you, your students, and the expectations of your district. However, we would like you to think about a portfolio as a work in progress and thus as formative rather than summative assessment. Portfolios should always be changing and growing just as your students do. There are many examples of portfolios on the Internet. Type "student portfolios" into your favorite search engine to see what's out there. It will be helpful to see various portfolios as you begin to develop ones for your classroom. Many things can go into

Table 10.1   Sample Rubric

Organization Within Science	+	Master of organization and organizational tools within science	+	Great potential for use of organization and organizational tools within science	+	Beginning to use organization and organizational tools within science
Groups		Uses many groups to make sense of information. EXAMPLE:		Uses two groups to make sense of information. EXAMPLE:		Uses one group to make sense of information. EXAMPLE:
Understanding		Talks about the groups, knows why different things go in groups, and can answer questions about the groups. EXAMPLE:		Talks about the groups and knows why different things go in the groups. EXAMPLE:		Talks about the group to the class. EXAMPLE:
Tools		Uses graphs, Venn diagrams, and drawings to show groups. EXAMPLE:		Uses Venn diagrams and drawings to show groups. EXAMPLE:		Uses drawings to show group. EXAMPLE:
Creativity		Creates own tools to organize things.		Uses Venn diagrams and drawings in new ways.		Uses own drawings rather than teacher made.

portfolios including pictures, work, or journal entries. Organization can vary as well. You could have students make science portfolios, or science material could be a part of a bigger "first grade" portfolio. As with any of these tools, portfolios can ultimately become ways to develop summative assessments. For example, you could develop portfolios around your district objectives, and students could receive points for the number of objectives they could show as completed.

When creating portfolios consider the following:

- Be specific about the portfolios' purpose. How will you use them? Who will see them?
- Students should be a big part of creating their portfolios. Depending on their maturational level, you might have them decide what to share with parents, decide everything that goes into the portfolio, or even decide how to organize their portfolios.
- Students should have opportunities to share their portfolios. They can share everything from one important piece of the portfolio to each item. They can write a summary of what's in the portfolio or talk about how they organized it.
- Portfolios should show growth. Don't take out the work that needs improvement because it will help you show growth later!
- Coordinate your rubrics with portfolios. Portfolios are great places to show examples of rubric work!

■ SUMMATIVE ASSESSMENTS

Summative, evaluative tests provide a picture of how students perform (how they answer specific questions) at a particular time in a particular place. The results of these tests are presumed to be a fair representation of what students know and are capable of doing. In contrast to formative assessments, evaluative tests are not used to improve the instruction or learning of the students who take them; because an evaluative test comes at the conclusion of a unit of instruction or time period (for example, the end of a quarter, semester, or year), the results cannot alter instruction that preceded it. However, the results of such tests can and should be used to affect instruction in similar programs that follow, perhaps the next year's or semester's material.

Most summative assessments assign values to student responses and therefore are ego-involved assessments. As we mentioned earlier, value-laden assessments tend to inhibit the development of intrinsic motivation. They actually support extrinsic motivation for some students and, when used often enough, can contribute to declines in long-term achievement and motivation for many, as reported in the published research literature. Less able students tend to fall further and further behind with the use of ego-involved assessment, and even good students do less well than they would have without ego involvement (see, for example, Butler, 1987). These effects are the opposite of those that teachers wish to see.

Summative, high-stakes tests have become very popular among some segments of society. They can be readily given and the results used for political or administrative purposes—to "reward" and "punish" both teachers and students. Thus, they are a reality that most teachers must face. Although the results of evaluative tests should not be used to judge individual students, teachers, or schools, such judgments will undoubtedly occur among those unfamiliar with what statistics from this type of test actually indicate.

However, we can minimize the detrimental effects that are associated with evaluative tests. One way is to use as much formative assessment as possible and to strengthen and enhance intrinsic motivation, hence the emphasis in the first part of this chapter. In addition, learning material well is one of the surest ways for students to perform well on high-stakes tests, and formative assessments help students learn well when the results are used as we described earlier.

A second way to minimize negative effects of evaluative tests is to develop some formative assessment questions in the same style as summative assessment questions. For example, you might create "tests" that include multiple-choice questions, fill-in-the-blank questions, and order-a-sequence-of-steps questions (either in practice or in pictorial form). This will give students practice with the test format, so they will be comfortable when taking high-stakes tests. Of course, the answers on the formative assessment "tests" will be used to plan lessons, so they do not need to be graded and returned to students.

A third way to minimize the detrimental effects of high-stakes evaluative tests is to emphasize the learning *community*—that is, students learning from one another and being encouraged to share information. Recall the importance placed on adult support and the community of learners in our discussion of active learning. A study of the role of genetics and the role of the environment in determining adult characteristics indicates a substantial role for both factors (Pinker, 2002). While we cannot yet direct or improve genetics, we can and do exert considerable environmental influence on students. Peer culture in particular is important; indeed, some argue that, in the long run, peers are the most important "environment" that nurtures the developing child (Harris, 1998; Pinker, 2002).

Harris (1998) also ascribes substantial developmental influence to teachers, noting that

> Teachers have power and responsibility because they are in control of an entire group of children. They can influence the attitudes and behaviors of the entire group. And they exert this influence where it is likely to have long-term effects: in the world outside the home, the world where children will spend their adult lives. (p. 241)

The way we consciously and unconsciously structure the classroom can greatly influence the types of peer-group subcultures that develop in it. For example, if students are segregated into "ethnic" groups, each may develop its own subculture, with students striving to maintain recognition and status in their group. Cliques of various types will likewise result in a fragmented classroom community. Students identify with a smaller social division, and they strive to excel in the criteria valued or demanded by a particular subculture. The same occurs when tracking groups of high and low achievers in the classroom. Low achievers often downplay the particular norms used to define their group and fail to do those things that would help them improve; thus, they fall further behind. You can have a substantial, positive effect on students by influencing the formation of these subcultures, by adjusting the norms of each subculture that does develop, and by influencing the image each peer group has of itself.

By stressing that the class (and the school, if possible) is a *single* community of young scientists pursuing knowledge, we can minimize the detrimental effects of evaluative judgments.

■ THE WHY OF ASSESSING

One of the most important ideas about assessment that you can take from this chapter is that you need to be a part of creating and implementing the assessments you use. Whether you are giving formative or summative assessments, you need to ask yourself

- What is the purpose of this assessment?
- How will assessing in this way affect student learning?
- How will I manage this information?
- Are the students involved in creating this assessment?

As with anything, there are benefits and limitations to using each of the kinds of assessment we have mentioned in this chapter. Once again, you need to do the work of thinking about the topic you are teaching, the students in your room, and why you are assessing so that you can assess using the best tool available. The best tool may be one we have suggested here, but you may have to modify it or possibly develop your own tool. Building a community of learners requires trust in yourself and in your students. It is important to remember that you both need to be a part of assessment within a community.

Conversation Starters

- Think of different ways to manage formative and summative assessments. What tools will help you best help students learn and continue to learn?

- What would you say to someone who believes assessment can only be tests?

- How can you give grades based on the kinds of assessments we've discussed in this chapter?

- What are the benefits and limitations of each kind of assessment?

- How can you incorporate some of the assessment tools we have shown here when your district has required assessment tools?

11

Access to Science in a Classroom

You have discovered how to help children actively do real science through the key science experiences supported by social interaction and learning structures like workshops and thinking routines. In this chapter, we will discuss building a science community that will facilitate this goal. Such a community includes, of course, the physical classroom itself, but it also includes emotionally safe spaces and access to materials, people, and the world. Building a science community requires you to understand the children you work with and what it means to do real science.

Take a moment to imagine a scientist in his or her laboratory. What does the scientist look like? What kinds of tools and materials is he or she using? What is the scientist doing? Are there any other people there? What might they be talking about? What do the walls and floor look like? Take out some paper and sketch your vision of a scientist and his or her surroundings. Share your drawing, or at least your ideas, with someone else. It is quite interesting to look at different images of scientists; they are often portrayed as "mad scientists" with bubbling pots of unknown substances and white hair standing on end, or as brilliant professors babbling in a language that most of us can't understand. We don't often picture scientists as regular people going about their lives in much the way we do. Of course, there are many kinds of scientists and many kinds of laboratories. If you have the opportunity, make an appointment to visit a scientist. Inquire at your local university or college for one, talk to an engineer, or visit a hospital lab. Be sure to observe the scientist's work environment!

Thinking about what adult scientists do in their jobs will help you learn how to provide the young scientists in your classroom with the spaces they need for *their* science work to flourish. Young scientists need some of the same things as their adult counterparts, but they also need spaces that are unique to them as individual learners. Using your image of a laboratory or considering a lab that you have actually visited, make a chart of things that were in it that you would *need* in a science space for children, things you would *like to have* in the space, and, finally, things that might not be appropriate for children. Think beyond just the physical aspects. What kind of science community is formed in a laboratory—that is, what is the "feel" of a laboratory that you would like to recreate in an elementary classroom? What kinds of people and ideas need to be available? Make sure you take some time to think about the reasons behind each of your ideas. For example, if you believe that microscopes are a definite must in a science classroom, ask yourself why. If you put microscopes in the *not appropriate* category, do the same.

■ SCIENCE STUDIOS

At the 2002 American Educational Research Association (AERA) National Conference in New Orleans, Kevin Pugh and Mark Girod asked the audience to consider classrooms as art studios rather than laboratories. This statement caused us some disequilibrium at first. After all, if we want students to do real science, shouldn't we promote classrooms as laboratories, with test tubes and lab coats and microscopes? Don't we want students engaging in problems, questions, and observations? These things all sound like characteristics of a laboratory not an art studio. What did Pugh and Girod mean?

Of course, classrooms shouldn't look, sound, or feel exactly like laboratories *or* art studios. However, there are ideas, moods, and materials characteristic of each that could help create a better environment for students to learn science. We might call it a *science studio*. What would a mixture of the best parts of a science laboratory and an art studio look, sound, and feel like?

From science laboratories, perhaps, we could take tools. For example, students should have access to microscopes, petri dishes, eyedroppers, lab coats, and slides. If your budget doesn't allow for these kinds of items, borrow them from a local service unit or library. Ask at a local laboratory for old items you can use, or ask for parent donations.

Besides tools, you'll want to use the scientific language of laboratories with students. When students get ready for science workshops, ask that all "scientists" get ready for workshop time and have them write in "logs" rather than notebooks. Use the words *hypothesize, observe, data, experiment,* and other scientific vocabulary. Make sure students understand what these terms mean, and encourage them to use such language themselves.

From art studios, we need the creative space and peaceful atmosphere in which great ideas can be nurtured without hurry. We need items that inspire great thinking and spark questions. For example, something as simple as a plant can stimulate interest and discovery. Art studios are places of collaboration, and our classrooms need to be designed to promote this as well.

One characteristic that laboratories and art studios share is *access*—access to materials, space, people, and the world. Our science classrooms need to provide the same.

ACCESS TO SCIENCE   ■

In many classrooms, students learn science by reading textbooks, listening to lectures, and watching demonstrations. You understand by now that our approach to science is about personal wondering, hands-on inquiry, and problem solving coupled with access to scientific information from others. The kind of classroom you design affects how children perceive science, how they engage in it, and what they learn from it. Certainly, children can learn science facts as they sit at desks, reading from textbooks and filling out worksheets. Perhaps this is how you learned science. However, in order to encourage the disposition to learn and love science, to cultivate the ability to ask questions and design projects of inquiry, and to help students gain the metacognitive knowledge necessary to learn effectively, teachers must provide a classroom environment with access to science.

What does having access to science mean? Does it depend on the kinds of lessons teachers plan? Does it depend on the materials and arrangement of the room? Does it depend on the emotional safety needed to take risks? If you had access to science during your own school experience, what made this access possible? If you had experiences that turned you off to science, what caused you to feel that way?

We believe that four aspects of classroom experience shape student access to science: materials, people, physical and emotional space, and the outside world. These pieces of a puzzle, when put together, create opportunities for students to learn and to have access to science.

ACCESS TO MATERIALS   ■

If you recall the chapters on the nature of science, active learning, and the key science experiences, you can see why materials are so important in elementary classrooms. Observing, organizing, representing, experimenting, patterning, questioning, and sharing are actions that require materials. Even maturation and materials are interdependent. Think back to Jerry and his encounter with one-celled animals. Being able to investigate pond water with a microscope advanced his understanding in a way that could not have happened without these materials. If children are to have access to science, they must have materials that they are encouraged to manipulate.

Types of Materials

What materials should be in a classroom environment? Sometimes, the best materials are those that do not have a specific purpose, ones that can be used and combined in a variety of ways. For example, recyclable materials like boxes, toilet paper rolls, and pop bottles can become star dioramas, telescopes, and boats in the hands of eager learners. Materials such as these require creativity, imagination, and thoughtful consideration of ideas. Reflect on the thinking necessary for a child to learn about a telescope and to create one using toilet paper rolls, magnifying glasses, and tape. Think about what this child would learn and how she would feel after making the telescope and trying it out.

Commercially available materials—microscopes, models, and other tools and equipment—are also important. These materials might be purchased for the classroom for several years' use or borrowed for just a few weeks. They are often used in connection with a particular unit of study and exchanged as students move on to new subjects. Some school districts have commercial materials available in kits for specific science topics, for example, models of the eye, ear, skeleton, and lungs for studying the human body or a grow lamp for growing plants.

Don't limit yourself or your students to materials found indoors— bring the outside world in! Making a rock collection, studying a variety of leaves, or sifting through dirt from different places can help children understand the world much more effectively than just reading about these things. If they never feel rocks, children will have trouble understanding their hardness. A caution about using outside materials for science: When using live animals, including insects and animals of any size, make sure children understand what it means to be humane. They might view pulling the wings off flies as an interesting exploration, but this is not a humane way to learn science.

In addition, you must not forget literature as a material. Not just textbooks! There are outstanding nonfiction and fiction books available for children that provide pictures, information, and questions dealing with science. Check them out!

Photo 11.1   Science Materials

In this classroom, students are testing how long ever-lasting jawbreakers last in different liquids.

Collecting and Organizing Materials

Gathering the types of materials we've talked about is a lot of work, and keeping up with students' interests and changing topics takes time. Enlist the help of parent volunteers or students to organize and care for materials. Materials can be organized in many different ways depending on the age of the children, available space and layout of the classroom, and storage facilities. However, materials need to be easy to find and easily reached by students. Attach labels or pictures to containers or storage shelves for different materials. This will help students find materials easily and encourage cleanup. Students are often willing to help you organize materials and should be encouraged to take care of them by putting them back where they belong.

You will also need to organize materials when planning a specific topic of study. Gathering materials for topics early on will help you plan activities and provide for individual interest and exploration. Whether you are creating a single lesson or unit or are stocking your room for the year, provide students with both familiar and unfamiliar materials. For example, when you study the different parts of plants, bring in familiar materials, such as celery (stem), carrots (roots), and cauliflower (flower). Also, encourage students to explore and compare unfamiliar materials, such as kale (stem), turnips (roots), and capers (flowers), to really stretch their thinking. Choose materials based on student interest, availability, and curricular objectives. Switching materials after a few months helps to revitalize enthusiasm and spark curiosity throughout the year. There is no need to change materials every week or even every month, and changing every material in the room is not necessary.

Creating a space in which students have access to materials requires much organization and planning for safety concerns. Materials that are

Photo 11.2   Shelves

Science materials that are clearly marked and easily accessed by students.

unsafe for children to use without supervision should be stored so that students don't have access without asking for help. Students should be aware that these materials are available but not have immediate access to them. For example, when making crystals, students may need to use materials such as ammonia, bluing, food coloring, and charcoal. For the safety of the children and the room furnishings, these materials need to be stored separately from materials like salt, cotton balls, boxes, and milk jugs.

Make sure all your materials are stored safely and that students know how to access them. Also, discuss which materials they can cut, glue, tear, or otherwise alter and which need to be kept in their original condition. I once had a student named Josh who was carrying out a wonderful water project. He was trying to siphon water in clear tubes all the way across the classroom. Unfortunately, I hadn't talked to the students about not altering some materials, and Josh drilled holes in many of my water tubs in order to fit the tubing into them! Although my tubs were destroyed, think about all the things Josh learned from his project! (It was worth the tubs.)

Why Is Access to Materials Important?

Many classrooms have a variety of materials. However, they are stored so that teachers, not students, have access to them. Having access to organized materials helps students feel that their ideas are valued and worthy of further exploration, and it keeps the classroom environment safe and orderly. Also, materials need to be accessible to all students so that, when ideas spark in their minds, students have the opportunity to act on them. The reverse is also true; students need to have opportunities to act on materials to spark new ideas. For example, if children have access to many different kinds of rocks, they may sort and classify them into different categories. While doing this, they may find that some rocks are dustier than others. The students may form questions about why some are dusty and some are not. If they actually have the rocks in front of them, they can begin to explore this question by rubbing the rocks to see what happens. By having access to the rocks, students are able to use the materials to form ideas about them and can also begin to ask questions and test for answers. Materials provide opportunities for both raising questions and answering them. Students need to be able to act on hunches, questions, and ideas. If they have access only to certain materials, acting on their ideas might be difficult. Children generally have a much better ability to see materials in unique ways than adults do. They can visualize a toilet paper roll as a telescope, a box as a backdrop for stars in the sky, and a pop bottle as a boat. By restricting access to materials or giving students only conventional tools and materials, you restrict students to far fewer possibilities.

Richard Feynman, a famous physicist, told a story in *Surely You're Joking, Mr. Feynman* (1985) that illustrates the importance of having access to science materials. Feynman described the difference between the environment surrounding a piece of science equipment at one college compared to the environment around the same piece at another college.

> MIT had built a new cyclotron when I was a student there, and it was just beautiful! The cyclotron itself was in one room, with the controls in another room. It was beautifully engineered. Now I had

read a lot of papers on cyclotron experiments, and there weren't many from MIT. Maybe they were just starting. But there were lots of results from places like Cornell, and Berkeley, and above all, Princeton. Therefore what I really wanted to see, what I was looking forward to, was the Princeton cyclotron. That must be something! So first thing Monday, I go into the physics building and ask, "Where is the cyclotron—which building?" "It's downstairs, in the basement—at the end of the hall." In the basement? It was an old building. There was no room in the basement for a cyclotron. I walked down to the end of the hall, went through the door, and in ten seconds I learned why Princeton was right for me—the best place for me to go to school. In this room there were wires strung all over the place! Switches were hanging from the wires, cooling water was dripping from the valves, the room was full of stuff, all out in the open. Tables piled with tools were everywhere. It reminded me of my lab at home. Nothing at MIT had ever reminded me of my lab at home. I suddenly realized why Princeton was getting results. They were working with the instrument! (p. 62)

Although we are not talking about materials as sophisticated as a cyclotron or about prestigious science laboratories like the ones at MIT or Princeton, Feynman's point is important for all educators. Fancy equipment and materials that remain out of reach don't produce many results. It is the same for elementary children!

Materials are often the first things to spark student interest in ideas. In addition, materials are often valuable resources for deeper conceptual understanding. Having many different materials can help children discover new interests and ask questions that they hadn't thought about before. Materials can help children make connections to previous experiences as well as provide instances of disequilibrium when an experience with a material is different from a previous experience.

Supporting Students' Work With Materials

Providing access to materials is only the first step in helping students engage in science. You also need to support the use of the materials and teach children how to use them. In many cases, children must be taught to use materials either as part of specific lessons or by modeling. This is an excellent opportunity to provide some scaffolding. For example, Jerry's first experience with a microscope didn't involve pond water. Before he had the opportunity to use the microscope, the class had conversations about microscopes, discussing what they are used for, how to use them, and safety concerns. Then the students observed everyday objects like newspaper, string, salt, and so on to learn to make slides and observe materials that were familiar. Students probably don't need a lesson on other materials such as petri dishes, tubs, or eyedroppers, but you do need to model correct usage. For example, students in my room learned how to use petri dishes to hold their mealworms by watching me use them in this way.

You may be wondering whether showing students how to use materials is a wise use of time when there is so much during the school day for them to learn. Remember that science is about procedural as well as factual knowledge, and materials like lab coats, petri dishes, test tubes, and microscopes facilitate the understanding of both process and fact. Using materials like these helps students understand that science is real, relevant to their lives, and interesting. Scientific materials make them feel like scientists, giving them a sense of efficacy, of their ability to master scientific knowledge and skills, and the interest to learn more science!

■ ACCESS TO SCIENCE SPACES

In addition to accessible materials and tools for experiencing science, students need spaces where they feel free to explore science ideas. This concept of space includes not only the physical environment—the desks, materials, tools, and places where teachers and students gather to learn— but also the *emotional environment* in which students think, wonder, play with ideas, and create. Abundant materials and spacious classrooms don't really matter much if students' ideas are not encouraged, their understanding isn't probed, and they aren't given time to wonder and delve deeply into learning. Interesting materials invite experience, but space provides the freedom to explore. Earlier, we discussed laboratories and studios. The space where children learn science needs to be open and accepting, like an art studio where creativity is promoted.

How do you create such a space for children? Think about a time and environment in which you felt free to think and create. Think about the physical aspects as well as the atmosphere or feeling of this place. Why were you able to learn there? Think about the people who were present and what they did to assist you. Think about the lighting, the furniture, the sounds. How free were you to make choices? As you read on, apply these qualities as you develop a plan for creating an accessible space for science. The following pages should also spark some ideas for you.

Physical Space

Many physical aspects of a room affect student ability to access science. The lighting, furniture, colors, temperature, and sounds all need to be considered when designing a space. Although you may not be able to do anything about some of the physical aspects of your classroom, you probably do have control over the arrangement of the furniture, what goes on the walls, and the choices you give children about using the physical space.

At first thought, furniture arrangement may not seem very important compared to other aspects of teaching science. However, the way students' tables or desks are arranged, how materials are stored, and even the placement of your desk convey important messages to students about learning. For example, when students' desks or tables are grouped together, it conveys the message that conversation about science topics is important. Sometimes, a teacher tries all kinds of strategies to encourage students to talk to one another instead of *the teacher* during class discussions, when the reason students aren't talking to one another is that they are all facing the teacher!

Photo 11.3   Forest Mural

Students created this wall-sized forest mural as a part of a habitat unit.

In addition, the workspace needs to be large enough for students to spread out and see all of the possibilities. Small desktops don't always provide enough room to work. Sometimes, desks should be pushed aside completely. When my class worked on the habitat murals, we pushed all of the desks aside and spread out all over the floor. The kids took their shoes off, gathered their Internet information, books, and materials, and got on the floor to work! As you design workshops, be sure to consider the physical arrangement of the furniture. What will best help students learn? What messages are you conveying with the arrangement you choose?

In addition to furniture, the walls (and perhaps the ceiling) of your classroom can also help provide access to science. Many teachers dread "decorating" their classroom walls and bulletin boards. They picture hours of cutting letters, boarders, and cute pictures for every season or holiday. This is not what we are advocating. Make the walls of your room interactive and full of students' work, not yours. If you are studying insects, display pictures of different insects or calendars showing students' drawings of the changes they are observing. If you are studying space, display students' projects or hang black paper on the ceiling. One year, a parent donated some Saturn wallpaper and my students measured, cut, and pinned it over an entire wall of the classroom.

Another idea is to make a wall for all of the science topics you will study during the year. For example, we filled a board with several circles; as students discovered a different cycle of science throughout the year, they drew a diagram of it inside one of the circles. Find posters with information on the topic you are studying and hang them in the science area of your room or all over the room. Many organizations will give you free posters. For example, NASA has many educational programs from which you can receive space pictures. If you have a camera in the room, let students take pictures of animals, plants, solids, and so on. Pictures of science field trips make a nice display and are a visual reminder of what students learned. Have students arrange the photos on posters, with captions describing what they learned or what the pictures show.

These are just a few ideas. However, they all point to two very important aspects of the physical space students need for science. *First, students' work needs to be displayed.* This promotes pride in their efforts and a desire to work hard and do well. Displaying students' work also provides them an opportunity to share ideas with others. The students who created the murals in my class invited other classes, their parents, and administrators to see their work. They explained the murals and described what they had learned, which was a great time of reviewing! *Second, the walls and the other objects in the room need to convey an excitement about learning.* One small poster on a bulletin board isn't going to do it. Fill the space with images and objects that spark imagination and the desire to learn more!

Although we have previously discussed the importance of giving students choices, we want to emphasize it again in the context of science spaces. For students to access science, they must have the freedom to create their own science spaces *and* know how to respect others' spaces. This freedom does not necessarily mean that students arrange the furniture however they want, but it does mean that they should be able to choose where they work and how that space feels. For example, if students are working on a project, they might choose to work at their desk, under a desk, on the floor, at a table, or in the hallway, as long as they are not disturbing anyone. Having the freedom to make decisions about physical space will help students learn respect for their classmates and their classroom. It will help them create, think, and understand, and it will help them learn about the kinds of spaces in which they learn best. Far from causing chaos or misbehavior, allowing children this choice will deter both. If students understand the expectations for the classroom, they will value the opportunity to choose, and if they have trouble working appropriately in their chosen spot, you can help them find a new one.

Of course, sometimes you do need to define the physical space in which students will work, for example, when they are working with messy or potentially harmful materials. You may also need to set some space parameters when students are sharing their work or you are having a class conversation. Because all students need to participate in these activities, allowing some students to sit under a desk or in a far corner of the room would not be appropriate.

Emotional Safety

Just as you create a physical space that invites students to explore, you must also create an atmosphere of emotional safety. That is, students need to feel free to explore their ideas and even to make mistakes. Not many of us can learn when we feel threatened or misunderstood, and science can often make us feel this way. Students who are afraid of making mistakes or answering incorrectly withdraw. You may have been one of those students. To avoid this happening with your students, create an environment that is open and welcoming to ideas.

How can you make a science space where students feel safe to try out solutions and where answers are "in the works" rather than right or wrong?

One solution that sounds easy but takes conscious effort is transforming the language you and the other students use in the classroom. Words should be welcoming and accepting, promoting conversation rather than stifling it. Instead of telling students that an answer is wrong, ask them to explain further, or tell them that you had a different experience or outcome.

For instance, imagine that Jerry tells you the moving objects in the water under the microscope are pieces of moss. You have several options for responding. You could tell him that he's wrong and that the objects are actually one-celled animals. This would give Jerry the correct answer, but it might be one that he is not developmentally ready to understand. Additionally, doing so would deprive him of the opportunity to discuss his thinking and eventually arrive at the real answer for himself. It might also make him conclude that science is a bunch of facts that he does not understand and shouldn't bother trying to figure out, because he will probably be wrong and an adult will tell him the right answer anyway.

Another option would be to ask him to explain his conclusion and open up a conversation about the moving objects. Then you might say, "Hmmm, I had not thought about that. Have you talked to Mike? He has a different idea." Doing this not only gives you an opportunity to understand Jerry's thinking but also creates an atmosphere of inquiry and debate. Whenever possible, offer students activities that involve reasoning, the core science processes, and creativity rather than finding one correct answer. For example, you might have students put a variety of solid objects into categories of their choosing. Here, there are no wrong answers, only possibilities. If students' categories or reasoning processes don't make sense to you, ask them to explain, or have them try again with different categories. Go back to the sample workshops in Chapter 9 and notice that most of the activities require students to think, create, and wonder rather than to arrive at a right answer, and yet they are wonderful learning experiences.

Of course, there are lessons or situations in which students *do* need to understand what conclusions are accepted as being correct. Workshop lessons and sharing time should include closure on ideas that have been debated. However, *be careful not to make the end of every lesson or sharing session a time when you reveal the right answer to students.* Students will realize that you will be giving them the right answer at the end and may come to feel that their ideas and investigations and struggles to make sense of what they've observed don't really matter. Although it will be difficult, you must suspend what you know to be true about science and become a learner with the students, working *together* to find some answers.

As you learn to use language that promotes an atmosphere of acceptance and experimentation, help your students learn to use this language with one another as well. The classroom won't be a safe space for learning science if students are ridiculing others' ideas. Part of learning science is learning how to disagree in a constructive way. Safe language needs to be modeled and directly taught. For example, during an activity in which students are grouping solid objects into categories without telling their partners what the categories are, you might encourage partners to tell each other that his or her idea was a "good possibility, but not the one I used" rather than to say the partner was dumb or wrong. Students will probably need prompting and practice with this. You could ask students to "say it differently" or ask them to use "kind language."

While scientists may not be as kind to each other as we are promoting here, they do have opportunities to present and explain their ideas to others. Laboratories are places where scientists disagree, wonder aloud, and ask for feedback. There often aren't right and wrong answers in laboratories either because, most of the time, no one yet knows the "right" answer. Science is about looking at all the possibilities!

Adequate Time for Investigation

In addition to having the *freedom* to play with ideas in an emotionally safe science space, students need *time* to play with their ideas. It's very difficult to find adequate time for this "play," considering all the topics teachers must cover. However, when students don't have enough time to think and ponder, it is difficult for them to work and rework their ideas. You may not be able to increase the time you allot for science, but you can give students more time to work on their projects by possibly shortening the time you lecture and give directions. The school culture now emphasizes on-task behavior. However, students are often so concentrated on finishing a task that they don't have time to really think about what they are doing and why. Having space to learn science means having time to develop thoughts and pursue questions over time.

Celebrations of Accomplishments

Finally, having access to a safe science space means celebrating accomplishments and ideas! A celebration may be as simple as smiling with students when they come up with an idea they think is great or as complex as sharing discoveries with other classrooms. Insect fairs, space exhibits, and forest murals are wonderful ways to celebrate the learning happening in your science space. Celebrating as an individual, a class, or a school should not be about getting rewarded but about gaining feedback, spreading knowledge, and feeling good about one's hard work!

Creating a space in which children have choices, their work is celebrated, and they are safe to create ideas will help them learn not only science but also the social skills they need to do well in all areas of life. Learning social skills is a lot like learning science. It needs to be active. Sitting at desks in rows and never talking to classmates does not help students learn to respect and understand one another effectively. There will probably be more behavioral issues in a classroom in which students have access to the learning space, and just think what wonderful learning opportunities those issues will create! Having access to science spaces with the support of peers and teachers makes learning science *and* social skills possible.

ACCESS TO PEOPLE

As we've seen, to access science, students need autonomy through choice, problem solving, and decision making—but they also need a sense of community. They need people with more experience, knowledge, and maturation to help them move within their zones of proximal development.

They need people who can set boundaries for them, who ask questions that move them into disequilibrium, and who provide safe opportunities for them to grow. Indeed, we all need access to a community of people who inspire our thoughts and who support our growth and yet give us enough space to develop a sense of self. Think about the people you might find in a laboratory and in a studio. What are they doing? How are they helping one another? What questions are they asking? Students need access to people who offer emotional safety, like quiet wonderers in an art studio. They need people who are inquisitive, like the scientists in a laboratory. They need caring and understanding teachers! Students studying science need classroom resources such as teachers and peers (both older and younger) as well as outside resources such as families and scientists.

Support From Teachers

Teachers must be actively involved in all aspects of classroom life in ways that promote students' subject knowledge, process knowledge, metacognitive knowledge, and social skills. Although teachers using an active learning, shared-control approach may look different from teachers standing in front of the classroom giving information and assignments, they still have a high level of involvement with students. Instead of being removed from students at the front of your room or at your desk, you can walk around to check on students, ask them individual questions, and listen. Instead of lecturing to an entire class of students, you can work with smaller workshop groups to individualize learning. You will have more access to the students, and the students will have more access to you. This kind of care and nurturing facilitates not only learning but also assessment of what students understand. Of course, there are situations in which it is entirely appropriate for you to address the class as a whole. Having access to the teacher is not about where the teacher is positioned but about how students and their ideas are valued and nurtured.

Teachers must work in ways that allow authentic relationships to grow and in ways that allow students to have access to them for questions, help, and support. This means having a genuine interest in students, their work, and their lives outside of school. It means trusting students to make decisions and helping them learn from those decisions. It means celebrating accomplishments and supporting them in times of need. Perhaps most important, it means treating them as any person in the world would want to be treated.

Collaboration With Peers

Part of the nature of science is the collaborative work among scientists. Peer collaboration is valuable for students as well. Therefore, teachers must not only make themselves accessible to students but also make students accessible to one another. Students should be encouraged to ask one another questions, collaborate on projects, and share their ideas and findings with the class. One way to encourage students to rely on one another is to require them to ask two peers for help before they ask you. Before students share ideas with the entire class, ask them to share with one other person. All of this may be difficult if students have not had the opportunity

Photo 11.4   Kids Working Cooperatively

Students work together to hang their beanstalk experiments.

to collaborate in the past. However, if you discuss expectations at the beginning of the year and teach students how to interact appropriately with their classmates, things will go much more smoothly.

Although it is much easier, from the standpoint of classroom discipline, to keep students at their desks during lessons, in the end, it is more beneficial for everyone if students can access one another. If students are having a class debate or conversation about a science topic, make sure to discuss the expectations for listening and commenting ahead of time. If students are working in cooperative learning groups and are sending unkind messages to one another verbally or physically, make sure you review and practice with them how to show respect to others. Help students see how beneficial working together can be!

When creating opportunities for peer collaboration, don't forget to include younger and older peers. Everyone benefits from cross-age interaction. For example, if you invite other classrooms for a presentation, your students gain confidence in presenting material, and the audience of younger students learns about science. If older peers come to your room to help students in small groups or individually, or you send your students to help younger peers, all of the children gain a sense of responsibility and caring as they learn content. Building this kind of community of learners requires you to collaborate with other teachers and show students how to interact with peers who are on a different social and cognitive level. One way to include students from other classrooms is to hold a science fair, one that combines features of a typical science fair with a lecture-style presentation. For example, my students created space projects and set them up around the room. Students from other classes came through to watch different presentations and ask questions. Projects weren't judged as in a traditional science fair, and all the students were proud to display and explain their projects. There are many ways to share great science work. Do some collaborating right now to brainstorm ways to include older and younger peers in your science classroom!

Family Involvement

Families are another important group of people that students should access when learning science, both in the classroom and at home. There are many ways for parents to be involved in the classroom. They may help with a science workshop or provide expertise on a topic. They may attend a class presentation or donate science supplies to the class.

I loved having parents help each year when we made taffy as a culminating experience for our unit on solids, liquids, and gases. We could not have done this experiment without the parents who loaned us their pots and pans, potholders, candy thermometers, and wooden spoons or those who led a group of students as they watched the ingredients change from solids to liquids to gases and back to solids. These parents got into the experiment as much as the children did. They let the children choose the flavoring to add, watched carefully as the children stirred, helped pull the taffy, and even cleaned up the mess.

To take advantage of the assistance families can provide in the classroom, you must get to know them. I knew that Noah's and Nathan's dad was a chemist, and he came in and mixed liquids together while the students ooohed and aaahed. I knew that Kayla's mom worked three days a week but could come in on Mondays. She helped me cut fruits and vegetables for an experiment and then stayed and asked the students wonderful questions. It is important that families know they are welcome any time and that they will be of great help. Ask for volunteers by sending notes, by requesting help at conferences or during curriculum nights, and by chatting with parents as you see them in the community. Try to utilize family strengths in as many units of study as possible. Students will feel proud to have their families be part of the classroom, and parents will grow to trust you and will communicate more readily.

Some parents can't make it to school to watch a science presentation or to volunteer, but they can help students learn about science by discussing topics during dinner or by helping with homework. For example, you can ask students to observe any number of science phenomena at home. They might observe a family pet or make a list of the solids and liquids around the house. Students might obtain soil samples from their neighborhood and compare them with samples taken from other areas. Although parents may or may not be directly involved in such observations or experiments, projects like these can spark family conversations.

Often parents who work *want* to be involved in their children's learning but find it difficult to carry on conversations about school because they don't know what is currently being studied. When asked what they are learning in school, children often reply, "I don't know" or "Nothing." Assignments such as those suggested previously, however, can help students and families at least begin conversations about science! In addition, homework that extends learning from the classroom can be fun and help students connect science to their lives. It's satisfying to hear that

Sam's younger brother helped him collect rocks for class or that Ehren did an entire demonstration of the body's defensive weapons (mucus, white blood cells, cilia, and so on) for his mother and doctor during a medical appointment. Families are wonderful resources for learning, both in the classroom and at home. It is your job to utilize what they have to offer.

Community Resources

Finally, students (and teachers) should have access to the many knowledgeable individuals in the community. Scientists, business people, librarians, 4-H groups, educators at educational service units, and university faculty members can all offer valuable information, learning materials, and classroom support. It takes some effort on your part to contact and coordinate these services, but it is well worth it. Many people will gladly visit the classroom to give a presentation, which can leave a lasting impression on students. One year, while my class was studying habitats, someone from an animal shelter came to talk to the students. She brought several items often found in the garbage and had students go through them to determine how the trash could hurt urban wildlife. The students were very interested in this topic and came away with valuable information. For instance, they learned that the plastic rings from packs of soda pop can kill birds and other animals because their heads get stuck in them and they aren't able to eat. I'm sure all of those children cut apart those rings now before disposing of them.

Even if community members aren't able to come to the classroom, they may have valuable resources and materials to share with you and your students. Involve students in making phone calls and writing letters to request information or materials. This is a valuable skill for them to learn. And who can refuse a young student's request? Having access to a wide variety of people, both inside the classroom and outside, is important for you and your students. The more we collaborate with others, the more we learn.

■ ACCESS TO THE WORLD

In a sense, the world in the twenty-first century has shrunk. We have greater access to the world now than ever before because of technology and transportation. Yet many classrooms remain closed to world access. Many children read from science textbooks that, even though they are only a few years old, contain outdated information. Many children only read about waves, machines, and animals instead of observing, manipulating, and sharing information about them. We are not trying to downplay the importance of reading in science; students can learn a great deal about science from books and other printed information, and they should be a regular part of any science program. However, students also need to have access to the real thing whenever possible. This does not necessarily mean that you have to pile students into a bus and drive to exotic places. It does mean, however, that students need actual materials to study and technology that will take them to places they cannot go themselves. It means that students should get out of the classroom—for field trips or even just outside the school—to experience their corner of the world.

It means that students should have access to the best science education possible, so when they do have the chance to go to different parts of the world, they can go as educated people.

The outside world is both a great studio and a great laboratory. It is full of inspirational sights, sounds, and smells, like a studio, and it is full of wonderful opportunities to test, manipulate, and observe, like a laboratory. The world *is* science! How can your students experience it? Let's talk about technology, field trips, and the great outdoors.

Technology

Technology allows students to gather resources, access places they have never been, and work with ideas in new ways. Many topics, such as space, are difficult or impossible to study directly, but, with the help of computers, the Internet, cameras, and CDs, students can study these topics in meaningful ways.

- Informational CDs and the Internet, for example, provide fantastic three-dimensional models and illustrations for children. The sun, moon, and stars can be put into motion, so students can see why we have seasons, nighttime and daytime, and moon phases. Certainly, students cannot travel (yet!) to see space and experience it firsthand, but many cannot even travel out of their own neighborhood or city. Technology can transport them to new places and provide access to world experts.
- E-mail can facilitate dialogue between scientists and students or between students in classrooms in different cities or towns. E-mailing scientists or other community members about insects, farms, or oceans is a wonderful way for students to have their questions answered and to create new questions. E-mailing other students about the weather, soils, or habitats in their area can give them new data to represent, compare, and sort for patterns.
- Cameras of all kinds can be used to take pictures of different stages in an experiment. My class took pictures of mealworms every day to record the stages of development over time.

Although technology enhances the study of science, it should not be the sole tool students use. Scientists use technology, but it does not replace their active thinking, wondering, asking, and experimenting. In other words, students should not be learning about insects only through the Internet. They should also be observing real insects!

Using technology requires knowledge about how to use it properly. Teach your students how to use technology safely and be diligent in your monitoring. Students need to understand that they should never give personal information on the Internet or in an e-mail. They need to know the procedures for getting out of an Internet site that is inappropriate, and they need to know how to handle and care for technological equipment. Some safety issues can be avoided altogether. For example, you might have students use your personal e-mail account for dialoguing with experts so that you can screen what the students see. Require students to use search engines, such as Yahooligans, that filter adult sites. Students

Photo 11.5   Doing Science on Computer

Two students work at a computer station during science.

should always be supervised when working on the computer or with other technology, and they should understand that, if they misuse it, they will lose the privilege of using it. Your school probably has procedures for using technology; you might ask the technology coordinator or media specialist for more information.

Technology requires skill, time, and energy to use. It also can be daunting and expensive. However, technology is an important tool for learning science—so utilize it fully!

Field Trips

Field trips are another avenue to the world of science. We often think of museums and zoos, but don't forget parks, planetariums, and businesses too. In addition to resources and information, such places often have experts who can answer students' questions and offer inspiration for future learning.

When you plan a field trip, make sure you think of it as an extension of the classroom. Students should have opportunities to observe, plan, organize, collect data, represent, experiment, reflect, and share, just as they do in the classroom. Picking places that facilitate real science will help you to best use field trip opportunities. For example, while studying habitats, my class visited a recreational forest, where students looked for evidence of producers, consumers, and decomposers.

While field trips should incorporate what students have already studied, they should also extend students' knowledge and prompt new questions. It is tempting to schedule a field trip as a culminating activity of a unit. However, whenever possible, plan field trips in the middle of a unit, so students can follow up on new ideas after the trip. You want students to connect the world to ideas they have studied in the classroom and then move forward with new ideas. Instead of having them do a scavenger hunt (with "right" answers) to make sure they go to all of the exhibits, create logbooks for the trip and ask students to write down their observations and questions. You might have them make notes beforehand of what they want to find out during the trip and ask them to jot down their discoveries on the big day. Make sure students have time to reflect after they return from the trip, both on their own and as a class or small group.

The Great Outdoors

Many school districts do not have funding for field trips, which is unfortunate. Other schools are located in areas with few museums or nature centers. However, the fascinating world of science is just outside your classroom door. Even the playground can be a wonderful place to learn science! I once took my class outside to look for evidence of erosion all around the playground. We made sundial watches and tested them outside to get a better understanding of our position in relationship to the sun and the world. We put hula hoops on a spot on the grass and counted the number of insects we saw inside the hula hoops. This activity was great for observing, collecting, and organizing data; graphing; and imagining how many billions of insects there must be in the world. We even made four different types of mountains in the dirt next to our portable classroom. In doing these experiments and many more, the students got out into their world and made some sense of it.

The outdoors is also a good place to do experiments or play games that are too messy or too noisy to do in the classroom. For example, students might play a habitat game that helps them understand camouflage. Students hide within a specific area outside, trying to blend in with their surroundings, and one student calls out the names of those he or she can see. Afterward, students reflect about what they were wearing and how well they were hidden. After a few games, students wearing bright colors figure out that it is wise to hide near the bike racks! Messy experiments, like blowing up volcanoes, also work better outside than inside. Make sure students understand safety expectations during outside activities.

In some cases, you might want to bring the outdoors into your classroom! If you don't have close access to a pond, garden, or grassy area, bring samples from each to your classroom. For example, bring a jar of pond water, put it in a tank, and set it next to the window or under a grow light. Every few days, add water. (If you add tap water, leave it uncovered for a while to get the chemicals out before adding it.) If you don't have a grassy area, grow some grass in the classroom. Create a variety of weather situations indoors, too. Students can make clouds in baggies with steam, or rain in a terrarium. When the first snow fell, we always went outside to observe the flakes and bring some back to the classroom.

Photo 11.6   Outside Science

Ryan learns science in the great outdoors.

We made "snow keepers" and tested them to see how long we could keep the snow from melting.

As you can see, facilitating science learning out in the world is not such a difficult task in elementary school. Not only will students learn about science, they will be excited about it. As you plan workshops for different topics, ask yourself if you have included the outside world. How can you include technology, field trips, and outside projects in workshops?

■ THE BEST OF BOTH WORLDS: LABORATORIES *AND* STUDIOS FOR CHILDREN

By providing students access to materials, safe spaces for learning, people, and the world, you can create a classroom that is the best of both laboratories *and* studios. What pieces of a laboratory will you borrow as you design your science classroom? What pieces of a studio will you borrow? Classrooms are where students gather to learn. They contain materials and furniture, paint and paper. But remember that classrooms also have an atmosphere that will either encourage or discourage active learning.

As you can see, access is a main focus in this chapter. Students must have access to their classroom and the things in the classroom to learn science and to learn about life. Some classrooms seem created for adults rather than students.

- The desks are in nice straight rows, *so adults have control.*
- The students' work—all the same—is organized neatly on the walls *for adults.*
- Materials are locked away, *so they won't be damaged.*
- Assignments are given *for adult accountability.*

The classroom must be *for* and *about* children and their learning. This chapter is about creating a room that invites student participation, fosters social interaction, inspires creativity and individuality, encourages responsibility, and develops in children a deep understanding and love of science.

Conversation Starters

- What "walls" are keeping you from giving students access to science? How might you get around them?

- How might you plan for safety outside?

- Make a list of places where you could get information, materials, etc. from a scientist.

- Is your classroom a laboratory or a studio? Why?

- Why is access to science so limited in today's classrooms?

12

Connections to Curriculum

In a way, the children's book called *The Big Orange Splot* by Daniel Pinkwater sums up our goals in writing this book about teaching science and meshing our approach with your district curriculum. Mr. Plumbean, the star of *The Big Orange Splot*, lives on a tidy street in a house that looks exactly the same as his neighbors' houses. But then one day, a seagull drops a bucket of orange paint on his house, creating a big orange *splot* on his roof. Mr. Plumbean's neighbors, feeling badly for him because his house now looks different from theirs, comment that he will need to repaint it. But Mr. Plumbean has other ideas. He turns his house into the house of his dreams, with different colors of splots all over and an alligator in the front yard. Rather disgusted with Mr. Plumbean, the neighbors each try to reason with him, telling him they want a neat street again and that he has disrupted the entire neighborhood by being different. Mr. Plumbean talks his neighbors, one by one, into changing *their* houses into dream houses. (You must read the book yourself to get the full impact of the story!)

We see this story as a great metaphor for teaching science in a time when there is considerable pressure to meet specific standards and benchmarks. As you begin using this approach, you may feel like Mr. Plumbean. Because it is not a cookie-cutter approach, resulting in classrooms that look and sound the same, you may feel as if you don't fit in. That's okay. Mr. Plumbean's house was different, yet it was still a house. The way your students learn science concepts may differ, but they will learn the important broad concepts students in other classrooms learn. Just as Mr. Plumbean took a basic house and made it his own, you can implement your district curriculum and standards effectively while using your own and your students' creativity and ideas.

In the morning the other people on the street came out of their houses. Their houses were all the same. But Mr. Plumbean's house was like a rainbow. It was like a jungle. It was like an explosion.

Photo 12.1   Big Orange Splot

Daniel Manus Pinkwater's book **The Big Orange Splot** *is a great metaphor for this approach to teaching and learning science. (Copyright 1977 by Daniel Manus Pinkwater. Reprinted by permission of Scholastic Inc.)*

You may encounter people who think as Mr. Plumbean's neighbors did—or you may be one of them yourself. A classroom certainly looks and sounds more "tidy" when students are all doing the same thing! However, because students (and teachers) are not all the same, the learning *must* look different. This doesn't mean that you throw out district objectives and expectations. You make these your foundation and then add on, making your own "house." In this chapter, you'll discover how to connect everything you've learned to the curriculum that you are expected to teach. This will require you to relearn your district science objectives, ask yourself some important questions, and view yourself as both a teacher and learner. Mr. Plumbean started with a foundation—a house—and made it his own. Now it's your turn. Let's start with your foundation—the science curriculum—and make it your own.

■ YOUR FOUNDATION: THE SCIENCE CURRICULUM

Few of us have the freedom to create our own curricula. We have district, state, and federal objectives and expectations to meet. In some ways, this is unfortunate, because it prevents us from completely tailoring learning to our particular students' needs. However, using this approach will allow you to meet objectives while helping students construct their own knowledge in meaningful ways. In other words, meeting objectives should not keep you from creating science lessons and units that meet individual students' needs.

Study Your District Objectives

To combine district objectives and goals with this approach, take a close look at your science objectives. Studying them will secure the ideas in your own mind, so you can better create choices for workshops. It will also create a good foundation for you to build on as you find out what your students need. If you aren't currently in a district, check out the *National Science Education Standards* or obtain a copy of your local school district's science objectives. We have listed several of one school's kindergarten science objectives below as an example.

Kindergarten Science Objectives

- The learner will be able to begin to observe that earth's materials sustain life.
- The learner will be able to begin to identify and develop an understanding of the objects in the sky.
- The learner will be able to explain day-to-day weather alterations.
- The learner will be able to distinguish between living and non-living things.
- The learner will be able to begin to find similarities and differences in specific properties of animals.
- The learner will be able to begin to explain how organisms alter as they grow.
- The learner will be able to begin to comprehend the life cycles of living things.
- The learner will be able to investigate how organisms require food, water, and air to survive.
- The learner will be able to explain a healthy diet.
- The learner will be able to begin to observe and identify that living things live and survive in particular habitats.
- The learner will be able to begin to describe how organisms interact with their surroundings as a result of specific attributes.
- The learner will be able to describe how the weather changes based on the seasons.
- The learner will be able to begin to explain how roots, stems, and leaves have different roles in plants.
- The learner will be able to begin to describe that substances can enhance or harm how the body functions.

In addition to studying the objectives for your grade level, look through the science objectives of other grades to understand how they are connected. Remember that science learning doesn't begin or end in your classroom. Having a sense of what students learned in a previous grade level and what they will be learning in the next will affect how you design science experiences. What do all these goals and objectives have in common? How do they complement one another? How do the objectives at your grade level fit in?

Next, focus on your grade's objectives. Take some time to *really* understand what each objective means. Although objectives are usually written clearly, they are somewhat general and need to be fleshed out. What does each objective mean to you? For example, what does it mean that students should "understand objects can be categorized into two groups, natural and designed"? What should students understand regarding the objective "objects in the sky have patterns of movement"? As you proceed, rephrase each objective in specific terms. The first example could be rephrased like this: "Students can distinguish between objects that occur in nature and those that are human made." What are some of those objects? What kind of a list would you make? Why do students need to know this? The second example might be rephrased like this: "Students will understand that the earth goes around the sun in an orbit, along with the other planets. In addition, the moon orbits around the earth in such a pattern that causes us to see the different moon phases each month." What would students need to know before accomplishing this objective? Why would they need to know this?

Rephrasing objectives and thinking through why students need to know each objective will help you to design appropriate experiences for students and to start making the collections of materials we discussed in Chapter 9. It will also give you a deeper understanding of the concepts you'll be teaching.

Plan Units Around the Objectives

After you have rephrased the objectives, look for commonalities among them and note which objectives could be taught together. Group these by cutting them apart and putting them into piles, highlighting them in different colors, or labeling them with numbers or short phrases. For example, you might group the following three objectives:

1. Objects can be categorized into two groups, natural and designed

2. Objects have many observable properties including size, weight, shape, color, temperature, and the ability to react to other substances

3. Objects are made of one or more materials, such as paper, wood, and metal

These three objectives are all concerned with properties of objects and could be expanded into a study of the differences among objects.

Next, label each group of objectives as a broad unit of study. The three objectives above might be labeled Solids/Liquids/Gases. Because it is better to have fewer units to teach during the year, avoid creating a whole unit for each objective. Aim for five or six groups that encompass all the objectives. For example, you might have units on states of matter, insects, space, machines, the human body, and animals. You would study these topics in depth with your students over the school year and still "cover" your objectives. Some objectives might be covered in more than one unit of study. For example, the objective "the learner will be able to distinguish between living and non-living things" could be studied in a unit about animals, a broader unit about habitats, or in a unit about solids, liquids, and gases. This specific objective might fit nicely as a scaffold between units. The kindergarten objectives from the previous box have now been put into units of possible study.

Example of Kindergarten Science Objectives Within Units

Habitats

- The learner will be able to begin to observe that earth's materials sustain life.
- The learner will be able to distinguish between living and non-living things.
- The learner will be able to begin to find similarities and differences in specific properties of animals.
- The learner will be able to investigate how organisms require food, water, and air to survive.
- The learner will be able to begin to observe and identify that living things live and survive in particular habitats.
- The learner will be able to begin to describe how organisms interact with their surroundings as a result of specific attributes.

Weather

- The learner will be able to begin to identify and develop an understanding of the objects in the sky.
- The learner will be able to describe how the weather changes based on the seasons.
- The learner will be able to explain day-to-day weather alterations.

Plants

- The learner will be able to begin to explain how organisms alter as they grow.
- The learner will be able to begin to explain how roots, stems, and leaves have different roles in plants.
- The learner will be able to begin to comprehend the life cycles of living things.

Human Body

- The learner will be able to explain a healthy diet.
- The learner will be able to begin to describe that substances can enhance or harm how the body functions.

Note that you could go through the same objectives and find completely different units of study that would work nicely. How would you group the objectives listed previously?

It may be hard to distinguish between objectives and units of study. Objectives are the specific ideas students need to learn; units of study are topics that will help your students understand the objectives. For example, most science curricula have an objective about the life cycle of animals. According to the *National Science Education Standards,* students should learn the following: "Plants and animals have life cycles that include being born, developing into adults, reproducing, and eventually dying" (NRC, 1996, p.129). This objective could fit into a number of units of study, such as units on insects, plants, frogs, or humans. There are many ways to meet a given set of objectives; choose the best ways based on your students' interests and the other objectives they need to understand. Covering objectives in many different ways aids students in their processes of accommodation and assimilation (Chapter 4).

If your district relies on a textbook for science objectives and teaching units, go through the book and list the broad topics you will be teaching. From each unit of study, list the broad objectives. Don't list every objective from every page of the book; just determine the goals each unit meets. Once you understand the goals, you can move away from using the book for every lesson. For example, if the science book has a unit on butterflies and one of the objectives is about life cycles, you can expand the unit to include other insects that go through similar or different life cycles. Instead of reading and answering questions just about butterflies, students could observe mealworms, milkweed bugs, and waxworms. Tailor your district objectives to your students and to helping students utilize the key science experiences!

THE NEXT LAYER: INTEGRATION

If your curriculum is the foundation and frame for teaching science, everything you've learned in the previous eleven chapters are the walls, ceiling, and floors. Just as a lot of boards nailed together is not a house, the most detailed list of objectives, even grouped in units of study, is not yet your curriculum–and even the best curriculum cannot teach children science. Once you have gotten to know your district's science curriculum and have mapped out broad units of study that meet the objectives, you can expand and stretch the topics so they meet your needs and those of individual students. Here we will revisit the main ideas from each chapter and show you how to link them with your objectives and units of study.

Plan science lessons that address the whole child. Remember that active learning, social interaction, the key science experiences, workshops, thinking routines, and formative assessments help students develop not only cognitively but also socially. Your science objectives, then, should be covered in ways that allow for student choice, so students learn how to make decisions and feel empowered about those decisions. There should be room for making mistakes and learning the social aspects of science, such as communication, problem solving, and handling disagreements. Both cognitive and social goals are important and can be achieved simultaneously. As you develop science units, workshops, and thinking opportunities, make sure you create social objectives in addition to cognitive objectives. The following box shows some of the thinking needed as you create a unit of study.

Human Body—First Brainstorm

- The learner will be able to explain a healthy diet.
- The learner will be able to begin to describe that substances can enhance or harm how the body functions.

(It looks as though these objectives center on making choices about eating and about medicines or drugs that could either help or harm the students.)

What are the types of cognitive/science goals in these objectives?

1. They will need to know what a healthy diet is and means for them.
2. They will need to know how to look at food labels to help themselves make healthy choices.
3. They will need to know about what food does for their bodies.
4. A lesson on what water does for their bodies might be helpful.
5. Exercise will fit nicely into this unit.
6. They will need to know the difference between helpful (medicines) and harmful drugs.
7. They will need to understand the role of a doctor and a pharmacist.
8. They may need to know how they can tell the difference between medicines and candy.
9. They may need to know how to get help if someone they know is being harmed by a medicine or drug.

What are the social goals surrounding these objectives?

1. Choice is going to be a major social goal. Their choices really affect them within this topic.
2. Another good social goal might be about getting help from an adult.
3. Students need to know how they can help themselves. For example, if water helps the brain learn, they should know that in order to help themselves.

What are some objectives from other subjects to incorporate?

1. Social Studies: we need to learn about diversity.
2. Math: we need to do some measuring.
3. Writing: we could do some writing about self.

Enable students to do real science. In Chapter 2, "The Nature of Science," you saw that science is a process as well as a body of knowledge. You must help your students learn both rather than merely memorize facts. Use your science objectives to guide students in doing real science—asking questions, making hypotheses, and testing their ideas. Objectives are places to *begin* investigations rather than end them. You see, science objectives are meant to do much more than help students do well on tests or help them succeed at the next grade level. They should help students understand and question existing information about the world; help them learn problem solving, questioning skills, and other subjects like reading, math, and history; and help them become productive members of our democratic society.

Human Body—Second Brainstorm

What is "real science" about these objectives?

1. One "real science" question that we could talk about might involve why some foods are more healthful than others.
2. This unit will require some definite questioning and organizing, especially when it comes to food groups and the difference between medicines that are helpful and

those that are harmful. (The same medicines can be helpful *and* harmful, depending on their concentrations and one's state of health.)

3. We could experiment with some different foods to see how they affect the body. An experiment where one puts egg shells (representing teeth) into different liquids such as soda, juice, coffee, milk, and water might be a good one for this unit.

4. It might be important for the students to represent where food goes and what happens to it in the body.

5. This unit would be a good place for students to begin organizing their own meal plans. Portion size might fit nicely with math objectives.

Construct knowledge along with the students. We hope this book has begun to help you get around the walls keeping you from teaching science, the walls that we talked about in Chapter 3, "Prior Beliefs, Efficacy, and Teaching Science." Although understanding the content you need to teach will take time, the objectives are a great place to start. Begin with the small bit of information in the objective, and continue to add ideas from other sources. Learn along with the students, and do some investigating yourself. As helpful as objectives are for launching learning, they can sometimes get in the way of helping students construct their own knowledge. Objectives should inspire creativity and a variety of answers and solutions; they are not the endpoint of a step-by-step procedure. By challenging and questioning students' ideas, you can guide them in the direction required by district objectives.

Human Body—Third Brainstorm

What questions do I have about this unit? What do I really wonder?

1. I don't know if I really understand the new food pyramid. The students and I will need to look at it and see what we think about it and then look at some other resources.

2. Why does changing a food from its original form make it less healthy? Or does it? If you fry potatoes, do the nutrients go away, or does it just make them have too much fat and calories?

3. Why does everyone say that we have to drink eight glasses of water a day?

4. What do vitamins do for the body?

Balance success with disequilibrium. As you develop units of study, be sure to take into consideration individual students and their development, as discussed in Chapter 4, "Maturation and Learning." Although all students are expected to meet the same objectives, they may need different experiences in order to do so. Give them many opportunities to assimilate and accommodate ideas through investigating, writing, having conversations, and drawing pictures. Enable them to feel successful, but push them to reach new levels of development and understanding.

Human Body–Fourth Brainstorm

What do I know about the students I am teaching?

1. These are kindergartners, and some of them have just turned five. They will need to have experiences that connect heavily to their own life experiences. Acting ideas out and physically organizing food might help understanding. Food labels might be too hard for them. What if we came up with our own system?
2. I don't know what they already understand about how food, drink, medicines, and drugs affect the body. We will need to do a KWL chart before we begin this unit.
3. We live in an urban area, so many might not know where the food they eat comes from. This might be an excellent time to visit a farm.
4. In order to pass the district assessments for these objectives, the students will have to put certain foods in the food groups. I need to make sure that the students have some experiences doing this.
5. The students will probably be interested in their teeth at this age. That might be a good place to begin.

Remember that science learning is physical, mental, and social. Chapter 5, "Social Interaction and Learning," and Chapter 6, "Active Learning," have important implications for your science curriculum. To construct knowledge about science concepts, students need social interaction with peers, parents, and teachers. Science is full of both physical objects to manipulate and interesting ideas to contemplate. Remember to scaffold ideas using such tools as language, signs, and symbols, and remember that objectives each have important ideas that come before and after them, ideas that need to be emphasized. As you get to know individual students, support them within their own zone of proximal development by providing opportunities for active learning. Remember that active learning doesn't mean completing "cookbook" activities! It means asking open-ended questions, presenting authentic problems, and helping students find their own answers. Students need choice, materials, manipulation, language, and adult support.

Human Body–Fifth Brainstorm

What are active, social, and physical pieces of this unit?

1. Students will need to have some actual food, food labels, and medicine bottles to manipulate.
2. Students will need opportunities to debate what foods they think of as healthful.
3. It might be helpful for students to do some body modeling of the pyramid or some portion sizes. I have a book called *Body Battles* about germs and drugs we could act out. We could also act out what happens to food in our bodies.
4. We could invite a pharmacist to come and help us learn about drugs and medicines.
5. I need to include some diversity in this unit.

Plan activities around the key science experiences. Just as students need to work with content, they need to develop skill in the processes mapped out in Chapter 7, "Key Science Experiences." These experiences shouldn't be taught out of context; they are tools to help students learn the science objectives. Students at every level of thinking can observe, represent, organize, pattern/question, experiment, and share in every unit of study and for every objective. As you design study units, make sure your district objectives are covered by helping students engage in the key science experiences.

Human Body–Sixth Brainstorm

What key science experiences will be most utilized during this unit?

1. Representing and organizing will be important because there is a lot of information in this unit that lends itself to these experiences.
2. Sharing will also be important as students talk about what they eat and how they take care of themselves at home.
3. There will be some observing, patterning/questioning, and experimenting, as always, but I think the first two are going to be key.

Teach content through workshops and thinking routines. Chapters 8 and 9, "Thinking Routines" and "Planning Science Workshops," explained how to provide flexible structures that enable students to engage in science. Both of these structures can incorporate your district objectives and the key science experiences. There are many different ways to help students understand concepts and meet objectives, and it is important to design workshops so that students can work with concepts in ways that make sense to them. The order of events matters within a workshop! It will be tempting to give facts and then let kids explore. Make sure you are letting them explore and then helping them understand their explorations. Students who don't have many prior experiences with a particular topic should feel as successful and grow just as much as students who have had more experiences. Remember that learning is not just about declarative and procedural knowledge but also about metacognitive knowledge. Students who use thinking routines within the boundaries of a broad topic will develop all three kinds of knowledge and become life-long learners.

It is important to note, as well, that, while you are going to plan ahead of time for workshops you will use to help students understand the objectives, you need to think of planning as "anticipating the curriculum" rather than putting it in stone. You will need to be flexible about adding experiences based on students' needs while keeping in mind the objectives you must get to. The following "brainstorm" contains a few workshop ideas based on the work done to combine objectives into units of study. However, they are not planned workshops. They are only ideas that I can flesh out as I need them. They provide a direction, but not an exact road to travel.

Human Body—Seventh Brainstorm

What are some specific workshops that utilize thinking routines that I want to be sure to incorporate into this unit?

1. Students get into pairs and draw large-scale outlines of their bodies by lying on paper placed on the floor; then each partner will "color in" the other person's features noting differences between them. Discuss diversity and then connect that to the fact that we *all* need some things.
2. Students could plan and create with pictures healthful meals. This could be done in stations so that they would need to go to different food group areas to complete their meals.
3. In groups, students could make up their own color system for labeling foods.
4. Students need opportunities to organize food into groups.
5. Students could plan experiments with egg shells for dental health.
6. Students could represent what happens to food in their bodies by acting it out.
7. I could read *Body Battles* to the students and have them plan ways to represent germs and drugs.
8. Students need to see where food comes from. We could visit a farm. We could visit a grocery store.

How do these workshops scaffold together?

These workshops seem to have some sub-themes that might fit together:

- Diversity of bodies and yet similar needs—first

    (workshop ideas= #1)

- What do our bodies need? (Including our teeth, our fuel, our brains)—second

    (workshop ideas= #2, #4, #5, #6)

- What is harmful to our bodies?—third

    (workshop ideas= #7)

- How can we make decisions about how to help our bodies?—fourth

    (workshop ideas= #3, #8)

Provide an emotionally safe environment for learning. Most students can memorize objectives for a test and therefore meet the objectives. However, if we want them to truly *learn* and internalize objectives, we must provide a safe environment—one in which they can take risks, focus their energy, and use their emotions to learn effectively. Using this approach in science is not just about meeting a list of science objectives. It is about helping individual children learn science as a verb and noun. It is about helping them understand themselves as learners and grow into self-reliant, caring, persistent individuals who continue to learn long after they are out of school. Chapters 10 and 11, "Assessment" and "Access to Science in a Classroom," emphasize this. Assessment should bring students together rather than divide them by ability. It should provide students feedback and direction for improvement without attacking their ego or their differences. Use assessment to help students grow instead of to help them learn a single objective for the time being. And provide plenty of access to people, space, materials, and the world, so students can learn science objectives, as well as other life lessons, in a safe and caring environment where high expectations, flexibility, and risk taking abound.

Human Body—Eighth Brainstorm

What assessments will possibly be useful?

1. Anecdotal notes will be useful.
2. At the end of each sub-theme, I could make up a worksheet where students need to circle pictures about what they know.
3. I could take pictures as they act ideas out and have them write or tell about the picture.

What materials will students need?

1. Access to foods.
2. Access to some places including a farm or a grocery store.
3. Access to organizational tools such as hula hoops or graphs.
4. Access to books about health and wellness.

MAKING THE CURRICULUM YOUR OWN

Your "house" now has a sturdy foundation and framework (district objectives and units of study), and the framework has been filled in with walls, ceiling, and floors. The house is not finished yet, however. It needs the finishing touches that will make it uniquely yours—paint, carpet, furniture, pictures, and trinkets collected over the years. What are these unique touches? You and your students! Science units are not complete without your collective experiences, questions, and interests. This is what makes teaching and learning exciting and gives students a desire to learn more. It is what transforms objectives from something like "materials can exist in different states—solid, liquid, and gas; some common materials, such as water, can be changed from one state to another by heating or cooling" (*National Science Education Standards*) to "we observed solids, liquids, and gases when we made taffy." Believe me, making taffy was not an objective in my district curriculum! It was a vehicle for meeting the district objective in a way that made both students and teachers look forward to school and left a lasting impression. Hopefully, when you were reading the previous brainstorms about the human body, you noticed that they provide only a framework of what might happen in the classroom. If I were actually doing this unit, I would take that frame and fill it in with needs as we moved along in the unit.

Just as you might begin turning a frame into a home of your own by asking yourself questions such as what colors you like, who might be able to lay the bricks, and what furniture you need, you must begin expanding your district objectives with questions. You will continue to ask yourself questions throughout the year, not just at the beginning of the year and not just when you are learning this approach. As your students grow and change and as you begin to feel confident in using this approach, you will have different answers to the questions and perhaps additional questions. Below is an empty brainstorm box for you to use. If you are thinking, "How will I do this for *every* unit?" Don't worry. The more you use this approach, the more natural and spontaneous your answers to these questions will be. In order to get started, take some time to think about them.

_____ Brainstorm

(unit)

Objectives that fit in this unit:
What are the cognitive/science goals surrounding these objectives?
What are the social goals surrounding these objectives?
What are objectives from other subjects that fit with this science unit?
What is "real science" about these objectives?
What questions do I have about this unit? What do I really wonder?
What do I know about the students I am teaching?
What are active, social, and physical pieces of this unit?
What key science experiences will be most utilized during this unit?
What are some specific workshops that utilize thinking routines that I want to be sure to incorporate into this unit?
How do these workshops scaffold together? (What should go first, second, third...?)
What assessments will possibly be useful?
What materials will students need?

Making the curriculum your own means making students the focal point. Your job is to help them make connections to the topic. This doesn't mean that every workshop has to be fun—fun is not necessarily the goal of science. However, if the work is meaningful and relevant and the questions are real, science *will* be enjoyable and engaging for students. Find out what students' interests are and what they would like to study. Add some of your own interests too. Making the curriculum your own will benefit the students because you will be excited about teaching and about learning science along with them.

Making the curriculum your own also brings some responsibility. It requires that you continue to learn and grow yourself. You will learn along with the students, with other colleagues, and individually while completing your units of study. As you grow in knowledge about science, your students, and teaching, this process of learning science will become more and more your own. You have learned about all the necessary elements; now mix in your personality, teaching style, and students!

Finally, making the curriculum your own means building a community of support. There will probably be days when things don't go as planned, when the workshops don't work, when the students are too social. Be kind to yourself at these times. Take the time to write down your thoughts and feelings in a journal, or talk to someone. Implement the approach slowly if jumping in all at once seems to be too much. Ask for help from your administrators, parents, and colleagues. You, as well as students, need a supportive place to learn and grow.

Mr. Plumbean may have been afraid to change his house at first. It was probably very tempting for him to just cover the big orange splot so that his house would again look the same as neighboring houses. His house caused others to feel some disequilibrium, and he probably had to work hard to persuade neighbors that, underneath the many colors of paint, there were still sturdy boards that made his house stand as strong as any in the neighborhood. He probably had to convince his neighbors that diversity and individuality make a neighborhood richer. It may have taken Mr. Plumbean a while to feel comfortable with the changes he made. His story will probably be similar to your story of change in science education. You can do it! Good luck.

Conversation Starters

- What science objectives are unclear to you or don't make sense? Try to reword them, so they do make sense.

- What ideas do you need to consider if there are only one or two objectives that fit together to form a unit of study?

- Other than your students, what resources do you have that will help you make the curriculum "your own"?

- Think about ways to make collections of resources. How would a collection of resources be valuable in beginning to teach science objectives?

- In what ways are you like or unlike Mr. Plumbean?

PART V

Resources

The final section of this book contains resources that we hope will help you as you continue to launch learners in science! In Part V, you will find a safety section highlighting information important for the safe launching of those learners. There is a children's literature section designed to help you get started using literature in your science classroom. Finally, there is a bibliography listing all the resources we used to write this book, resources that might be useful if you want to continue to learn about teaching and teaching science.

Resource A: Safety

SAFETY IN THE CLASSROOM ■

Safety in the elementary science program is or should be a central concern for a number of reasons. First and foremost, we want to protect the children under our care. In so doing, we must make wise decisions regarding the materials we use, the manipulations of those materials by the students, and other factors. Second, we must recognize the legal responsibility we have on behalf of the school and school system. In a way, the legal responsibility is a stimulus for us to recognize more clearly our first stated goal—to protect the students.

Safety and Active Learning

Safety is one of the important things we should *teach!* Let's first think about human beings—about "us"—and about the opportunity teachers have to turn general safety issues into a way of learning about our basic biology.

In what ways can children (or any of us) be harmed? How are we endangered? We tend to answer these questions in terms of specific, identifiable risks, such as (1) poisons, (2) punctures, (3) infection with viruses or microbes (germs), or (4) being cut by glass or other sharp objects. Of course, there are a huge number of ways we can be injured. But they all come down to "breaching" our body's defense mechanisms! We would like to stress again that incorporating safety into the science classroom is really just extending a lesson or activity and enriching it. It places some aspects of experiments or workshops into a larger context, enriching experience rather than detracting from it. Considering safety in this way places it within the normal process of actually doing science, so it is not some additional thing to "frighten" students.

Our body is protected by a number of distinct, cooperating defense mechanisms. Our skin surrounds our body and physically protects us from being "invaded" by other organisms or chemicals. This defense can be breached by its being punctured or cut, and most of us realize this immediately. The skin can also be bypassed by chemicals that are "absorbed" through it and then enter the body. Occasionally, we recognize these dangers, especially when plant products enter in this fashion. Poison ivy, poison oak, and poison sumac all produce oils secreted onto leaf surfaces and present in sap that cause itching, skin redness, and blistering about 24 to 48 hours after contact. (These symptoms are actually a part of an immunological defense mechanism that we will discuss shortly.)

The skin is also an important sense organ with receptors for pain, temperature, and other environmental conditions. And the skin serves to keep us cool (via evaporation of water from sweat glands) and warm (by erecting body hair as a form of quilt). These processes must be appreciated and protected. Perhaps you are familiar with an old James Bond character named Goldfinger who "paints" victims with metallic gold paint that clogs the pores. This paint prevents the body from cooling (via evaporation), and the victim dies from excess heat.

The key point here is that the skin is a tough, first line of protection whose functioning and integrity must be preserved. Therefore, we should be aware of anything that can break that line of defense, for example, sharp objects, materials that can cut, solvents that can breach the skin, and materials that can block its functioning.

Other entry ports to our body are the eyes, ears, nose, mouth, air passages, and the "private" parts of the body. Some of these are direct entry or exit ways for materials that seem to enter or leave the body. For example, we seem to take food "in" through the mouth, although in reality we simply surround it there and in the digestive tract. The food stays "outside" our body until it is broken down into molecular-sized pieces that are brought in—or until there is a major breach of the digestive tract. However, all these areas are protected by a kind of tissue called an epithelium. The epithelia (plural of epithelium) act partly like the skin but have several other additional properties. For example, they tend to be moist and covered with mucous to protect them from mechanical abrasion. The mucous acts like "oil" in a machine and allows agents to slip and slide rather than abrade and slice. However, the moist mucous is also "water-based." This suggests that water may provide another means of breaching the defense system; water, acting as the universal solvent for agents that enter the cavities listed previously, may be absorbed by the tissues and simultaneously bring in the foreign chemicals. So another safety step we can consciously take is to keep chemicals away from these epithelia so that the chemicals do not dissolve and enter the body. Two simple safety measures, then, are to refrain from tasting and smelling foreign or unknown materials. Keep chemical solutions and chemical vapors away from the eyes for the same reason.

The epithelia contain another line of defense as well. They contain immunoglobulins—antibodies—that protect the body from foreign chemicals and foreign cells. The "immune system" is a set of chemical and cellular defense mechanisms designed to protect the body from an immense number of agents that manage to penetrate the body's defenses or that the body itself forms "accidentally." One part of the immune system specializes in releasing chemicals that "neutralize" the activity of chemical and biological intruders. These protective chemicals—immunoglobulins—can coat the surfaces of the foreign chemicals and intruders. Immunoglobulins often act as a kind of "sugar coating" so that other parts of the immune system can literally eat and digest the unwanted agents. In other instances, the immunoglobulins act as a scaffold for assembling molecular drills that put holes in foreign cells, hence killing them. Yet another part of the immune system specializes in forming cellular "assassins." These "killer T cells" are specialized for drilling holes in and killing foreign cells. They are responsible for the ability of the body to "reject" foreign cells and tissues, such as those involved in organ transplants.

Sometimes, the immune system cells can become more of a problem than a solution. Most of us, for example, are aware of the problems associated with organ rejections. Although foreign cells and tissues are normally "bad" and we want to stop their growth and functioning, occasionally we want such transplanted tissues to grow and function. Then we have to "trick" the body into accepting the foreigners.

Similarly, the antibodies are normally used to protect the body from foreign chemicals and cells. But, occasionally, while doing their job, the antibodies can do more harm to the body than would the foreign chemicals themselves. This unusual immunological response is called an allergy. Allergies can range in seriousness from annoying to dangerous. Some people develop a hypersensitivity to certain agents, and, when they are exposed to these agents, the massive responses of the immune system can be both very rapid and life threatening. For example, some people are very allergic to bee stings or to peanut butter. Exposure to these chemicals can cause mammoth immune responses leading to what has been called an "anaphylactic response." People with such hypersensitivity must receive prompt medical and first-aid treatment when exposed to the critical agent! As teachers, we must be aware of these responses and aware that such allergies are more common than we normally think.

So far, we have talked about the physical lines of defense (skin and epithelia) and the chemical line of defense (the immune system). We have also indicated how these systems can be "broken" and the steps we can take to protect against such breaches. There are also "unseen" ways that the body's defenses can be broken, namely, by electromagnetic radiation and by radioactivity. Electromagnetic radiation takes on many forms. We are probably most familiar with visible light because we use this form so extensively. Our vision depends on certain of our cells being sensitive to and responding to electromagnetic radiation that has a rather narrow range of energies. "Light" rays can be more energetic than the visible rays we see, and these energetic rays take on such forms as ultraviolet light, which is responsible not only for stimulating "tanning" (often sought by the young!) but also for causing genetic mutations, skin cancers, and blindness if viewed directly with the eye (hardly sought by anyone). Even more energetic radiation occurs in the form of "X-rays." X-rays can be beneficial medically by allowing us to "see" inside the body. But they can also be detrimental by causing genetic mutations and cancers! We should be aware of these types of radiation and avoid exposure to them. And we should remember that the eye can focus (that is, concentrate) radiation, making it even more dangerous because of its increased intensity. For example, a laser can be a pointer for a lecture, a scalpel for surgery, or a weapon of immense power depending on the laser's intensity.

Choose any lesson that involves materials, choices, or manipulation, and safety should be a consideration. For example, in the K–3 elementary grades, the students should be told explicitly not to put materials in their mouths for tasting or other purposes (except in special circumstances and the "specialness" of those circumstances should then be stressed). They should also be told of any potential risks and how to avoid problems from those risks. The students should be encouraged to think of potential problems themselves. As they get older, we want them to be responsible for their own safety and that of others as well.

Perhaps a story might be helpful here. One teacher decided to participate in a school fair designed to raise money for the school. You may know of these fairs, the ones in which teachers offer memorabilia for sale or do silly things as "fund raisers." As part of the "fun and funds," the teacher offered students the chance to purchase strips of duct tape and to use them to tape the teacher to a board. Sounded like fun—and it was a great way to observe the strength of the duct tape. What are some of the potential problems? One would want to control (1) how well the tape holds so that the teacher doesn't fall off the board, (2) how far off the ground the teacher is raised, and (3) how the teacher will be taken down. The teacher considered these possible difficulties. What the teacher didn't realize or think about was one of the basic biological principles we've already discussed. Can you see which one? (Duct tape is so dense it doesn't allow the skin to "breathe.") Like the victims of Goldfinger, the teacher became overheated. In fact, this was almost fatal to the teacher. The point is, one should *always review safety issues*—both before and after—to learn as much as possible for future reference.

■ SOME "ABSOLUTE MUSTS"

Here are a few absolute musts with respect to safety in the elementary classroom or, indeed, in any classroom:

- Have emergency phone numbers posted, and let the class know where they are; among the numbers you should have are those for emergency services (such as 911), the main school office, and a poison control center. Also have a policy for when they will be used.
- Read the school and school district safety manual. If the school or district does not have one, you may think about helping to create one.
- Have a first aid kit to which *only you the teacher* have access; this will ensure that materials are not missing or misused. One of the items in this kit should be at least a pair of latex or plastic examination gloves that are to be used whenever there is blood or other body fluids. This is for both your safety and that of the children.
- Know what other resources are available and how to use them. For example, if your school maintains a list of Material Safety Data Sheets (MSDS), know where they are kept and how to read them. By law, all chemical suppliers must include such a sheet with all chemicals that are distributed. In fact, such a sheet should be available for *every* chemical on hand. In the elementary school classroom, most such chemicals will be things you purchase at the grocery or hardware store, and the sheets will not be given when you purchase them. However, a number of web sites specialize in providing MSDS sheets. For example, http://www.msdssearch.com is a popular site with access to more than 2 million MSDS. There are several other sources, and you can identify your favorite by simply searching the Internet.

Resource B: Literature

CHILDREN'S LITERATURE

Literature is a great way to intrigue children about science, help them better understand the nature of science, and help them both answer and create questions about science. Indeed, there are many thousands of books we could list that would enhance any science unit or lesson. Both fiction and nonfiction books can be read aloud to introduce topics or used as classroom resources as children create projects, complete assignments, or experience workshops. Science poems and picture books take children to new places that they can't actually visit, such as a rainforest or a cave. Books of experiments can spark ideas for further investigation. Fictional stories can help children develop patterns and observational skills or merely see that science is everywhere! Finding the right book is as easy as asking your school librarian or science specialist, or just sitting down at the computer and searching different topics on the Internet. As you begin to make decisions about science units and lessons, make sure that children's literature titles are a part of your collections (Chapter 9)!

As with most of the ideas in this book, our list of literature for science is only a launching point. We hope that this list will encourage you to begin to utilize good children's literature in science and lead you to seek more literature for the topics that you teach. At first, it is difficult to take the time to find literature that fits into units, and this list may help you get started. Then it is up to you to keep scaffolding your book knowledge! Perhaps adding two or three books each year would be a manageable goal for you. Make sure to ask for help from other teachers and from school resource personnel. Remember that we are not suggesting you use literature for every science lesson. However, it *is* very important to have books available and displayed, so students have access to them at all times. For example, if you are studying coral reefs, take the time to find some great books on coral reefs and display them in your classroom!

The books that follow come from a variety of sources including our list of the favorites we have used in elementary classrooms, The National Science Teachers Association's yearly list of "Outstanding Science Trade Books for Students K–12" (www.nsta.org/ostbc), and suggestions from other classroom teachers. The books are categorized according to the six science standards, poetry, and experiment books. Indeed, the categories are quite broad and, in many cases, books could be placed into more than one category. For example, the book *The Lorax* could fit into Standard 4 of the *NSES* because it is about characteristics of organisms. However, it also fits into Standard 5 because it is about characteristics of the earth. We actually put this book in Standard 7 because it is about a human, or social, problem. Make sure to make children's science literature your own by considering your students, your objectives, and your interests as you choose books. Here is our list! We hope it helps you!

SCIENCE STANDARD 1: Unifying concepts and processes

- Systems, order, and organization
- Evidence, models, and explanation
- Change, constancy, and measurement
- Evolution and equilibrium
- Form and function

Aardema, V. (1975). *Why mosquitoes buzz in people's ears.*
Arnosky, J. (1995). *I see animals hiding.*
Hoban, T. (1971). *Look again!*
Hoban, T. (1981). *Take another look.*
Hoban, T. (1994a). *What is that?*
Hoban, T. (1994b). *Who are they?*
Quinlan, S. E. (1995). *The case of the mummified pigs: And other mysteries in nature.*
Rotner, S., & Olivo, R. (1997). *Close, closer, closest.*
Van Allsburg, C. (1988). *Two bad ants.*

SCIENCE STANDARD 2: Science as inquiry

- Abilities necessary to do scientific inquiry
- Understandings about scientific inquiry

Berger, M. (1980). *Mad scientists in fact and fiction.*
Jackson, D. M. (2002). *The bug scientist.*
Lehn, B. (1998). *What is a scientist?*

SCIENCE STANDARD 3: Physical Science

- Properties of objects and materials
- Position and motion of objects
- Light, heat, electricity, and magnetism

Ardley, N. (1984). *Force and strength.*
Ardley, N. (1992a). *The science book of gravity.*
Ardley, N. (1992b). *The science book of hot and cold.*
Berger, M. (1989). *Switch on, switch off.*
Bradley, K. B. (2001). *Pop! A book about bubbles.*
Branley, F. (1996). *What makes a magnet?*
Bulla, C. R. (1994). *What makes a shadow?*
Curtis, J. L. (2000). *Where do balloons go?*

Hoban, T. (1984). *Is it rough? Is it smooth? Is it shiny?*
Hoban, T. (1990). *Shadows and reflections.*
Jonas, A. (1989). *Color dance.*
Lange, K. (2002). *Magic school bus in concert.*
Macaulay, D. (1975). *Pyramid.*
Macaulay, D. (1977). *Castle.*
Macaulay, D. (1994). *The way things work.*
Macaulay, D. (1998). *The new way things work.*
Mayes, S. (1995). *Where does electricity come from?*
Pipe, J. (2002). *What does a wheel do?*

SCIENCE STANDARD 4: Life Science

- Characteristics of organisms
- Life cycles of organisms
- Organisms and environments

Amery, H., & Songi, J. (1994a). *Discover hidden worlds: The home.*
Amery, H., & Songi, J. (1994b). *Discover hidden worlds: The human body.*
Arnosky, J. (1994). *All about alligators.*
Base, G. (1992). *The sign of the seahorse.*
Bunting, E. (1999). *Butterfly house.*
Cannon, J. (1993). *Stellaluna.*
Cannon, J. (1997). *Verdi.*
Carle, E. (1977). *The grouchy ladybug.*
Carle, E. (1984). *The mixed-up chameleon.*
Cole, J. (1989). *The magic school bus: Inside the human body.*
Cummings, P. (1986). *Chadwick the crab.*
dePaola, T. (1997). *Mice squeak, we speak.*
Feldman, E. (1992). *Animals don't wear pajamas.*
Gibbons, G. (1984). *The seasons of Arnold's apple tree.*
Gibbons, G. (1991). *From seed to plan.*
Gibbons, G. (1997). *The honey makers.*
Gibbons, G. (2002a). *Giant pandas.*
Gibbons, G. (2002b). *Tell me, tree: All about trees for kids.*
Greenaway, T. (2001a). *Ants.*
Greenaway, T. (2001b). *Crabs.*
Greenaway, T. (2001c). *Snakes.*
Greenaway, T. (2001d). *Spiders.*
Greenaway, T. (2001e). *Whales.*
Greenaway, T. (2001f). *Wolves, wild dogs, and foxes.*
Guiberson, B. Z. (1994). *Spotted owl: Bird of the ancient forest.*
Hirschi, R. (2000). *Salmon.*
Jenkins, S. (1995). *Biggest, strongest, fastest.*
Kaner, E., & Stephens, P. (1999). *Animal defenses: How animals protect themselves.*
Keller, H. (1995). *Who eats what? Food chains and food webs.*
Korman, S. (2001). *Box turtle at Silver Pond Lane.*
Lauber, P. (1994). *Earthworms: Underground farmers.*
Lerner, C. (2002). *Butterflies in the garden.*
Miller, M. (1994). *My five senses.*
Nelson, K. (2002). *Clever raccoons.*
Oliver, C. (2002a). *Life in a pond.*
Oliver, C. (2002b). *Life in a tide pool.*

Pascoe, E. (2001a). *Leaves and trees.*
Pascoe, E. (2001b). *Pill bugs and sow bugs.*
Pfeiffer, J. (2001). *Leaping grasshoppers.*
Pratt, K. J. (1994). *A swim through the sea.*
Ryan, S. J. (2001). *Esmeralda and the enchanted pond.*
Sandeman, A. (1995). *Bones.*
Staub, F. (1994). *America's prairies.*
Wilkinson, V. (1994). *Flies are fascinating.*
Yolen, J. (1987). *Owl moon.*

SCIENCE STANDARD 5: Earth and Space Science

- Properties of earth materials
- Objects in the sky
- Changes in earth and sky

Apfel, N. H. (1995). *Orion, the hunter.*
Barrett, J. (1981). *Cloudy with a chance of meatballs.*
Branley, F. M. (1985). *Volcanoes.*
Branley, F. M. (1990). *Earthquakes.*
Bundy, N. (2000). *Ice and earth.*
Carle, E. (1996). *Little cloud.*
Christian, P. (2000). *If you find a rock.*
Cole, J. (1995). *The magic school bus: Inside a hurricane.*
dePaola, T. (1985). *The cloud book.*
Dewey, J. O. (2001). *Antarctic journal: Four months at the bottom of the world.*
Gans, R. (1997). *Let's go rock collecting.*
Gibbons, G. (1983). *Sun up, sun down.*
Gibbons, G. (1995). *The reason for seasons.*
Gibbons, G. (1997). *The moon book.*
Goble, P. (1988). *Ikitomi and the boulder.*
Hooper, M. (1998). *The drop in my drink: The story of water on our planet.*
James, C. (2001). *From the Artic to the Antarctica.*
Johnson, R. L. (2001a). *A walk in the desert.*
Johnson, R. L. (2001b). *A walk in the prairie.*
Johnson, R. L. (2001c). *A walk in the rainforest.*
Kramer, S. (1995). *Caves.*
LeBeau, S. (2002). *American deserts.*
Oxlade, C. (2002a). *Cotton.*
Oxlade, C. (2002b). *Glass.*
Oxlade, C. (2002c). *Life in a cave.*
Oxlade, C. (2002d). *Life in a flowerbed.*
Oxlade, C. (2002e). *Life in a tree.*
Oxlade, C. (2002f). *Metal.*
Oxlade, C. (2002g). *Plastic.*
Oxlade, C. (2002h). *Rock.*
Oxlade, C. (2002i). *Rubber.*
Pfeffer, W. (1995). *Marta's magnets.*
Polacco, P. (1990). *Thundercake.*
Pope, J. (1995). *The children's atlas of natural wonders.*
Rushton, K. (2002). *Backyard stars: A guide for home and the road.*
Sattler, H. R. (1995). *Our patchwork planet.*
Simon, S. (1994a). *Comets, meteors, and asteroids.*
Simon, S. (1994b). *Mountains.*

Simon, S. (1994c). *Winter across America.*
Skurzynski, G. (1994). *Zero gravity.*
Steele, C. (2001a). *Ice storms and hailstorms.*
Steele, C. (2001b). *Landslides and avalanches.*
Steele, C. (2001c). *Thunderstorms.*
Steele, C. (2001d). *Tsunamis.*
Steig, W. (1969). *Sylvester and the magic pebble.*
Sywilok, A. (2001). *Crab moon.*
Tripp, N. (1994). *Thunderstorm!*
Watts, J. F. (1994). *Deep-sea vents: Living worlds without sun.*
Whisenant, T. (2002). *Weather watch.*
Yolen, J. (1995). *Before the storm.*
Zoehfeld, K. W. (1995). *How mountains are made.*

SCIENCE STANDARD 6: Science and Technology

- Abilities of technological design
- Understandings about science and technology
- Abilities to distinguish between natural objects and objects made by humans

Branley, F. M. (1987). *Rockets and satellites.*
Cole, J. (1986). *The magic school bus at the water works.*
Gates, P. (1995). *Nature got there first: Inventions inspired by nature.*
Gibbons, G. (1979). *Clocks and how they go.*
Gibbons, G. (1997). *Click! A book about cameras and taking pictures.*
Kramer, S. (2001). *Hidden worlds: Looking through a scientist's microscope.*
Markle, S. (1994). *Science to the rescue.*
Romanek, T. (2001). *The technology book for girls and other advanced beings.*

SCIENCE STANDARD 7:
Science in Personal and Social Perspectives

- Personal health
- Characteristics and changes in populations
- Types of resources
- Changes in environments
- Science and technology in local challenges

Berger, M. (1986). *Germs make me sick!*
Berger, M. (1991). *Ouch! A book about cuts, scratches, and scrapes.*
Cherry, L. (1990). *The great kapok tree.*
Coombs, K. M. (1995). *Flush! Treating wastewater.*
Getz, D. (1994). *Frozen man.*
Gibbons, G. (1984). *Tunnels.*
Golden-Gelman, R. (1992). *Body battles.*
Hadingha, E., & Hadingha, J. (1990). *Garbage!*
Parker, S. (1995). *Medicine.*
Pemberton, D. (2001). *Egyptian mummies: People of the past.*
Showers, P. (1994). *Where does the garbage go?*
Stokes, J. (2002). *A dinosaur named Sue: The story of the colossal fossil.*
Suess, D. (1971). *The Lorax.*
Tagliaferro, L. (2001). *Galapagos Islands: Nature's delicate balance at risk.*

SCIENCE STANDARD 8: History and Nature of Science

- Science as a human endeavor

Bortz, F. (1995). *Catastrophe! Great engineering failure and success.*
Briggs-Martin, J. (1998). *Snowflake Bentley.*
Cobb, V. (1970). *Gases.*
Delano, M. F. (2002). *Inventing the future: A photobiography of Thomas Alva Edison.*
Heligman, D. (1994). *Barbara McClintock: Alone in her field.*
Hurst, C. O. (2001). *Rocks in his head.*
Jackson, E. (2002). *Looking for life in the universe.*
Lessem, D. (1994). *Jack Horner: Living with dinosaurs.*
Marrin, A. (2002). *Dr. Jenner and the speckled monster: The search for the smallpox vaccine.*
McPherson, S. S. (1995). *Ordinary genius: The story of Albert Einstein.*
McPherson, S. S. (2001). *Jonas Salk: Conquering polio.*
Mullane, R. M. (1994). *Liftoff! An astronaut's dream.*
Poynter, M. (1994). *Marie Curie, discoverer of radium.*
Ptacek, G. (1994). *Champion for children's health: A story about Dr. S. Josephine Baker.*
Thimmesh, C. (2002). *The sky's the limit: Stories of discovery by women and girls.*
Van Meter, V., & Gutman, D. (1995). *Taking flight: My story.*
Yount, L. (1994). *William Harvey, discoverer of how blood circulates.*

EXPERIMENT BOOKS

Cobb, V. (1994). *Science experiments you can eat!*
Gardner, R. (1978). *Moving right along: A book of science experiments and puzzlers about motion.*
Gardner, R. (1982). *Kitchen chemistry.*
Markle, S. (1996). *Icky, squishy science.*
Potter, J. (1995). *Science in seconds for kids: Over 100 experiments you can do in ten minutes or less.*
Raferty, K., & Raferty, D. (1989). *Kid's gardening: A kid's guide to messing around in the dirt.*
Rohrig, B. (2002). *39 spectacular experiments with soda pop.*
Wood, R. W. (1991a). *39 easy meteorology experiments.*
Wood, R. W. (1991b). *39 easy plant biology experiments.*
Wood, R. W. (1991c). *Science for kids: 39 easy astronomy experiments.*
Wood, R. W. (1991d). *Science for kids: 39 easy geology experiments.*
Wood, R. W. (1992). *39 easy engineering experiments.*
Wyler, R. (1987). *Science fun with mud and dirt.*

POETRY

Bennett, J. (1987). *Noisy poems.*
Brown, M. W. (1993). *Under the sun and the moon and other poems.*
Goldish, M. (1999). *101 science poems & songs for young learners.*
Graham, J. B. (1994). *Splish splash.*
Graham, J. B. (1999). *Flicker flash.*
Kuskin, K. (1980). *Dogs and dragons: Trees and dreams.*
Moore, L. (1992). *Sunflakes: Poems for children.*
O'Neill, M. (1961). *Hailstones and halibut bones.*
Yolen, J. (1997). *Once upon ice and other frozen poems.*

References

Akerson, V. L., Abd-El-Khalik, F., & Lederman, N. G. (2000). The influence of a reflective activity-based approach on elementary teachers' conceptions of the nature of science. *Journal of Research in Science Teaching, 37,* 295–317.

Allison, L. (1977). *Blood and guts.* New York: Scholastic.

Ashton, P. (1994). Teacher efficacy: A motivational paradigm for effective teacher education. *Journal of Teacher Education, 35*(5), 28–32.

Atherton, J. S. (2005). *Learning and teaching: Experiential learning.* Retrieved August 31, 2006, from http://www.learningandteaching.info/learning/experience.htm

Ball, D. L. (1988). Unlearning to teach mathematics. *For the Learning of Mathematics, 8*(1), 40–48.

Bandura, A. (1981). Self referent thought: A developmental analysis of self-efficacy. In J. H. Flavell & L. Ross (Eds.), *Social cognitive development: Frontiers and possible futures* (pp. 202–239). New York: Cambridge University Press.

Bandura, A. (1997). *Self-efficacy: The exercise of control.* New York: Freeman.

Beeth, M. E., & Hewson, P. W. (1999). Learning goals in an exemplary science teacher's practice: Cognitive and social factors in teaching for conceptual change. *Science Education, 83*(6), 738–760.

Beisenherz, P., Dantonio, M., & Richardson, L. (2001). The learning cycle and instructional conversations. *Science Scope, 24,* 34–38.

Bergan, J. R., Sladecezek, I. E., Schwarz, R. D., & Smith, A. N. (1991). Effects of a measurement and planning system on kindergartners' cognitive development and educational programming. *American Educational Research Journal, 28,* 683–714.

Berk, L. E., & Winsler, A. (1995). *Scaffolding children's learning: Vygotsky and early childhood education* (Vol. 7). Washington, DC: National Association for the Education of Young Children.

BioQUEST Curriculum Consortium. (2003). *BioQUEST.* Retrieved August 28, 2006, from http://bioquest.org

Black, P., & Wiliam, D. (1998). Assessment and classroom learning. *Assessment in Education, 5*(1), 7–74.

Blackwell, F., & Hohmann, C. (1991). *Science.* Ypsilanti, MI: High/Scope Press.

Bliss, J. (1995). Piaget and after: The case of learning science. *Studies in Science Education, 25,* 139–172.

Boardman, L. A., Zembal-Saul, C., Frazier, M., Appel, H., & Weiss, R. (1999). *Enhancing the "science" in elementary science methods: A collaborative effort between science education and entomology.* Paper presented at the Annual International Conference of the Association for the Education of Teachers in Science, Austin, TX. (ERIC Document Reproduction Service No. ED444820).

Boud, D., Keogh, R., & Walker, D. (1985). *The reflective process in context.* London: Kogan Page.

Bransford, J. D., & Donovan, M. S. (2005). *How students learn: Science in the classroom.* Washington, DC: National Academies Press.

Brickhouse, N. W. (1990). Teachers' beliefs about the nature of science and their relationship to classroom practice. *Journal of Teacher Education, 41*(3), 53–62.

Brooks, J. G., & Brooks, M. G. (1999). *The case for constructivist classrooms.* Alexandria, VA: Association for Supervision and Curriculum.

Bruner, J. S. (1972). Nature and uses of immaturity. *American Psychologist, 27*(8), 687–708.

Bruner, J. S. (1986). Play, thought, and language. *Prospects: Quarterly Review of Language, 16*(1), 77–83.

Bruning, R. H., Schraw, G. J., & Ronning, R. R. (1999). *Cognitive psychology and instruction* (3rd ed.). Columbus, OH: Merrill.

Bullough, R. V., Knowles, J. G., & Crow, N. A. (1989). Teacher self-concept and student culture in the first year of teaching. *Teachers College Record, 91*(2), 209–233.

Butler, R. (1987). Task-involving and ego-involving properties of evaluation: Effects of different feedback conditions on motivational perceptions, interest and performance. *Journal of Educational Psychology, 79*(4), 474–482.

Cahill, L., Prins, B., Weber, M., & McGaugh, J. (1994). Adrenergic activation and memory for emotional events. *Nature, 371*, 702–704.

Caine, R. N., & Caine, G. (1991). *Making connections: Teaching and the human brain.* Parsippany, NJ: Dale Seymour Publications.

Carmody, B., Hohmann, C., & Johnston, D. J. (2000). *Training resource materials: The High/Scope Elementary Approach.* Ypsilanti, MI: High/Scope Press.

Cash, T., & Parker, S. (1990). *175 More science experiments to amuse and amaze your friends.* New York: Random House.

Christianson, S. (Ed.). (1992). *The handbook of emotion and memory: Research and theory.* Hillsdale, NJ: Lawrence Erlbaum.

Christianson, S., & Loftus, E. (1990). Remembering emotional events: The fate of detailed information. *Cognition and Emotion, 5*, 693–701.

Clark, E.T. (2002). *Designing & implementing an integrated curriculum: A student centered approach.* Brandon, VT: Holistic Education Press.

Covey, S. R. (1989). *The seven habits of highly effective people: Powerful lessons in personal change.* New York: Simon & Schuster.

Crowther, D. T. (1996). *Science experiences and attitudes of elementary education majors as they experience Biology 295: A multiple case study.* Unpublished doctoral dissertation, University of Nebraska–Lincoln, Lincoln, NE.

Csikszentmihalyi, M. (1996). *Creativity: Flow and the psychology of discovery and invention.* New York: Harper Collins.

Dantonio, M., & Beisenherz, P. (2001). *Learning to question, Questioning to learn.* Needham Heights, MA: Allyn & Bacon.

Davis, B. (1996). *Teaching mathematics towards a sound alternative.* New York: Garland Publishing.

Dewey, J. (1934). *Art as experience.* New York: The Berkley Publishing Group.

Dewey, J. (1938). *Experience & education.* New York: Touchstone.

Dewey, J. (1964). *John Dewey on education: Selected writings.* New York: Modern Library.

Dockett, S., & Perry, B. (1996). Young children's construction of knowledge. *Australian Journal of Early Childhood, 21*(4), 6–11.

Driver, R. (1994). Constructing scientific knowledge in the classroom. *Education Researcher, 23*(7), 5–12.

Duckworth, E. (1996). *The having of wonderful ideas and other essays on teaching and learning* (2nd ed.). New York: Teachers College Press.

Duckworth, E. (1997). Spotting active learning. *The Active Learner: A Foxfire Journal for Teachers, 2*(2), 24–27.

Elkind, D. (1981). *Children and adolescents* (3rd ed.). Oxford: Oxford University Press.

Ernest, P. (1989). The knowledge, beliefs and attitudes of the mathematics teacher: A model. *Journal of Education for Teaching, 15*(1), 13–33.

Feynman, R. P. (1985). *"Surely you're joking Mr. Feynman!"* New York: W.W. Norton.

Franklin, J. (2005). Mental mileage: How teachers are putting brain research to work. *ASCD Education Update, 47*(6), 1–3, 7.

Freire, P. (1998). *Teachers as cultural workers: Letters to those who dare to teach* (2nd ed.). Boulder, CO: Westview Press.

Fulghum, R. (1995). *All I really needed to know I learned in kindergarten: Uncommon thoughts on common things.* New York: Villard Books.

Gadamer, H. (1964). *Psychology, the philosophy of art, history, and politics.* Evanston, IL: Northwestern University Press.

Gardner, H. (1983). *Frames of mind: How children think and how we should teach.* New York: Basic Books.

Gardner, H. (1999). *Intelligence reframed: Multiple intelligences for the 21st century.* New York: Basic Books.

Gibson, S., & Dembo, M. H. (1984). Teacher efficacy: A construct validation. *Journal of Educational Psychology, 76*, 569–582.

Ginns, I. S., & Watters, J. J. (1995). An analysis of scientific understandings of pre-service elementary teacher education. *Journal of Research in Science Teaching, 32*(2), 205–222.

Glasson, G. E., & Lalik, R. V. (1993). Reinterpreting the learning cycle from a social constructivist perspective: A qualitative study of teacher's beliefs and practices. *Journal of Research in Science Teaching, 30*(2), 187–207.

Goatly, R. (1999). *Developing skill of reflection.* Hatfield, UK: University of Hertfordshire.

Goble, P. (1988). *Ikitomi and the boulder.* New York: Orchard Books.

Gudmundsdottir, S. (1990). Values in pedagogical content knowledge. *Journal of Teacher Education, 41*(3), 44–52.

Harris, J. R. (1998). *The nurture assumption: Why children turn out the way they do.* New York: Free Press.

Hausfather, S. J. (1996). Vygotsky and schooling: Creating a social context for learning. *Action in Teacher Education, 18*(2), 1–10.

Hawkins, D. (1974). What it means to teach. *Outlook, 12*, 6–13.

Henniger, M. L. (1987). Learning mathematics and science through play. *Childhood Education, 63*(3), 167–171.

Hewson, P. W., Tabachnick, B. R., Zeichner, K. M., Blomker, K. B., Meyer, H., Lemberger, J., Marion, R., Park, H., & Toolin, R. (1999). Educating prospective teachers of biology: Findings, limitations, and recommendations. *Science Education, 83*(3), 247–273.

Hodson, D., & Hodson, J. (1998). From constructivism to social constructivism: A Vygotskian perspective on teaching and learning science. *School Science Review, 79*(289), 33–41.

Hohmann, C. (1991). *Mathematics.* Ypsilanti, MI: High/Scope Press.

Hohmann, C., & Buckleitner, W. (1992). *Learning environment.* Ypsilanti, MI: High/Scope Press.

Hohmann, M., & Weikart, D. P. (1995). *Educating young children.* Ypsilanti, MI: High/Scope Press.

Holt-Reynolds, D. (1992). Personal history-based beliefs as relevant prior knowledge in course work. *American Educational Research Journal, 29*(2), 325–349.

Jensen, E. (2005). *Teaching with the brain in mind* (2nd ed.). Alexandria, VA: Association for Supervision and Curriculum Development.

Kamii, C. (2000). *Young children reinvent arithmetic: Implications of Piaget's theory* (2nd ed.). New York: Teacher's College Press.

Katz, L. G., & Chard, S. C. (1989). *Engaging children's minds: The project approach.* Norwood, NJ: Ablex.

Kenda, M., & Williams, P. S. (1992). *Science wizardry for kids.* New York: Barron's Educational Series, Inc.

Kliebard, H. M. (1995). *The struggle for the American curriculum* (2nd ed.). New York: Routledge.

Knowles, J. G., & Holt-Reynolds, D. (1991). Shaping pedagogies through personal histories in preservice teacher education. *Teachers College Record, 93*(1), 87–111.

Kohn, A. (1993). *Punished by rewards: The trouble with gold stars, incentive plans, A's, praise and other bribes.* New York: Houghton Mifflin.

Kolb, D. A. (1984). *Experiential learning: Experience as the source of learning and development.* Englewood Cliffs, NJ: Prentice Hall.

Krasnow, M. H. (1993). *Waiting for Thursday: New teachers discover teaching.* Paper presented at the American Educational Research Association, Atlanta, GA.

Labinowicz, E. (1980). *The Piagetian primer.* Menlo Park, CA: Addison-Wesley.

Langdon, P., Weltzl-Fairchild, A., & Haggar, J. (1997). Co-operating teachers: Concerns and issues. *Canadian Review of Art Education, 24*(1), 46–57.

Leamnson, R. (1999). *Thinking about teaching and learning: Developing habits of learning with first year college and university students.* Sterling, VA: Stylus Publishing, LLC.

Levine, M. (2002). *A mind at a time.* New York: Simon & Schuster.

Littky, D. (2004). *The big picture: Education is everyone's business.* Alexandria, VA: Association for Supervision and Curriculum Development.

Lockett, N. (2006). Introduction to teaching strategies. *Instructional Framework.* Retrieved August 28, 2006, from http://www.aea267.k12.ia.us/framework/strategies

Moll, L. (1990). *Vygotsky and education: Instructional implications and applications of sociohistorical psychology.* Cambridge, MA: Cambridge University Press.

Moshman, D., Glover, J. A., & Bruning, R. H. (1987). *Developmental psychology: A topical approach.* Boston: Little, Brown.

National Research Council. (1990). *Fulfilling the promise: Biology education in the nation's schools.* Washington, DC: National Academy Press.

National Research Council. (1996). *National Science Education Standards.* Washington, DC: National Academy Press.

National Research Council, Committee on the Foundations of Assessment. (2001). *Knowing what students know: The science and design of educational assessment* (J. W. Pellegrino, N. Chudowsky, & R. Glaser, Eds.). Washington, DC: National Academy Press.

Packard, V. O. (1957). *The hidden persuaders.* New York: D. McKay.

Pellegrino, J. W., Chudowsky, N., & Glaser, R. (Eds.). (2001). *Knowing what students know.* Washington, DC: National Academy Press.

Penick, J. E., Crow, L. W., & Bonnstetter, R. J. (1996). Questions are the answers. *The Science Teacher, 63*(1), 26–29.

Pinker, S. (2002). *The blank slate: The modern denial of human nature.* New York: Viking Penguin.

Pinkwater, D. M. (1977). *The big orange splot.* New York: Scholastic.

Poole, M. B. G., Okeafor, K., & Sloan, E. C. (1989). *Teachers' interactions, personal efficacy, and change implementation.* Paper presented at the annual meeting of the American Educational Research Association, San Francisco, CA.

Pugh, K., & Girod, M. (2002). *What Dewey's aesthetics has to offer education.* Paper presented at the annual meeting of the American Educational Research Association, New Orleans, LA.

Reed, E. W. (1997). Projects and activities: A means not an end. *American Educator, 21*(4), 26–27.

Ritchhart, R. (2002). Intellectual character: What it is, why it matters, and how to get it. San Francisco: JosseyBass.

Santrock, J. W. (2000). *Children* (6th ed.). Boston: McGraw-Hill Higher Education.

Schempp, P. G., Sparkes, A. C., & Templin, T. J. (1993). The micropolitics of teacher induction. *American Educational Research Journal, 30*(3), 447–472.

Schön, D. A. (1983). *The reflective practioner: How professionals think in action.* New York: Basic Books.

Schweinhart, L. J., & Wallgren, C. R. (1993). Effects of a follow through program on school achievement. *Journal of Research on Childhood Education, 8*(1), 43–56.

Schweinhart, L. J., & Weikart, D. P. (1993). Success by empowerment: The High/Scope Perry preschool study through age 27. *Young Children, 49*(1), 54–58.

Schweinhart, L. J., & Weikart, D. P. (1997). The High/Scope preschool curriculum comparison study through age 23. *Early Childhood Research Quarterly, 12,* 117–143.

Schweinhart, L. J., & Weikart, D. P. (1998). Why curriculum matters in early childhood education. *Educational Leadership, 55*(6), 57–60.

Small, M.Y. (1990). *Cognitive development.* San Diego: Harcourt Brace Jovanovich.

Smith, R. W. (1991). *Obstacles to student teacher reflection: The role of prior school experiences as a barrier to teacher development.* Paper presented at the annual meeting of the American Educational Research Association, Chicago, IL.

Smylie, M. A. (1988). The enhancement function of staff development: Organizational and psychological antecedents to individual teacher change. *American Educational Research Journal, 25,* 1–30.

Steig, W. (1969). *Sylvester and the magic pebble.* New York: Aladdin Picture Books.

Stiggins, R. (2002). Assessment crisis: The absence of assessment FOR learning. *Phi Delta Kappan, 83,* 758–765.

Stoddart, T., Connell, M., Stofflett, R., & Peck, D. (1993). Reconstructing elementary teacher candidates' understanding of mathematics and science content. *Teacher & Teacher Education, 9*(3), 229–241.

Tilgner, P. J. (1990). Avoiding science in the elementary school. *Science Education, 74,* 421–431.

Van de Walle, J. A. (2001). *Elementary and middle school mathematics* (4th ed.). New York: Addison, Wesley, Longman, Inc.

Wasserman, S. (1988). Play-debrief-replay: An instructional model for science. *Childhood Education, 64*(4), 232–234.

Watson, B., & Konicek, R. (1990). Teaching for conceptual change: Confronting children's experience. *Phi Delta Kappan, 71*(9), 680–685.

Weikart, D. P. (1988). A perspective in High/Scope's early education research. *Early Child Development and Care, 33,* 29–40.

Weikart, D. P. (1989). Hard choices in early childhood care and education: A view to the future. *Young Children, 44*(3), 25–30.

Weikart, D. P., Bond, J. T., & McNeil, J. T. (1978). *The Ypsilanti Perry Preschool Project: Preschool years and longitudinal results through fourth grade.* Ypsilanti, MI: High/Scope Educational Research Foundation.

Weikart, D. P., Hohmann, C. F., & Rhine, W. R. (1981). *High/Scope cognitively oriented curriculum model.* In W. R. Rhine (Ed.), *Making schools more effective: New directives from follow through* (pp. 201–247). New York: Academic Press.

Wheatley, G. H. (1991). Constructivist perspectives on science and mathematics learning. *Science Education, 75*(1), 9–21.

Williams, K.C. (2004). *Preservice teachers' perceptions of plan-do-review: A thinking routine.* Unpublished doctoral dissertation, University of Nebraska–Lincoln, Lincoln, NE.

Wood, E., & Bennett, N. (1998). Teachers' theories of play: Constructivist or social constructivist? *Early Child Development and Care, 140,* 17–30.

Woolfolk, A. E., & Hoy, W. K. (1990). Prospective teachers' sense of efficacy and beliefs about control. *Journal of Educational Psychology, 82,* 81–91.

Zembal-Saul, C., Blumenfeld, P., & Krajcik, J. (2000). Influence of guided cycles of planning, teaching, and reflection on prospective elementary teachers' science content representations. *Journal of Research in Science Teaching, 37*(4), 318–339.

Index